THE

BIRTH AND DEVELOPMENT OF ORNAMENT.

THE MIRADOR DE LINDARAJA.

THE

BIRTH AND DEVELOPMENT OF ORNAMENT

BY

F. EDWARD HULME, F.L.S., F.S.A.

Author of Suggestions in Floral Design, Principles of Ornamental Art,
History, Principles, and Practice of Heraldry, History, Principles, and Practice
of Symbolism, etc.

With 12 Plates and 168 Text Illustrations

"All common and useful things may be refined into objects
of beauty, and all that is beautiful or high in art is merely an
elaboration and refinement of what is fundamentally a useful
and a necessary art."—FERGUSON

ARDVA·QVÆ·PVLCRA

𝔏𝔬𝔫𝔡𝔬𝔫

SWAN SONNENSCHEIN & CO

NEW YORK: MACMILLAN & CO

1894

TABLE OF CONTENTS.

" Order gave each thing view."—SHAKESPEARE.

CHAPTER I.

CHAPTER II.

CHAPTER VI.

LIST OF ILLUSTRATIONS.

"Look here, upon this picture, and on this."—SHAKESPEARE.

The Birth and Development of Ornament.

"By your gracious patience
I will a round unvarnish'd tale deliver."
—OTHELLO.

CHAPTER I.

The Birth of Ornament—Distinction between pictorial and decorative
art—Impossible to draw a sharp line between them—What
styles of ornament are—All changes gradual and continual—
Value of a knowledge of the ornament of the past—Sir Joshua
Reynolds and Guizot thereupon—The study of principles—
Art at second hand—Decoration a necessity—Utility the first
consideration—Difference between design and decoration—
Difference between symbolic and æsthetic ornament—The
limitation imposed by imperfect means—The appropriate use
of materials.

THE Birth of Ornament! Countless centuries before
man appeared upon the earth, the Creator of the universe
had gazed upon the works of His hands, and declared
that all had reached His lofty ideal. Some people hold
the mistaken idea that ornament is all very well perhaps
for those who like it, but that what they want is some-

B

thing practical; but the works of Nature gently rebuke this cold utilitarian spirit, and afford us countless illustrations of beauty wedded to use. The painting of the petals of the commonest wayside weed, the exquisite markings on shells so minute that only the microscope enables us to appreciate their beauty, the gorgeous colouring of the peacock's feathers, the rich markings on the wings of the butterfly, the splendour of colour of the ruby and topaz, the graceful forms of the evanescent snow crystals, are but a few instances that at once rise to our minds.

Man made in the image of God shows in some degree His attributes, and appreciates in some measure the perfection of His work. Hence the cannibal savage and fetish worshipper of Central Africa who carves his weapons or weaves his basket work into bands and chequers, the ancient Greek who decorated with such refinement of art the funereal urn or the water vessel of daily use, and the mediæval workman who wreathed his capitals and mouldings with sculpture of hawthorn and maple, all alike testify that man liveth not by bread alone, all alike, consciously or unconsciously, working under the influence of the Spirit breathed into them as children of the great Father of all. Hence we claim for our subject nothing short of infinite antiquity, nothing less than Divine authority.

As in the biography of some famous man two lines may suffice to give all needful particulars of his birth and parentage, while a volume of a thousand pages may scarcely do full justice to his after career, so a couple of paragraphs have sufficed to give us our starting point, while the after development of ornament in all its ramifications would need more volumes for its elucidation than we can at present give pages.

In these latter days a distinction has been made between fine and decorative art, the man who paints a picture esteeming himself an altogether superior person to a designer of ornament. There is no sharp line that can possibly be drawn between decorative art and fine art, though in many cases one finds no difficulty in assigning to one or the other a given example ; hence it is an utter mistake to regard decorative art as necessarily on a lower footing. Much harm has of course been done to the latter by many who in the present day call themselves " decorators," but this is a disadvantage that almost all callings are liable to, and we do not ordinarily judge any body of men by the worst examples.

Decorative art and fine art merge imperceptibly into each other, and the same thing may receive one or the other name according to circumstances. If, for example, we see a group of lilies painted on canvas, put into a gold frame and hung on the wall, we call the result a picture, an example of fine art, the work of an artist; but if the same flowers, equally well painted, are placed in the panel of a door, the result is a decorative design. When we come to figure subjects the distinction is still more difficult. In Rome, Paris, and elsewhere in the large public galleries and government buildings, we find the work of the first artists adapted to fill certain recognised spaces in the architectural construction, and they are thus far decorative, though one would never dare to question their claim to be considered works of fine art as well.[1] Many an old altar piece and fresco that was essentially decorative art in its original home becomes a choice example of this, that, or the other old master when put into a gold frame and hung in some national picture gallery.

Throughout the preceding centuries we find no such dividing line, the choicest work of Phidias or of Michael Angelo being frankly decorative in character. The grandest sculptures of the finest period of Greek art were units in the magnificent decoration of the Parthenon, and the work of the great Florentine sculptor and painter in the Sistine Chapel and elsewhere fills its allotted space in the grand general scheme of decoration [2] of the build-

---

[1] Perhaps the happiest effort to draw a clear line of distinction will be found in the following definitions by Palgrave : —

" In pictorial art we have the representation of natural objects selected and combined, supplemented by the imagination and invention of the artist; for without this imagination—this ideal within himself—the artist would only produce a dead mechanical copy, more or less accurate according to his technical skill.

" In ornamental or inventive art as applied to decoration and industry, we have the adaptation of the representation of natural objects selected and combined, applied in geometric proportions, and in some styles based on geometry only, the specific application being governed by application to some useful object, or given space, and controlled by the material in which the design is to be wrought out, and the means, handicraft or mechanical, by which it is to be produced."

[2] The word decorative is derived from the Latin word *decorous,* a root that also supplies us with our English word decorum. Decorative art is therefore primarily what may be used in a certain position with propriety ; that which is seemly, becoming, and fitting. That such work should naturally be pleasing and attractive to the

ing it ennobled. In the same way the artists of Egypt carved with wonderful power the long avenues of sphinxes, or drew with rich profusion countless incidents of the daily life of the people on the walls of the temples and the tombs. The triumphs in war or in the chase of the monarchs of Assyria were recorded in the mural decoration of the palaces of Khorsabad and Kyonjik.

Hence, therefore, we must enter upon our subject with no narrow prepossessions or prejudices. To understand any phase of art requires a far wider study than appears on the surface, and a far-reaching sympathy—a sympathy that can at least teach respect even where it cannot mature into appreciation. The history of ornamental art covers an immense area, and it is impossible to satisfactorily isolate any section of it. Even if a man would desire to confine his attention to some one style or period, as for example Greek or Gothic, he would speedily find that to comprehend its *motif* he must go back possibly for centuries, and see its beginnings developing in countries far remote. The fall of Rome, the rise of Byzantium, and the Eastern influence that then arose may all be recorded, to those who can read the signs aright, in a capital in the cathedral of Lincoln, and the art of Greece was no merely local growth, but a development and outcome of many foreign influences that Thebes and Memphis, Tyre and Sidon may be taken as illustrations of.

---

eye follows almost as a matter of course; but this we see was not the fundamental idea, and no matter how charming a thing may be in itself, if it be not fitted to its position, it is not truly decorative.

Persons often speak of styles of ornament as though
each had a distinct individuality, or quite definite beginning and ending; as if they sprang into existence in
full development, and then, for some reason or other,
ceased to be, and were at once supplanted by something
else.   Books on ornament are largely responsible for this,
as they naturally, in dealing with any period of art, deal
with its leading characteristics, but they omit to show us
those transitional forms and modifications of type that
are continually changing it and developing it into something else.   Hence we are taken, for example, at once
from Early English or thirteenth-century Gothic to fourteenth-century or Decorated, and the turning over of a
page lands us in an entirely new set of forms.   We do
undoubtedly find in almost every age and in every nation
a certain type of ornament that is more or less local and
individual, and which for the time being may be called a
style, as it contains certain characteristic developments
and broad distinctive features, and it may hence very
conveniently be given a distinctive title; but, after all,
in this world nothing continueth long in one stay, and
everything that has healthy life in it has also growth, and
growth is change.

The rainbow has its seven distinctive bands of colour,
all easily recognisable and capable of being exactly
named, yet each merges imperceptibly into its neighbour,
and all blend together into one glorious whole; and in
like manner each period of art has its rise, its period
of splendour, and its passing away, when, phœnix-like,
another rises from its decay.   Ornamental art is not like

a series of isolated and more or less stagnant lakes, but as it comes down through the centuries is rather a flowing river that gathers contributory streams from either side, and is ever changing, ever growing.

All the so-called styles are not of equal importance; thus the Roman is little more than a modification of the Greek. In Egypt the art of the Pharaohs was for centuries magnificent, while the admixture of Greek elements under the Ptolemies sullied its purity, and its degradation became complete under the sway of Rome. Gothic art, again, as a primary style, has its distinctive and secondary modifications in England, France, Germany, and Spain. Mohammedan art, though it has a very distinct character, has no less distinctly marked phases in Spain, in Persia, and in India ; while the Renaissance period of art has its equally clearly marked local developments in Italy, France, and England. Hence it is impossible to draw sharp dividing lines, and the study of any one period necessitates, as we have said, a far-reaching investigation that quickly takes us in ever-widening circles far from our starting point.

Soon after Thorwaldsen had sent some of his sculptures from Rome to Copenhagen, the meadows round the northern city were gay with strange Italian wild flowers that sprang from seeds in the hay that had been used as a packing. When the industrious coral insects have reared another island amidst the waves of the Pacific, the new creation rapidly grows verdant with the palms and other vegetation from seeds that are drifted, blown, or transported by birds to its shores. So in less visible and

material fashion are ideas conveyed into new soil ready
for their reception ; and we shall see, later on, how great
an influence the two potent factors of war and commerce
have had in this dissemination.   Nothing short of Chinese
exclusiveness can suffice to isolate a style from external
influences.

A knowledge of the ornament of the past is of great
value, historically and artistically.   Historically, because
it often by its character furnishes us with the date of
that whereon it is found, and tells us of the incursion of
various races, a piece of Samian ware dug up in Kent or
Sussex being practically as good a proof of Roman
occupation as a confirmatory passage in the writings of
Cæsar.   Artistically, because even though now-a-days
we are little likely to re-introduce Egyptian or Assyrian
designs into modern work, there has been a considerable
revival of other styles, such as Greek and the various
periods of Gothic ; and it seems but reasonable that if we
go in for the reproduction of this past art, it should be
done thoroughly and with knowledge.   Hence the modern
designer should be a good archæologist, a man of wide
reading, of keen observation, a lover of all that is beautiful
-—alike in the whole realm of nature and in the wide field
of art.   The specialist should be a man whose knowledge
and powers far exceed his speciality, and whose sympathies extend beyond its routine.   For the requirements
of the designer are so diverse that occasions will frequently arise to test his versatility, and his knowledge
should be both deep and wide.   It is the first test of a
true artist that he should sympathise with all art.

Sir Joshua Reynolds, in his various "Discourses on Art," is very emphatic on this point; thus in his second Discourse he asserts that "It is indisputably evident that a great part of every man's life must be employed in collecting materials for the exercise of genius. Invention, strictly speaking, is little more than a new combination of those images which have been previously gathered and deposited in the memory:—nothing can come of nothing; he who has laid up no materials can produce no combinations. The more extensive, therefore, your acquaintance is with the works of those who have excelled, the more extensive will be your powers of invention, and, what may appear still more like a paradox, the more original will be your conceptions." In the sixth Discourse he reverts to the matter in the following words: "The greatest natural genius cannot subsist on its own stock. He who resolves never to ransack any mind but his own, will be soon reduced from mere barrenness to the poorest of all imitation; he will be obliged to imitate himself, and to repeat what he has before often repeated. When we know the subject designed by such men, it will never be difficult to guess what kind of work is to be produced." While not to needlessly multiply illustrations we may conclude our extracts with the following quotation from his seventh Discourse: "Those who, either from their own engagements and hurry of business, or from indolence, or from conceit and vanity, have neglected looking out of themselves, as far as my experience and observation reaches, have from that time not only ceased to advance and improve in their performances, but have gone backward. They may be compared to men who have lived upon their principal till they are reduced to beggary and left without resources." In all these extracts alike it will be seen that the urgent necessity of the study of past art is most powerfully and persistently dwelt upon.

It is painful to see the hurrying crowds of people who are utterly bored in our museums and galleries in the midst of things of surpassing interest, but which from a want of knowledge on their part convey no meaning to them. Thousands hurry past the Nineveh bas-reliefs, the Halicarnassus sculptures, or the Rosetta stone in the British Museum, ignorant of the wealth of interest they are missing; and in the South Kensington Museum the great majority of people merely peep into a certain big room full of casts and then hurry out again, though this court contains the whole history of Greek art, from the archaic examples through all the intermediate steps to those masterpieces of art that make the sculpture of Hellas a wonder and delight throughout all time, and supplies superabundant material for hours of study. The venerable stones of Westminster Abbey again speak to us of the whole history of architecture in England for many centuries; but while they speak in a language clear enough to those who have studied the subject, to many it is evidently an unknown tongue, and lack of knowledge necessarily results in lack of interest.[1]

---

[1] "The study of art possesses this great and peculiar charm, that it is absolutely unconnected with the struggles and contests of ordinary life. By private interests, by political questions, men are deeply

Past art should be studied for its principles; the mere copying of old work is entirely useless. It is invaluable for analysis, for criticism, a spur to emulation, a guide to success, and sometimes for warning; but its adaptation as a substitute for thought is an entirely false use of it. Thus the Greeks rarely if ever made two series of capitals alike, those of any one temple differing somewhat from those of all others; while modern writers, selecting some one beautiful example of an order, have measured it carefully into so many modules and parts, and to these a slavish and most prosaic compliance has been given; thus all originality has been crushed out, and in striving for the letter they have lost the spirit. Art at second hand is already art in its decay. Art that is unreal goes the way of all other shams, and history affords us many examples of this. Greek art was as noble in its simplicity as any that the world has ever seen; while Roman art, inferior as it was, had yet a certain virile strength; but the debased Græco-Roman is feeble, unreal, hastening to its fall. Hence each healthy period of art has asserted its own individuality. Local peculiarities and all specialities, such as the influence of a particular form of religious

divided and set at variance; but beyond and above all such strifes, they are attracted and united by a taste for the beautiful in art. It is a taste at once engrossing and unselfish, which may be indulged without effort, and yet has the power of exciting the deepest emotions —a taste able to exercise and to gratify both the nobler and softer parts of our nature—the imagination and the judgment, love of emotion and power of reflection, the enthusiasm and the critical faculty, the senses and the reason."—GUIZOT.

belief, die out; and if these causes cannot be recalled, the revival of any ancient style must be to a great extent a sham; but all that is founded on abstract principles of art and beauty is enduring, and can never really grow old and out of date.

Decoration has at all times been felt to be a necessity. Man liveth not by bread alone, and there is a hunger of the mind as truly as there is a hunger of the body. It is the first essential that utility be not sacrificed,[1] but this point once secured it is a natural instinct and propensity to add to this crude material form the refinement of decoration. Wherever there is an opening for handiwork there is room also for brainwork, and this brainwork should assert itself in two different directions—first in the determination of the absolute fitness of the form to its purpose, and then in the addition of such adornment as may make it attractive to the eye and the mind.[2] The veriest savage who carves his club or paddle is not oblivious to these two great considerations. Even to him beauty of form and colour

---

[1] " The primary consideration of construction is so necessary to pure design that it almost follows that, whenever style and ornament are debased, construction will be found to have been first disregarded ; and that those styles which are considered the purest, and the best periods of those styles, are just those wherein constructive utility has been rightly understood and most thoroughly attended to."—REDGRAVE.

[2] " The useful is a vehicle for the beautiful."—OWEN JONES.

" Decoration is not a substantive, but an adjective. It does not stand alone. It is not a thing of itself ; it decorates something else. It follows; it does not lead the way. It enhances ; it does not originate. This is its restricted province."—JOHN BELL.

is an attraction, but the stern necessities of warfare will effectually prevent his so carving his club or paddle that they will break in his hands in the stress of fight. The shield of Achilles in all the beauty of its workmanship and art was not the less an effective defence against the javelins of his foes. The tempered blades of Toledo or of Damascus were not one whit the less keen and trenchant for the exquisite inlays that adorned them. Utility without adornment is too barbarous even for South Sea Islanders, but in all true work we see that decoration is but the adjunct to utility.

Design and decoration are terms often employed as though they were equivalent, but it will be seen on a moment's reflection that the first of these covers a much greater area than the second, and may indeed include it. Design is the consideration of all the necessities of the case, utilitarian and decorative, and the man who devises a more practical form of fork or spoon is as much a designer as the man who chases its surface with flowing curves and graceful ornament. Hence the necessary limitation of our title. Had we substituted design for ornament, our labours would have been a thousandfold increased, and Stephenson, Brunel, and Wren would have claimed as rightfully a place as Cellini or Grinling Gibbons. We should have found that the construction of the Forth Bridge had as full a right to our consideration as the mosaics of Byzantium or the pottery of Greece.

Having thus limited our field, what is left to us? To this we may at once reply, that what still remains

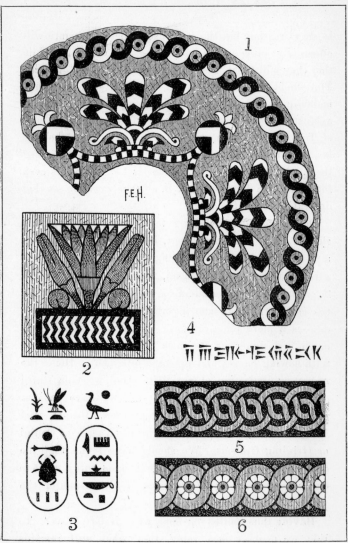

F.E.H.

is practically inexhaustible; and while we can but hope in so narrow a compass to deal but superficially with the fringe of the subject, we may at least enumerate some of the points that open out when we turn our thoughts to its broad consideration. The wide field of prehistoric art, the finds in the lake dwellings and burial mounds of these ancient peoples, the bizarre pottery and textile fabrics, the quaint architecture and mural decoration of ancient Mexico and Peru, and of Central America, and of the various savage tribes of the New World. The rock-hewn temples of India, the art of the followers of Buddha, Brahma, and Siva. The art of ancient Egypt and of Assyria, of Babylonia and of Persia. The art of Greece, Etruria, and Rome, the Romanesque and Byzantine outgrowth from classic art, with their derivatives, Lombardic, Norman, and Gothic. The Renaissance. The works of the Chinese, Japanese, and Persians, and the influence of Mohammedanism in Spain. And this artistic outcome, too, modified in every direction by the forms in which it is encountered in the grandest architecture and the noblest sculpture, or worked in elaborate mosaic, glowing in glorious stained glass, wrought in bronze and iron, woven at the loom, turned on the potter's wheel, carved in ivory or in marble, in wood and stone; the result of the patient labour of the lifetime of the monkish illuminator, the deft handiwork of the lace-worker, or the embroiderer, or the medallist, or the goldsmith. In all times and in all places, the love of Art! In some of its manifestations delightful and in others distasteful to us, but always full of interest.

FIG. 7. GREEK FIGURE TREATMENT.

All decorative art falls naturally into one or other of two great divisions, the symbolic and the æsthetic. In the first of these the forms have been chosen primarily for their significance, while in the second they have been selected solely for their beauty ; and we cannot adequately judge of any work until we clearly realize whether we must regard it as an appeal to our knowledge and understanding, or as an appeal to our taste. We must bear in mind, too, that imperfect means or inadequate knowledge may make a given work more or less grotesque to us where the designer intended no such suggestion, and in such a case we must endeavour to realize rather what he intended to convey than to dwell upon his shortcomings. Much Norman figure carving, for instance, is almost laughably quaint ; but the old carver had in most cases a very serious end in view, and nothing was further from his thoughts than that the ultimate result of his work would be that it should raise a smile. Over the Ecole des Beaux Arts in Paris is placed the inscription—" La critique est aisée, mais l'art est difficile ;" and it is in such spirit of appreciation that even the rudest work should be judged.

Means are rarely imperfect, after all, when a master hand deals with them, as such an one knows what is possible with them and does not attempt to pass beyond the legitimate limits imposed. A designer, for instance, who is required to produce work that will only be printed in one or two colours will eschew a naturalistic treatment ; and while much of the noblest work owes much to its suggestion of nature, this natural beauty must be foregone when the circumstances of the case necessarily show that the result must be a failure, for in that case the goodness of the intention does not excuse the imperfection of the result. Imperfection of means, whatever form this may take, must be frankly recognised together with the limitation it imposes.

In Greek art, for example, this conventionalism of treatment arising from imperfect means is very frankly accepted ; hence in the one or two flat tints that were available in their vases—red, buff, or black—we find no attempt to absolutely reproduce nature. The figure subjects in the centres of the pateras or upon the vases are treated in a bold and flat manner, as in Fig. 7, and the floral bands are suggestive, not imitative. The result is infinitely preferable to any laboured attempt to give a naturalistic representation with imperfect means, such as we often see in the floral groups printed in one colour on the lower class of some modern pottery goods.

The materials in which a design is worked have an important influence for good or evil. Any one, for instance, on looking at Fig. 8, will feel at once that " the human form divine " cannot be adequately rendered with the coarse tesseræ that nevertheless serve well enough for the less ambitious aim represented by Fig. 9. Both these examples are from Roman mosaic pavements. Any one studying any of the numerous examples available in our museums or as seen at Brading or elsewhere will, we think, feel with us that while the figure subjects introduced are deeply interesting they are artistically weak, and that the little cubes that have so admirably served for the fretwork or the guilloches and other minor details are not equal to the demands upon them in the more ambitious attempt to pourtray the wheat-crowned Ceres, rosy-rayed Aurora, or great Jove himself. Of course it may be said that with smaller tesseræ the work could be quite adequately done, but in this case the amount of

Fig. 8.

labour involved would be extreme, and it is better to recognise the fact that the means are imperfect, and not to strain them beyond just requirements.

Artistic work should bring out the distinctive character of the material employed, and one should never laboriously do in an intractable material what can be much more readily performed in another. "If," to quote

Ruskin, one of our greatest writers, "you don't want the qualities of the substance you use, you ought to use some other substance: it can be only affectation, and desire to display your skill that lead you to employ a refractory substance, and therefore your art will all be base. Glass, for instance, is eminently, in its nature, transparent. If you don't want transparency, let the glass alone. Do not try to make a window look like an opaque picture, but take an opaque ground to begin with. Again, marble is eminently a solid and massive substance. Unless you want mass and solidity, don't work in marble. If you wish for lightness, take wood; if for freedom, take stucco; if for ductility, take glass. Don't try to carve feathers, or trees, or nets, or foam, out of marble. Carve white limbs and broad breasts only out of that. So again, iron is eminently a ductile and tenacious substance—tenacious above all things, ductile more than most. When you want tenacity, therefore, and involved form, take iron. It is eminently made for that. It is the material given to the sculptor as the companion of marble, with a message, as plain as it can well be spoken, from the lips of the earth-mother, 'Here's for you to cut, and here's for you to hammer. Shape this, and twist that. What is solid and simple, carve out; what is thin and entangled, beat out. I give you all kinds of forms to be delighted in:—fluttering leaves as well as fair bodies; twisted branches as well as open brows. The leaf and the branch you may beat and drag into their imagery: the body and brow you shall reverently touch into their imagery. And if you choose rightly and work rightly, what you do shall be safe afterwards. Your slender leaves shall not break off in my tenacious iron, though they may be rusted a little with an iron autumn. Your broad surfaces shall not be unsmoothed in my pure crystalline marble—no decay shall touch them. But if you carve in the marble what will break with a touch, or mould in the

Fig. 9.

metal what a stain of rust or verdigris will spoil, it is your fault—not mine.' "

Many other general principles might be brought forward were we writing a treatise on the practice of design, but as our aim at present is somewhat different—a consideration of the ornament of the past rather than a

guide to the future—we now forbear, and we do so the
more willingly because, knowing their value and interest,
we shall have opportunity from time to time to elucidate
all necessary points by reference to the art of the past
centuries.   While therefore the reader escapes for the
time being any further preamble, and finds himself at
last fairly launched on the consideration of the art of
Egypt, Assyria, or Greece, we shall not ourselves be content to merely enumerate the various features as they
come before us, but shall also indicate in what way they
appear to us to illustrate and elucidate the leading laws
that underlie all sound work, not resting content with
being pleased, but endeavouring to find out how it is that
certain forms give this pleasure, and therefore appear and
reappear almost throughout the whole field of study.

CHAPTER II.

The antiquity and commercial greatness of Egypt—Chronological
details and sketch of history—Royal jealousy of the fame of
past sovereigns—The ruins of Karnak, Thebes, and Luxor—
The mural paintings—Authorities to consult—General spirit of
Egyptian art—Its religious character—Archaic and archeistic
work—Domination of the priesthood over art—Repetition and
alternation of simple units—The lotus—Deification of the Nile
—The Indian lotus or sacred bean—The papyrus—Columns
simulating bundles of stems—Colossal figure columns—Caryatides—Sacred animals — The winged globe — Sun-worship —
Massive character of Egyptian work—Obelisks—Cleopatra's
Needle—Rise of the Babylonian Empire—The Assyrians—Discoveries of Layard and others—Assyrian art—Arrowhead inscriptions — Colour — The sacred tree — Colossal bulls — The
Phœnicians—Influence of commerce and war upon art.

FROM the earliest period of which we have any record,
Egypt was far in advance of the rest of the world in
civilization, and a thousand years before the Christian
era it was a prosperous State, trafficking with all the then
known world,[1] of great commercial influence and warlike

---

[1] In the book of Proverbs we read of the "fine linen of Egypt,"
and in Ezekiel again of "fine linen with broidered work" from the
same source. Daniel writes of "the precious things of Egypt," and
many other allusions to the great commercial prosperity and skill of
the people may readily be found in the Bible and in other writings
of ancient authors. Some mummy cloth before us as we write is
of excellent texture, and as sound in fabric as the day it was made in
the far-off past.

power, and the seat of knowledge of all kinds. The city of Heliopolis was the great university of the ancient world, and thither flocked the scholars of all the surrounding peoples.[1] In architecture and in art Egypt was no less distinguished.

Our knowledge of Egyptian ornament is almost entirely derived from the architecture of the land. Mummy cases, pottery, glass and beadwork, furniture, and some few other means of information on the subject are open to us; but these are strictly subordinate sources, and even many of these are of architectural type, the pendant of a necklace being often of the form of a temple, while in the British Museum may be seen several small vases that are direct imitations in form and ornament of the columns, lotus or palm-crowned, so characteristic of Egyptian architecture. Abundant examples of grand architectural work may be found throughout the valley of the Nile for a distance of more than a thousand miles.

It is foreign to our present purpose to give anything like the history of Egypt, but all the temples bear the names of their builders, and by this means much valuable chronological knowledge is gained, and it is manifest that the study of the art of this ancient people is rendered immensely more interesting by this knowledge. We may therefore indicate some few salient points. The

[1] So that the writer of the book of Kings (1 Kings iv. 30) could give no more graphic idea of the wisdom of Solomon than to say that it excelled " all the wisdom of Egypt "; while Moses, the great leader of Israel, we are specially told " was learned in all the wisdom of the Egyptians."

history of Egypt can be traced back for over four thousand years before the dawn of our era.[1] From about B.C. 4400 to 2466 the seat of government was chiefly at Memphis. From 2466 to 1200, the period of Egypt's greatest splendour, it was generally at Thebes, though in each period the extension of the kingdom, revolution, or disaster in war, led to various changes in the seat of government. The magnificent temples at Thebes, Karnak, and Luxor were chiefly built by the monarchs of the eighteenth dynasty, B.C. 1700 to 1400, Ahmes, Amen-hotep, and others. Rameses I. (B.C. 1400 to 1366) was also a great temple-builder at Karnak, Memphis, and else-where—an example that was followed by his son Rameses II., otherwise Rameses the Great, though we must not accept his cartouche upon these great buildings as an entirely sufficient proof, as he was not above the mean-ness of erasing from older structures the names of their founders and substituting his own.[2] The great rock-hewn temple of Abou-Simbel in Nubia is of this period. This Pharaoh was the oppressor of the captive children of Israel, and their labours were largely utilised in his great

---

[1] We naturally associate Abraham in our minds with a very early period, yet at the time of his sojourn in the land Egypt had been a great nation over a thousand years.

[2] From the same feeling of jealousy of the grandeur and powers of his predecessors, the Chinese Emperor Tsin-Chi-Hoang-Ti demolished, A.D. 246, every building of importance, so that practically nothing now remains in that ancient land of any higher antiquity. We can perhaps realize this better if we imagine a decree going forth next month that Windsor Castle, Westminster Abbey, all our old cathedrals, and everything in fact of any historic value was to be ruthlessly de-stroyed.

works. Shishak, who is also referred to in the Bible, was an alien, and from this period, B.C. 966, Egypt was almost entirely under foreign sway, Ethiopian or Assyrian, until Psammetichus, B.C. 666, came to the throne, and achieved the independence of the land from the foreigner. The ancient cities were restored, and much excellent artistic work was produced. In B.C. 527 the Persians subdued the country, and for more than a century Egypt was but a province of Persia. The Persians in turn were vanquished, B.C. 332, by Alexander the Great, and the once mighty Egypt again exchanged masters. Later on it became a Roman province, and on the break up of the Roman State was overrun by the Arabs, then passed into the hands of the Turks, A.D. 1517, and is now garrisoned by British soldiers. An altogether wonderful history, full of striking pictures and contrasts.[1]

The great temples of Egypt grew for centuries, and by the labours of generations of monarchs were made what they ultimately became. The magnificent temple at Karnak was thus growing for two thousand years. Its erection had already commenced when Joseph was sold into Egypt, and thereafter all that wealth, skill, art, and the sovereign will of successive monarchs could command was lavished upon it.[2]

---

[1] As for instance, but two out of hundreds, the little ark bearing the infant Moses on the bosom of the Nile, and the same current bearing on its surface the Canadian voyageurs speeding to Khartoum.

[2] "From the time of Joseph to the Christian era, through the whole period of the Jewish history and of the ancient world, the splendour of the earth kept pouring into that space for 2000 years." —STANLEY. In one of its halls, a very small portion of the immense

In close proximity to Karnak, and, like it, within the area once covered by "hundred-gated"[1] Thebes, are the almost equally grand ruins of Luxor. All early art deals with profile only, the figures of men or animals being always rendered in side view, whatever the action may be. We may see this very well shown in the Greek example already given in Fig. 7, and it is equally characteristic of Egyptian, Assyrian, and other early work.

All the walls and columns of these temples are covered with brilliantly coloured figure subjects, figures of the gods or of the Pharaoh who built the monument in question, with representations of his warlike prowess and other incidents that redounded to his glory, the monarch, as in most early work, being represented by a figure much larger than any of the subordinate actors in the various scenes depicted. The hieroglyphics again, though primarily inscriptions, greatly aid in the general decorative effect from their quaint animal or other forms and from the richness of their colouring, a richness that yet remains practically unimpaired in the dry climate of Egypt.

On these and other monuments, and especially in the tombs, we get a wonderfully interesting series of illustrations of the whole life of the people, their religious ceremonies, their daily work and play. We see the potter shaping the clay, the musicians with harp and pipe, the shoemaker sewing his work together, the mason dressing

---

fabric, there is ample space to deposit the cathedral of Our Lady of Paris.

[1] "Thebes, where through each her hundred portals wide
Two hundred charioteers their coursers guide."—HOMER.

the block of stone, the progress of the banquet, the game of ball, the fisherman with his net, barbed spear, or rod and line, and all the labours of the husbandman, such as sowing, ploughing, reaping, treading out the corn with oxen, plucking the figs, watering the vines, and gathering in the vintage. Elsewhere we see the glass-blower at the furnace, the confectioner making sweetmeats, or the brickmaker at work, while standing by the latter is the taskmaster with formidable whip. All these and many more may be seen in Rosellini's magnificent work on the monuments of Egypt, published in three folio volumes at Pisa in 1832–44.[1] The first deals with the monuments of the Pharaohs, the second with the civil monuments, and the third with the religious worship of the Egyptians. This may be seen in the library at South Kensington Museum, and elsewhere; but to those who find any difficulty in seeing it, Wilkinson's "Ancient Egyptians" will prove a very good substitute, as it is very freely and excellently illustrated.[2]

---

[1] "I Monumenti dell' Egitto e della Nubia, disegnati della spedizione scientificolitteraria Toscana in Egitto : distribuiti in ordine di materie, interpretati ed illustrati dal Dottore Ippolito Rosellini." The text is published separately in an octavo volume, and is in Italian ; but the illustrations are themselves so graphic, that it is a matter of very little moment whether one's knowledge of the language is up to full standard or not; the subjects tell their own story by whatever name they are called.

[2] Wilkinson, Sir J. G., " The Manners and Customs of the Ancient Egyptians, including their Private Life, Government, Laws, Arts Manufactures, Religion, Agriculture, and Early History, derived from a Comparison of the Paintings, Sculptures, and Monuments still existing, with the Accounts of Ancient Authors." The following may

The general spirit of Egyptian art was profoundly religious and symbolic. All was under the dominion of the priesthood, and was bound with rigour to adhere to certain orthodox requirements. The influence of religion upon art, pictorial and decorative, must not be overlooked. Throughout Egyptian work its claims are paramount. Its influence in Greece was most potent; in all the peoples of Islam its power was supreme; the symbolism of the

---

also be consulted :—Gau's "Antiquités de la Nubie, ou Monumens inédits des Bords du Nil, situés entre la première et la seconde Cataracte, dessinés et mesurés en 1819. Ouvrage faisant suite au grand ouvrage de la Commission d'Egypte." Large folio. Paris.——"Description de l'Egypte, ou Recueil des Observations et des Recherches qui ont été faites en Egypte pendant l'Expédition de l'Armée Française. Publié par les ordres de sa Majesté l'Empereur Napoléon le Grand." The great work of the French Expedition, treating of the Antiquities, Arts, Natural History, and Modern State of Egypt. 23 vols. folio, atlas folio, and elephant. Paris.——Canina's "L'Architettura Antica, descritta e dimostrata coi Monumenti," 3 vols., royal folio, containing 705 engraved plates of the famous Monuments and Edifices of Greece, Rome, and Egypt.——Fergusson's "History of Architecture in all Countries, from the Earliest Times to the Present Day," gives most interesting material, and may be consulted freely for all periods of art, as may also the excellent "Grammar of Ornament" of Owen Jones. The great book of Prisse d'Avennes should also be seen. This valuable work was published under the auspices of the French Government. Its title is as follows : "Histoire de l'Art Egyptien, d'après les Monuments depuis les temps les plus reculés jusqu'a la domination Romaine." There are two folio volumes, containing 159 plates, a large number of which are executed in chromolithography. These treat of the Architecture, Sculpture, Paintings, Designs, and Industrial Arts of Egypt. The 4to volume of text, with numerous woodcuts interspersed, forms a complete History of Egyptian Art. The price of the book was originally £45, a sum that indicates that no expense was spared in making it as perfect as possible by the enlightened Government that honours itself by the production of such a work.

mediæval glass painter and carver is based almost entirely
upon it. One cannot understand the art of any people
without a recognition of this fact, and a knowledge of
how much or how little they allowed their lives and
actions to be swayed by their belief.[1] All the grandest
work that has ever been done springs from man's sense
of the need to propitiate some greater power outside himself; hence the glorious temple of Athene Parthenos, in
which all that was noblest in art was dedicated to the
Virgin goddess,—hence the glorious minsters of mediæval
days that speak so eloquently of the piety of our forefathers,—hence the splendour of the temple of Solomon
and the grandeur of Luxor and Karnak. It may be
pointed out that in these latter the exploits of the earthly
monarch occupy a very prominent position; but we must
remember that the belief in the divinity that was held to
hedge about a king and that made him the Lord's anointed
was emphatically held in ancient Egypt, where the
monarch was deemed to be specially beloved of the gods
and their vicegerent on earth. Great Osiris, therefore,
was honoured in the person of his pontiff and earthly
representative.

This domination of the priesthood, however, cramped
the artistic faculty, as certain types were alone permissible under this religious censorship, and it was penal and

---

[1] Benham's Dictionary of Religion may very advantageously be
studied by the student, as it gives a sufficient account of each cult
to enable the reader to see a meaning in what otherwise would in
many cases be obscure, without overburdening him with theological
refinements.

heretic to deviate from them. Hence even in the period
of highest culture the archaic treatment [1] was adhered to,
though doubtless those who did such noble work under
these hard limitations would have produced still finer
had they not thus been fettered. One point, slight in
itself, but characteristic, may be mentioned in illustration
of this rigid conservatism—the prescribed position for the
representation of walking was that the left leg should
be the forward one. Amongst all the hundreds of statues
and paintings, no example has ever yet been seen of a man
advancing with his right foot in advance of the left!

On the mummy wrappings, cartonnage, or coffins, the
ornament, apart from various religious emblems, is ordinarily of a very simple character, being chiefly bands,
an inch or so wide, of simple floral forms, each row
or band being quite independent in treatment of those
adjacent to it. This continuous repetition of simple units
is a very marked characteristic of Egyptian ornament.
The lotus flower, or its bud, or its fruit, or detached
petals of it, are the most favourite forms.

Repetition as a principle in design is very freely met
with in the ornament of all peoples, as there is a certain
charm in the regular sequence of units, even though these
units in themselves have very little to commend them.
One sees this even in the commonest wall paper or chintz
of to-day, and it may be equally well seen in the diapering

---

[1] Archaic work is the early and imperfect work, the immature
production of beginners. The deliberate imitation of this early work,
with all its shortcomings, should be distinguished by the term
Archeistic.

of Gothic work, the egg-and-tongue and other mouldings
in classic work, and, in fact, throughout the art of every
period.   Fig. 10 is a very good illustration of this, as the
richness of effect in the Indian things therein represented
is entirely produced by the repetition over their surfaces
of a few very simple forms.   Other characteristic instances
may be seen in Figs. 99, 100, 101, 133, 134, 175, 176.

Though ordinarily it is only the simpler forms that
submit happily to this repetition, the Egyptians, in their
colossal figures of the king and their avenues of sphinxes,
did not scruple to avail themselves of it, and, it must be
admitted, with grand effect.

Alternation is an agreeable variation on the absolute
repetition of a single form.   The Greeks were well aware
of this, and we see examples of it in much of their work,
as, for example, in the anthemion patterns, Figs. 40, 63,
and we may see other good illustrations of it in Fig. 1,
an Assyrian tile design, and Figs. 61 and 62.

The Egyptians made a considerable use of diaper patterns, but they were always based on a very simple geometrical foundation, ordinarily in chequers, like a chessboard, and are quite wanting in the richness of treatment
that many later styles have developed.

The dull mechanical uniformity of machine repetition
is hostile to the best art, and we must here point out that
all the Egyptian examples we have ever seen illustrated
in any books on the subject are drawn far too carefully
and regularly.   In real Egyptian work, as any one may
satisfy themselves by a visit to the British Museum, the
repetition of the forms is ordinarily not at all exact.

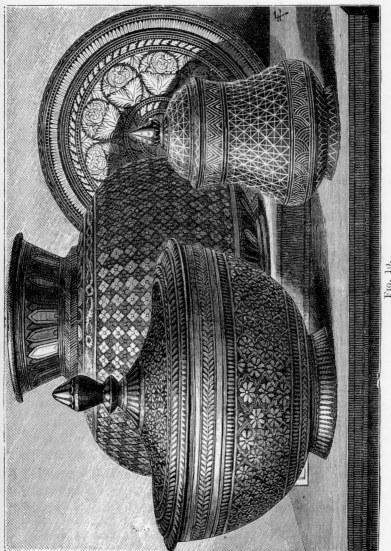

Fig. 10.

33

D

The lotus, the beautiful lily of the Nile, is one of the most characteristic forms in Egyptian ornament. It was dedicated to Isis and Osiris, and was also an emblem of fertility from its association with the great river that, by its annual overflow, brought plenty to the land, and made Egypt the granary of the ancient world. This mysterious and life-sustaining river, flowing they knew not from whence, they deified as Hapi, the hidden one, and worshipped as the giver of all good. At the period of inundation great festival was made, sacrifices offered, and hymns of praise chanted to the beneficent being who poured in rich abundance his blessing on the thirsty land. The following lines are a portion of one of these poems of rejoicing :—

> " Hail to thee, O Nile !
>   Coming in peace, giving life unto Egypt,
>   And, without ceasing, watering the land.
>   Lover of good, bestower of corn,
>   Offerings are made to thee,
>   Oxen are slain to thee,
>   Shine forth in glory, O Nile ! "

Thus the lotus, from its beauty and its intimate connection with the Nile, became the symbol of Hapi, the life-giver, and entered freely into the decoration of almost everything. The columns of the temples had ordinarily their capitals in the form of the lotus bud or of the fully expanded flower, and we find the same beautiful symbol again in the pottery, jewellery, and, in fact, everything susceptible of decoration.[1]

---

[1] We learn from various old writers that the lotus was also an article of food. " The Egyptians," says Herodotus, for example, " who

A certain amount of confusion has arisen from the fact that a plant somewhat similar in form, and often called the lotus, is very freely introduced into Indian, Chinese, and Japanese art. This is, however, the sacred bean, the attribute of Ganga, the goddess of the Ganges. On the creation of the world by Vishnu we are told that he first produced the lotus, and that from its expanding flower sprang Brahma. With the Buddhists it is the emblem of life-giving fertility and the throne of Buddha. This deity is by his reverent followers referred to, not by name, but as " he who sits upon the lotus," and in all statues of Buddha the petals of this flower may be seen around the base. Hence, in all countries where Buddhism prevails, the sacred bean, the so-called lotus, is an ever-recurring symbol. Both the Egyptian and the Indian types of lotus flower freely in the Royal Botanic Gardens at Kew ; and as they are both in the same conservatory, com-

---

live in the marshy grounds, make use of the following expedient to procure themselves more easily the means of subsistence. When the waters have risen to their extreme height, and all their fields are overflowed, there appears above the surface an immense quantity of plants of the lily species, which the Egyptians call the lotus, and which they cut down and dry in the sun. The seed of the flower, which resembles that of the poppy, they bake and make into a kind of bread ; they also eat the root of this plant, which is round, of an agreeable flavour, and about the size of an apple." The same plant is thus described by Theophrastus : " The lotus of Egypt grows in the inundated fields. Its flowers are like those of the lily. They grow close to one another in great numbers. The flowers close at the setting of the sun, and sink below the water, but when the sun rises they again open and reappear. The fruit is equal to that of a large poppy, and contains a large number of grains resembling those of millet."

parison becomes very easy. Botanically, the Egyptian plant is the *Nymphœa Lotus*, and the sacred bean the *Nelumbium speciosum*.

The paper reed or papyrus, the *Cyperus Papyrus* of science, is also freely introduced in Egyptian work. It may be seen growing luxuriantly at Kew in the same house as the lotus and sacred bean. As the lotus symbolised the satisfaction of bodily wants, so the papyrus was an emblem of the provision of sustenance for the mind, since it supplied the paper upon which all records were made. Many of these MSS. still exist in almost perfect condition. Strabo, Pliny, and other old writers give a full description of the method of preparing the paper from the plant.

In the great hall of the temple of Karnak columns forty-two feet high and nine feet in diameter are copied from the papyrus, and their capitals are the unopened bud, while at their bases are conventionalised representations of the scales met with in that position in the real plant. The stem of the papyrus is three-angled, in order that it may resist the pressure of the current, and in all papyrus columns the Egyptians always carefully preserved the three lines down their shafts that represented these edges. Often the columns are composed of eight or more of these reeds bound together,[1] and in this case a series of horizontal bands just below the capital represent the cord that binds them together. Wood of any considerable size

---

[1] A very good example of one of these clustered columns may be seen in the British Museum. It is from the temple of Luxor.

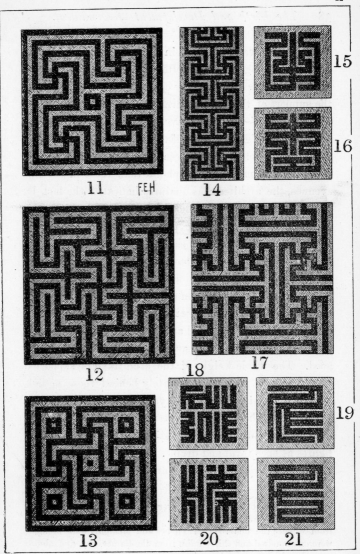

15

16

19

VARIOUS FORMS OF FRET-PATTERNS.

and strength was very rare in Egypt, so that bundles of
papyrus tied together were often used instead, and these
makeshift posts were gravely copied in stone, and became
the support of the massive architrave reared upon them.[1]
The columns of the central avenue in this hall at Karnak
are yet more gigantic, being sixty-six feet high and twelve
feet in diameter; and as these may be considered to be
still finer and more mature plants than those in the side
avenues, the architect has quaintly indicated the fact by
representing the capitals, not as buds, but as fully expanded. In the Ptolemaic period we find a considerable
use of the palm leaf on the capitals and elsewhere.

Another marked characteristic of Egyptian work was
the great use made of human and animal forms. The
façade of the hall of columns already referred to shows
us colossal figures thirty feet high represented Rameses
as Osiris, holding the flail and crook as emblems of his
power to punish the evil, and to protect and guide the
good. The whole weight of the architrave is supported
on the square pillars immediately behind these figures.
In Greek architecture the caryatid figures actually support on their heads the superstructure, but the Egyptian
architect shrank from suggesting such a duty for his
figures at once royal and divine.

The best example of these anthropomorphic pillars is

---

[1] One of the horizontal blocks over a doorway at Karnak is over
forty feet long and five feet square. The great quarries of Syene,
from whence the materials for Thebes and Memphis were brought,
were one hundred and thirty miles from the former city, and almost
seven hundred from the latter!

seen in the Erechtheum at Athens. When male figures
are introduced, they are ordinarily shown as bearing their
burden at the expense of considerable muscular effort.
Such figures are termed Atlantes or Telamones.[1] Female
figures, termed Caryatides, are represented as tranquil
and quiescent, bearing their burden with ease and quiet
dignity. As our field of study is a very large one, we
can scarcely stay to explain the various technical terms
that arise; but students will find either Fairholt's "Dictionary of Art" or Gwilt's "Encyclopædia of Architecture" excellent books of reference. Both are freely illustrated. The latter has over fifteen hundred figures.

The Isis-headed columns of the temples at Dendera,
Edfou, and elsewhere may also be referred to. The
various deities represented are almost invariably given
the heads of animals; thus Anubis has the head of a
jackal, Thoth that of the ibis, Khnum that of the ram,
Ra that of the hawk.[2] We also find figures with the
heads of the ape, lion, wolf, dog, cat, and many other
creatures. It is impossible to assign any precedence of
power or dignity amongst these, as each principal city
had its local group of divinities. Several other animals,
such as the bull, cow, shrew-mouse, goose, crocodile,
beetle, and eel, were sacred as the incarnations of various

---

[1] "If the end of art is to please, the impression produced by figures
standing in uncomfortable positions, supporting weights which would
crush them in reality, is, to say the least, very unpleasing, and
therefore must be artistically untrue."—Mayeux's "Decorative Composition," a book from which the student may derive some useful
hints.

[2] Ra being the Sun-god, bears on his head the circular solar disk.

deities, and all may be freely met with in Egyptian sculpture, mural decoration, charms, articles of personal adornment, and so forth.

The winged globe is a very characteristic Egyptian form. The globe is supposed to represent the Sun, and the wings the shielding protection of the deity, while the asps on either side imply dominion. This symbolic ornament is generally placed over doors and other openings, and is very commonly painted on the mummy cases. The asp alone is also very freely met with, a long series of these being often the only decoration of a frieze or other band of ornament. As symbols of sovereignty they are often placed again on either side of the cartouche that bears the name and titles of the Pharaoh.

An attempt was made by Amenophis III. and his immediate successors to substitute for the polytheistic national creed the worship of the Sun alone, but the change was not an enduring one. Those holding it endeavoured to efface the effigies of the other gods, but without avail; and revolution, followed by a new dynasty, resulted in the restoration of the ancient religious usages and beliefs.

Sun-worship is one of the oldest forms of religion and one of the most widespread. The following hymn from the Rig-Veda of the Hindus is very striking: " In the beginning there arose the Golden One: as soon as he was born he alone was the Lord of all that is. He established the earth and heaven. Who is the God to whom we shall offer sacrifice? He who gives breath, he who gives strength, whose command all the bright gods revere, whose

shadow is death." The Rig-Veda is of unknown antiquity. Hindu tradition gives 3101 B.C., or nearly 5,000
years ago, as the date of its composition. The Vedic
cult was in force long before the rise of Buddhism in the
sixth century B.C. Professor Max Muller, an authority
of immense weight on such matters, thinks it cannot well
be more modern than 1000 B.C.

The Israelites, who came much beneath the influence of
the Egyptians, were repeatedly warned against this form
of idolatry.[1] Manasseh, we read in 2 Kings xxi. 3, "worshipped all the host of heaven," and in chapter xxiii. we
read of the idolatrous priests of Judah "that burned
incense unto Baal, to the sun, and to the moon." Other
interesting confirmatory passages may be found in 2 Kings
xvii. 16 and xxiii. 4, Jeremiah viii. 2 and xix. 13,
Zephaniah i. 5, and Acts vii. 42.

One of the most marked features of Egyptian art is
massiveness. The figure of Rameses the Great prostrate
before his royal palace-temple is twenty-two feet from
shoulder to shoulder, and a toe is three feet long; the
pyramid of Khufu[2] covers over thirteen acres of ground.
Herodotus tells us that its construction necessitated the
continuous labour of a hundred thousand men for twenty
years, while the obelisks carved from one solid block of
stone are in their degree as wonderful. There are no
less than twelve of these Egyptian obelisks in Rome, the

---

[1] As for example—"Lest thou lift up thine eyes unto heaven, and
when thou seest the sun and the moon and the stars, even all the
host of heaven, should be driven to worship them."

[2] B.C. 3733-3700.

largest being a gigantic monolith of red granite one hundred and six feet high. It originally stood in front of the Temple of the Sun at Thebes, but was removed to Rome by the Emperor Constantius. Another of these was brought by Augustus Cæsar after his victory at Actium. It came from the Temple of the Sun at Heliopolis. The well-known obelisk in the centre of the piazza of St. Peter's Cathedral was brought to Rome by Caligula. Our own so-called Cleopatra's Needle was one of a pair that were set up by the great temple builder Thothmes III. about B.C. 1600 at On, or the City of the Sun, better known perhaps under its Greek name of like significance, Heliopolis. The hieroglyphics upon it point to its consecration to solar worship, and to these, two centuries later, Rameses added others commemorative of some of his victories. Its association with Cleopatra is a comparatively modern affair, as it was not removed by her to her royal capital at Alexandria till some sixteen centuries afterwards. Some eighteen centuries again after this, A.D. 1878, it was again removed to grace the capital of another royal lady. *Sic transit gloria mundi.* The companion obelisk, after a similar break of the journey for centuries at Alexandria, has travelled from Heliopolis to New York. When the Assyrian kings came into contact with Egypt, they seem to have been greatly impressed with these obelisks; so that when Ashur-bani-pal, the Sardanapalus of the Greek historians, invaded Egypt, he carried away two of these massive monoliths from Thebes to Nineveh. No traces of them have been found, and it was probable that they were broken up during one-of the sieges of Nineveh, though it is quite possible that they may yet be found, as much excavating still remains to be done. It is recorded in the Ninevite inscriptions that they were covered with hieroglyphs, and were esteemed as very curious and valuable works of art. Cleopatra's Needle is sixty-nine feet high, while that of Luxor in the Place de la Concorde, in Paris, is a little over seventy-two.

This feature of massive bulk is characteristic of much early work: in illustration of this we need only refer to the great chryselephantine statue of Zeus, the Colossus of Rhodes, or in our own land to the mysterious stone circles of Avebury and Stonehenge.

Egyptian art, after a duration of centuries, finally declined on the accession of the Ptolemies, the Greek influences then introduced being altogether alien in spirit to those that had hitherto ruled supreme. In some work of this period the style is wholly Greek; while in one example that has come under our notice, the capital is a strange compound of the lotus and the acanthus.

All knowledge of the rise of the Babylonian empire is lost in the mists of far-reaching antiquity. The earliest kings of Babylon that are mentioned in the inscriptions are Entenna, who reigned about B.C. 4200, and Sargon I., who dates approximately B.C. 3750. This kingdom gradually extended northwards along the Tigris, and Ashur, Nineveh,[1] and other cities were built; but about B.C. 1700

---

[1] "Out of that land went forth Asshur and builded Nineveh" (Gen. x. 11).

this northern extension of the old Babylonian empire re-
volted, and not only secured its independence as the kingdom of Assyria, but turned its arms against Babylonia
and subdued it. Almost constant conflicts were waged,
however, with varying success; but into these details it
is foreign to our present purpose to go, as the Assyrians
were for centuries victorious, and became the great dominant race of Western Asia. In the year 885 B.C., Ashur-
nasir-pal, one of the greatest of the Assyrian monarchs,
ascended the throne, and under the reign of this great
warrior and law-giver the arts greatly flourished. Sargon
II., B.C. 722–705, built the great palace of Khorsabad, of
which so many interesting relics have been brought to the
British Museum, while his son Sennacherib erected a still
grander palace at Kyonjik. His son, again, Esarhaddon,
was a great builder, and the excavations at Nimroud and
Nineveh have revealed much of his work. About B.C. 609
the Medes and Babylonians invaded Assyria, and after a
two years' siege of the capital, Nineveh was destroyed,
and the once mighty empire was divided amongst its
many adversaries and passed out of existence. The
Assyrians were ruthless conquerors,[1] and in their sculptures we see abundant proof of their prowess and their
cruelty. The measure that they had meted out to the
men of Babylon, of Judah, of Israel, of Syria, Egypt,

---

[1] In the prophecy of Nahum we read, " Woe to the bloody city ! "
Hence after his declaration that the city shall be destroyed by fire,
he adds that all that hear of the final downfall of Nineveh shall clap
their hands in glad rejoicing, " for upon whom hath not thy wicked-
ness passed continually ? "

Media, and Phœnicia, at last became their own lot, and Nineveh disappeared in blood and flame and righteous vengeance, and was for centuries but a name.

> " To my soul
> The days of old return : I breathe the air
> Of the young world: I see her giant sons
> Like to a gorgeous pageant in the sky
> Of Summer's evening, cloud on fiery cloud
> Thronging unheaped : before me rise the walls
> Of the Titanic city : brazen gates,
> Towers, temples, palaces, enormous piled ;
> Imperial Nineveh, the earthly queen !
> In all her golden pomp I see her now ;
> Her swarming streets ; her splendid festivals ;
> Her sprightly damsels to the timbrels' sound
> Airily bounding, and their anklets chime ;
> Her lusty sons, like Summer morning gay ;
> Her warriors stern ; her rich robed rulers grave ;
> I see her halls brightly at midnight shine,
> I hear the music of her banquetings.
> Again I look: and lo ! before the walls
> Unnumber'd hosts in flaming panoply ;
> Chariots like fire,—horsemen with flashing arms !
> I hear the shouts of battle—like the waves
> Of a tumultuous sea they roll and dash !
> In flame and smoke the imperial city sinks !
> Her walls are gone : her palaces are dust :
> Within and around her lies the desert:
> Oh, how like shadows have all passed away ! " [1]

The entire disappearance of Nineveh arose from the materials employed. While the Egyptians and Greeks built their temples of granite, marble, and such-like durable material, the Assyrians built with sun-dried brick, and only used alabaster, marble, and kiln-burnt

---

[1] Atherstone.

tiles to a slight extent as ornamental details. The roofs
and pillars were of wood ; and when the place was given
to the flames, the upper walls soon fell in and buried
everything. The imperfectly burnt bricks reverted in
time to their natural clay, and for something like two
thousand years these mounds and heaps have grown grass
and corn, and been the sites of peasant dwellings, while
the palaces of mighty kings were buried beneath.

> " Those golden pallaces, those gorgeous halles,
>   With fourniture superflouslie faire,
> Those statlie courts, those sky-encountring walles
>   Evanish all like vapours in the aire. " [1]

In the year 1842, M. Botta, a Frenchman, made several
excavations on the site of the ancient city and at Khorsabad, a few miles north of Nineveh ; while a year or
two later Layard began investigations in a great mound
at Nimroud, some miles to the south. M. Botta was successful in finding the palace of Sargon, and sent off many
interesting sculptures to Paris ; while our countryman,
Layard, discovered at Nimroud the palaces of Ashur-
nasir-pal, of Shalmaneser II., and of Esarhaddon, and
dispatched a goodly store of material of great historic
and artistic interest to the British Museum. Later on,
at Kyonjik, the site of ancient Nineveh, many other
most interesting discoveries, associated with Sennacherib,
Ashur-bani-pal, and other monarchs, were made. Of the
palace of Sennacherib, " no less than seventy-one halls,
chambers, and passages were explored, whose walls,
almost without an exception, were panelled with slabs of

---

[1] Stirling, 1604.

sculptured alabaster, recording the wars, the triumphs, and other great deeds of the Assyrian king." Thus wrote Layard, and he adds that in this vast and magnificent building the bas-reliefs would, if placed in one line, have reached nearly two miles. Though the Biblical account itself gives many details that indicate a marked similarity between the great buildings of Solomon and those of the sovereigns of Nineveh, Josephus adds a very character- istic feature when he states that Solomon built some of these with stones of ten cubits in length, and wainscotted the walls with other stones that were sawn. This latter clause at once recalls to our minds the marble slabs on the palace walls of Nineveh. In 1854, Rawlinson com- menced excavations at Babylon, some three hundred miles to the south, and in the great mound at Birs Nimroud found the remains of the palace of King Nebuchadnezzar. Since this period several other explorers have been busily at work, and sculptures, tiles, and written records of immense interest have been unearthed.

After the destruction of Nineveh the Babylonian em- pire lasted some seventy years, but in the reign of Belshazzar, Cyrus, B.C. 539, conquered the country, and it remained beneath the Persian sway until Alexander the Great destroyed the Persian empire and brought all beneath the dominion of Greece. The Persians succeeded to the arts as well as the empire of the Babylonians, and their sovereigns maintained palaces in Babylon, though their capital city was at first Passargadæ. This was later on supplanted by the far more magnificent Perse- polis, the regal residence of Darius, Xerxes, and other

monarchs. The British Museum has acquired by the
labours of Mr. Cecil Smith an excellent series of examples
from the magnificent sculptures of Persepolis, most interesting artistically, and also as illustrating many passages in the Bible and in the writings of Herodotus.

Egyptian art, we have seen, quickly reached a point
when no further progress in it was possible. It became
bound in the iron fetters of a rigid conventionalism imposed upon it by the priesthood, and certain canons were
laid down and adhered to for many centuries from which
neither the representations of gods nor men might differ.
No healthy art growth, therefore, was possible to them
within these limitations, though we see by their representations of the lower animals—of dogs, birds, and the
like—that there was a greater artistic power in them
than the tyranny under which they were held would ever
allow them scope for. In the art of Assyria, on the contrary, there was abundant life and liberty; and though
we rarely, if ever, find it except as ministering to the
pomp of the monarch, so far as it goes it is full of power.
The king plunges with vengeful cruelty his javelin into
the eyes of his suppliant foe, pours out libations to his
gods, or engages with fierce energy in the chase, and in
every case the story is admirably told. In the lion hunts
we see the great savage animals creeping with stealthy
steps for the final spring, dragging their wounded bodies,
arrow-transfixed, along the ground, or clutching at the
chariot wheels in intensity of despairing rage; while in
others the relaxed limbs testify that death has ended
their sufferings. A lioness that drags herself slowly

along, her hinder limbs paralysed by an arrow, while she snarls defiance at her foes, lives especially in our memory. The attitudes of the animals are varied in the extreme. The huge hunting dogs are also finely portrayed, animals of most ferocious aspect. No bear hunt of Snyders or stag hunt of Landseer could give more fully the spirit and resolution of the animals than we find them rendered in these ancient slabs, the sculptured decorations of the long buried palaces of ancient Assyria, and no other antique remains can at all compare with them for vigour and power. The representations of the chase of the wild bull or the antelope are equally graphic, the expression of art free to do its uttermost, and ever seeking its inspiration where alone it should be sought— not in rules and formulæ, but in the presence of living nature. The Egyptian artists undoubtedly attained to a certain stately dignity of repose; while the Assyrians, in trying for much more than this, naturally made some failures, but they were the failures of honest endeavour; and while the art of Thebes was art-death, that of Kyonjik was art-life.

It has been held that the art of Assyria was merely an off-shoot of that of Egypt; but while the Assyrians undoubtedly borrowed some ideas from the valley of the Nile, the architecture, sculpture, and decoration of the palace-temples of Nineveh and Babylon had a strong individuality of its own. The Assyrians, like the Romans later on, were not themselves an artistic people, but they were prompt in utilising the art of others, and they largely employed foreign artists in their buildings, much

E

of the Assyrian work being produced by Phœnicians or Egyptians, sometimes as honoured guests, but more frequently as captives of war. Some of the ivory carvings found at Nimroud have distinctly Egyptian ornamentation—a proof of an intimate connection between Egypt and Assyria at a very early period—while others bore Phœnician inscriptions. These may be seen in the British Museum.

One interesting evidence of the intimate political intercourse between Egypt and Assyria is that amongst the collection of clay seals found by Layard at Kyonjik is one with two impressions of royal signets, one being that of Sennacherib and the other that of Sabaco. The treaty of peace or other state document to which this attestation was attached has perished ages ago, but the clay seal still remains to testify to this association of the two monarchs. This Sabaco is the " So, King of Egypt," of the Bible record.

From the earliest ages of which we possess any records, the employment of inscriptions has been a conspicuous feature—a feature extending chronologically from the childhood of the world throughout the intervening centuries to the present day; and geographically from the mysterious buildings of bygone races in Mexico and Peru, to the work of the teeming millions of Hindustan, and yet more distant China. Such inscriptions are found not alone on the stately monuments reared at the command of some ambitious ruler, or on the massive tomb that marks his resting-place, but on all the multiplicity of objects that come beneath the hand of the art-worker.

III

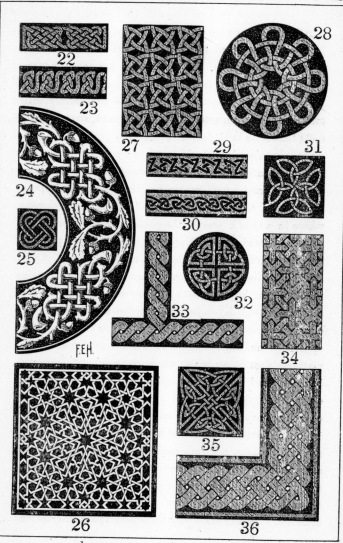

INTERLACINGS FROM VARIOUS SOURCES.

51

All inscriptions for our present purpose may be divided into two broad and distinct classes—those that are primarily decorative, and those that are not. A great many of the inscriptions that we come across, we need scarcely point out, are thoroughly and exclusively utilitarian in their character and motive, mere statements of facts that it is held desirable that the reader should be made acquainted with, but neither possessing nor professing artistic merit. As an instance of these, we may quote one from a well-known building in the metropolis. The style of the building is classic, and in the pediment, where in a Greek temple the noblest sculpture would be placed, we read, " Corn Exchange, erected 1828, pursuant to Act of Parliament, 7th Geo. IV. cap. 55."

The long lines of arrowhead characters, rich and quaint in effect as they are, that run across the sculptures of Khorsabad and Kyonjik belong to the former of our two classes; for decorative in appearance as the characters appear to us, the inscriptions, when translated, are the matter-of-fact records of victories won, catalogues of besieged and conquered cities, enumerations of vanquished peoples, details of the spoil of war, or perchance the narrative of the successes of the royal hunter, whose achievements in the battle-field, or in pursuit of the wild beasts, are represented in the sculptured slab across which the long lines of cuneiform writing are thrown. Our illustration, Fig. 4, gives the name and titles of King Darius, from a cylinder in the British Museum.[1]   In the same way the hieroglyphic inscriptions

---

[1] Sir Thomas Herbert, in his book entitled " Some Yeares Travels

FIG. 37.

on the temples of Egypt were not primarily decorative
in motive, however decorative they are actually in effect.
Their distinct intention was to inform the reader, and to
appeal to the mind rather than to the eye, though to the
great bulk of mankind nowadays the forms convey no
meaning, and only impress us from their quaintness of
form and the brilliancy of their colouring, and one might
therefore very naturally, but erroneously, regard them as
being essentially decorative in intention. Fig. 3, the
name and titles of Amunothph II., affords us a good idea
of their general character.

The Assyrians made a very great use of colour in their
architecture, sculpture, and wherever else in decoration it
was practicable to employ it, and from the remains of gold
leaf abundantly found amongst the ruins it is evident
that a profuse use of gilding was also made. The Jews
had much intercourse with Assyria, and any one reading carefully the description of the Temple of Solomon—
a building contemporary with the best period of Assyrian
art—will really derive a very good idea of much of the

into Africa and Asia," the edition of 1677 being before us as we write,
says of the arrowhead : "How inconceivable soever these characters
be to us, yet doubtless in the age these were engraven they were both
legible and intelligible, and not to be imagined that they were there
placed either to amuse or to delude the spectators. I have thought
fit to insert a few of these for better demonstration, which, nevertheless, whiles they cannot be read, will in all probability, like the Mene
Tekel, without the help of a Daniel hardly be interpreted ; " a surmise that the skill of many learned scholars has since rendered
entirely out of date. For centuries the world has evidently been on
the verge of the discoveries that the excavations of Layard, Botta,
and others have only in these latter days brought to light.

detail of the palaces of Nineveh. Solomon too, like the Assyrian monarchs, availed himself of Phœnician aid ; the men of Hiram, king of Tyre, cutting cedar trees in abundance, and providing a man " skilful to work in gold, and in silver, in brass, in iron, in stone, and in timber, in purple, in blue, and in fine linen, and in crimson ; also to grave any manner of graving." Portions of charred cedar beams from the roofs of the palaces are abundantly found in the excavations in Assyria, and in the Ninevite inscriptions the king is described as going, as the men of Tyre did for Solomon, to the forests of Lebanon for the cedar required for his palace. Solomon, we read, ceiled his temple with cedar, and " overlaid also the house, the beams, the posts, and the walls thereof with gold " ; and the beams had " set thereon palm trees and chains." These palm trees were doubtless the radiate form that is termed the anthemion ; while the chains would be the interlacing circle pattern known as the guilloche. Both these forms may be very well seen in Fig. 1, a piece of pure Assyrian work from a tile now in the British Museum. The cherubim have been described by commentators as mystic figures having the head of a man conjoined to the body of an ox or lion, and having the wings of an eagle ; and therefore of the same nature as the colossal figures so abundantly met with in the palaces of Assyria. " The molten sea," supported on figures of bulls, and the brim of it adorned " with flowers of lilies," is another illustration, and that these flowers of lilies were doubtless the conventional lotus we may very reasonably conclude.

The colours found in the ruins of the Assyrian temples are blue, red, yellow, white, green, and black. All these are pigments having a mineral base. If they employed others having a vegetable origin, the more fugitive nature of these has led to their entire decay. One conspicuous feature in Assyrian ornament is the very strong black outline : this may be seen very well in Fig. 1. The Assyrians delighted in strong contrasts, the colours in the tile referred to being pure white and dense black on a buff ground; and they were also very partial, as here, to confining themselves to two colours in a piece of ornament, often even in an elaborate design combining them very happily and producing a very rich effect.

The geometrical patterns seen in pavements, metal-work patterns, and so forth, are of a considerably richer character in Assyrian than in Egyptian work.

The form known as the Sacred Tree (Fig. 37) is abundantly met with; and it is always accompanied by winged deities, standing or kneeling, one on either side. It probably represents the Tree of Life, a mysterious symbol that is found in many religious systems. In primæval Eden stood the Tree of Life,[1] and in the Paradise of God it re-appears; and it is not improbable that the impor-

---

[1] " In this pleasant soil
His far more pleasant garden God ordained ;
Out of the fertile ground He caused to grow
All trees of noblest kind, for sight, smell, taste.
And all amid them stood the tree of life,
High, eminent, blooming, with ambrosial fruit
Of vegetable gold."

—MILTON.

FIG. 38.

tance thus given to this mysterious form subsequently developed into tree worship.[1] The oak under which Abraham received his celestial guests was for centuries regarded with veneration, while the Jews were constantly being rebuked by the prophets for their idolatrous worship in groves. One need only name, too, the great oracle of the Oak of Dodona, and the sanctity of the oak with the Druids. The peepul, or bo-tree (*Ficus religiosa*), is in the East associated with Buddha ; [2] and in Africa the fetish-tree is an object of much veneration and awe.[3]

The colossal human-headed and eagle-winged bulls are another very marked characteristic of Assyrian art. They were ordinarily placed as though guarding the entrances. They were doubtless emblematic figures—the human head signifying wisdom, the body of the bull power, and the wings of the eagle ubiquity. The prophet Ezekiel saw in his wondrous vision living creatures, winged, and having respectively the heads of

---

[1] " With all their poetry and all their usefulness, we can hardly feel astonished that the primitive races of mankind should have considered trees as the choicest gifts of God to man, and should have believed that their spirits still delighted to dwell among their branches, or spoke oracles through their rustling leaves."—DR. FERGUSON : " Tree and Serpent Worship."

[2] See Knighton's book on " Forest Life in Ceylon," for much interesting matter thereon.

[3] The word Coomassie means " the town round the tree," the houses being all built around this fetish. On the day, during the war with Ashanti, that Sir Garnet Wolseley sent his ultimatum to the king, a bird of ill-omen was seen to perch upon this tree ; and half an hour afterwards a violent gale sprang up, and the fetish was levelled to the ground. This caused a profound sensation among the Ashantees.

a man, a lion, an ox, and an eagle—the four sacred types of the Assyrians. His auditors could well realize the imagery, as both he and they had been carried away captive by Shalmaneser, and must have been very familiar with these typical forms in Assyrian symbolism.

The magnificent ruins of Persepolis, the capital of the ancient kingdom of Persia, recall at once to us the well-known types of Assyrian work, though it is not necessary to assume that they were copied from them. Nineveh was already but a heap of forgotten ruins when Persepolis arose. The influence of commerce on the one hand, and war on the other, had largely affected the individuality of the various nationalities ; and though we find certain characteristic and localised forms, there is no doubt but that there was a general art tradition that influenced all, and a continuous passing to and fro of cunning workmen that more or less blended into one the art of the Egyptians, Jews, Assyrians, Babylonians, Phœnicians, Medes, and Persians.

The Phœnicians were a great mercantile people, and their vessels traversed every sea of the then known world. The shores of the Mediterranean were studded thickly with their colonies.[1] The woad-stained Celts of Britain exchanged their tin for the productions of the East, and long before the Christian era they had circumnavigated Africa. Their merchants were equally at home in the markets of Egypt and Ethiopia, of Persia and India, and the riches of the world were poured into Tyre and

---

[1] Carthage, founded about B.C. 1800, being the most important.

Sidon.[1]   They were distributors perhaps rather than producers, though Homer frequently refers to their artistic skill.   Thus we read of the Queen of Troy intending to offer a mantle or robe to Pallas :—

> " Herself, the while, her chamber, ever sweet
> With burning odours, sought.   There stored she kept
> Her mantles of all hues, accomplished works
> Of fair Sidonians, wafted o'er the deep
> By God-like Paris, when the galleys brought¦
> The high-born Helen to the shores of Troy.
> From these the widest and of brightest dyes
> She chose for Pallas : radiant as a star
> It glittered."

Achilles at the funeral games for Patroclus offers as a prize—

> " A silver goblet, of six measures: earth
> Own'd not its like for elegance of form.
> Skilful Sidonian artists had around
> Embellish'd it : and o'er the sable deep,
> Phœnician merchants unto Lemnos' port
> Had borne it, and the boon to Thaos given."

In the Odyssey we meet—

> " A fair Phœnician, tall, full-sized, and skilled
> In works of elegance,"

who on interrogation by the wanderers, affirms—

> " I am of Sidon, famous for her wealth,
> By dyeing earn'd."

When Telemachus expressed his surprise and delight at the art treasures of gold and silver, brass and ivory

---

[1] " Tyre, the crowning city, whose merchants are princes, whose traffickers are the honourable of the earth."—Isaiah xxiii. 8.

that he saw in the palace of Menelaus, his host informed
him that they were gathered from Cyprus, Phœnicia, and
Egypt. Much of the Phœnician work, as in the examples of pottery in Fig. 38, is quaint and bizarre, and
one finds in it little of the dignity and beauty of that of
the nations—the Egyptians, Assyrians, and Persians—from
whom they freely borrowed. The Greeks, later on—a
people as energetic and far more artistic—supplanted
them, and took from them their mercantile supremacy.
Thus, to take but one instance, the prosperity of the
ancient Greek colony of Samos arose almost entirely from
its pottery. The Samians carried on a most important
trade in this, and their beautiful productions are found
everywhere amongst the *débris* of the great cities of
Greece, Rome, and other centres of ancient civilization.
Its merchants became princes, and this little island of
the Mediterranean, in thus directing its energies to the
cultivation of the arts, attained mercantile and political
pre-eminence and undying fame.[1]

The world of art is curiously knit together. One striking example of the curious distribution that has always
been going on may be seen in the antiquities found in a
tomb near Volci, in Etruria. These—terra-cotta vases and

---

[1] "Art-knowledge is of value to the individual and to the country
at large. Take, for example, clay as a natural material : in the
hands of one man this becomes flower-pots, worth eighteen pence a
cast (a number varying from sixty to twelve, according to size) ; in
the hands of another it becomes a tazza or a vase, worth five pounds,
or perhaps fifty. It is the art which gives the value, and not the
material."—DRESSER.

figures, etc.—may be seen in the British Museum, and amongst them may be observed an Egyptian porcelain scarab bearing the name and titles of Psammeticus I. (656–611 B.C.). How that got there it would be very interesting and instructive to know. Many of the things found at Etruria, a district in North-west Italy, are very Assyrian in character.

With the Romans, as we shall see more fully later on, art was practically an exotic, and they drew their supplies in a great measure from the foreigner. In our own country the influence of commerce has been most marked, as, like the Phœnicians of old, our merchants have supplied the markets of the world, exporting in some directions, importing in others, and thus distributing and circulating art, good, bad, and indifferent, the wide world over.[1] By means of this commerce we have gone far to vitiate the wonderful art instinct of the millions of India and Japan, and through its aid we have brought to ourselves the choicest examples of all kinds of art products from every art centre, north, south, east, and west.

Political events have also had their influence in this circulation of art. Thus persecution in a land has driven out thence many capable workers who have enriched by their skill the countries to which they wandered;

---

[1] We remember, when going over a large warehouse in Manchester, seeing thousands of coarse white plates for the African trade. Each had one splash of bright red colour and one of crude blue on it, these ragged blotches of raw colour falling anyhow and anywhere on the plates. We also saw there an immense variety of beads for use amongst the various tribes. All things to all men, so long as money could be made—a very Phœnician view!

and in France, Italy, Britain, and elsewhere, powerful monarchs and wealthy nobles have invited men accomplished in the various arts to take up their abode with them. Thus Jean de Mabuse came at the invitation of Henry VII.; and during the reign of Charles I., again, many distinguished foreigners took service in our midst. France in like manner invited many famous Italians, and Primaticcio, Cellini, and many others accepted the call. Royal marriages have in like manner spread art knowledge. When Edward I. married his Spanish queen, Spanish pottery and many other articles from the home of the bride were first largely seen ; and Oriental carpets —a luxury borrowed from the Moors in that country— were introduced. Through this introduction of foreign consorts, many of the accomplishments of other countries became known to Englishmen, and were practised either by foreigners or native craftsmen.

The Moorish influence in Western and Southern Europe was also a notable factor. Sicily, from the ninth to the thirteenth century a Mohammedan country, was a great centre of artistic industry, the metal work, ivory carving, and weaving being all of the choicest description. Hence, in looking through any collection of objects, or representations of them in books, we are at once struck by their Oriental character. All Italy felt the influence, and the fabrics produced at Lucca and elsewhere are just such as were being woven in Bagdad or Cairo. The great commerce of Venice also and her outlying colonies brought her into close intimacy with the choicest Oriental art, and she cordially invited the craftsmen of the East to make their

abode with her.[1]　Few countries have a sea-coast so extended in proportion to the size of the country as Italy,
hence commerce with other lands touched her shores at
almost every point, and left its mark everywhere.　Hence
Italy was nearly as Greek as Greece, and as Arab as
Alexandria or Damascus.　To Persia we must look for
the origin of the brilliant golden or ruby lustres which,
passing with the Arabs into Spain and Italy, make the
Majolica ware of Gubbio so resplendent.

Even in the far East, amongst peoples that we have
deemed most conservative, commercial intercourse has
influenced the arts; and though the art of Japan has
travelled in excellence far beyond its parentage in China,
this relationship is undoubted.　It is curious that the

---

[1] "I stood in Venice, on the Bridge of Sighs;
　　A palace and a prison on each hand:
　　I saw from out the wave her structures rise
　　As from the stroke of the enchanter's wand:
　　A thousand years their cloudy wings expand
　　Around me, and a dying Glory smiles
　　O'er the far times, when many a subject land
　　Look'd to the winged Lion's marble piles,
　Where Venice sate in state, throned on her hundred isles!

　　She looks a sea Cybele, fresh from ocean,
　　Rising with her tiara of proud towers
　　At airy distance, with majestic motion,
　　A ruler of the waters and their powers:
　　And such she was; her daughters had their dowers
　　From spoils of nations, and the exhaustless East
　　Pour'd in her lap all gems in sparkling showers.
　　In purple was she robed, and of her feast
　Monarchs partook, and deem'd their dignity increased."
　　　　　　　　　　　　　　　　—Byron.

Chinese work of the twelfth and thirteenth centuries
much more nearly resembles the freedom of Japanese
design than does that of later date, when a purely conventional style has reigned supreme. Hence, starting
from a common standpoint, one has become more and more
naturalistic, the other more and more conventional, till at
last it is hard to realize that both were once under the
same influence. Our great-grandfathers were highly
appreciative of the work of the Celestials, and tried to
imitate it; while we, on the other hand, have found in
the art of Japan a power and character that has largely
influenced for good our designs and manufactures.

The English potters had for many years but little
higher ambition than to produce work of similar character
to that on the Chinese pottery. On the doubling of the
Cape of Good Hope by the Portuguese in 1497, Chinese
porcelain began to find its way to Europe freely. The
early productions of Worcester were chiefly imitations of
Chinese things, and they went so far as to place on
them counterfeit imitations of the marks found on the
real thing. Many pieces thus falsely marked may be
seen in collections of ceramic ware. The porcelain works
at Bow were originally called New Canton. Much of the
early Dutch pottery shows this strong Chinese influence,
and our readers will doubtless remember the popular old
" willow pattern " that has survived amongst ourselves in
all its foolish hideousness till almost the present day.

The influence of war has been another potent factor in
the dissemination of art ideas. Into the historical details
on such a point it is foreign to our present aim to go

F

at any length, interesting as it would be to do so; but we may just glance at the almost continuous struggles for supremacy that have been going on. About B.C. 1630 we find the armies of Egypt under Thothmes crossing the Asiatic frontier, and presently returning home with the spoil and tribute of a victorious campaign; while his warriors, after a reign of over fifty years of almost ceaseless war, subdued Syria and Assyria. A little later on we find Rameses I. at war with the Syrians again, and victorious over the Phœnicians and Libyans. In the year 672 we see the victorious Assyrians under Esarhaddon masters of the whole land of Egypt, and the Pharaoh a fugitive fleeing for his life to Nubia. B.C. 527 we find the Persians under Cambyses overrunning the Delta and Egypt again under the rule of the conqueror. In Assyria we have Shalmaneser master of the whole of Western Asia; Jehu, king of Israel, being one of those whom we find paying tribute. The reign of Sargon again was one long series of foreign campaigns, and in fact the same thing may be said of monarch after monarch, Egypt, Assyria, Babylonia, Media, Phœnicia, Persia, and the kingdoms of Judah and Israel being almost continuously seething in fierce and barbarous conflict. On one side or other we find the sovereign and his people carried away captive into the land of the enemy, and it is inevitable that in such constantly recurring experiences the knowledge of the sciences and arts of their conquerors must have borne fruit. The thousands of exiles that toiled for years beneath the lash of the taskmaster in rearing the temples of the conqueror had at least a very good lesson in architecture, however unwillingly they may have imbibed it.

Later on we find the States of Greece in almost constant conflict with each other or with the Persians and other powers; while the Romans have left us in their wide-spreading empire many proofs of their influence over the conquered peoples. The custom of decreeing a triumph on the return of the victor was itself an art education as well as a great patriotic festival,[1] as the conqueror paraded through the streets of Rome the choicest art treasures of the conquered race. The triumph of Paulus Emilius, B.C. 168, on his victory over Perseus, king of Macedonia, has been very fully described by Plutarch. It was the first of those magnificent spectacles with which Rome was afterwards familiar. The triumph lasted three days, and every variety of costly "loot" was displayed to the citizens, including the richest armour, vases, and other art treasures. "The first day," we read, "was scarcely sufficient to see the passing by of the images and pictures and statues of wonderful size, all won and gotten of their enemies, and drawn in the show upon two hundred and fifty chariots." The second day, to quote the quaint translation of Sir Thomas North, "there was carried upon a number of carts all the fairest and richest armour of the Macedonians, as well of copper as also of iron and steel, all glistering bright, being newly furbished, and artifici-

---

[1] It was also a valuable object lesson in science, as the natural products of the conquered territory, including possibly elephants, crocodiles, apes, giraffes, and ostriches, were made a feature of the show.

ally laid in order (and yet in such sort as if they had been cast in heaps, one upon another, without taking any care otherwise for the ordering and laying of them), fair burganets upon targets; habergions, or brigantines and corslets, upon greaves; round targets of the Cretans, and javelins of the Thracians, and arrows amongst the armed pikes; all this armour and carriage being bound one to another so trimly (neither being too loose nor too straight) that one hitting against another as they drew them upon the carts through the city, they made such a sound and noise as it was fearful to hear it : so that the only sight of these spoils of the captives being overcome made the sight so much more terrible to behold.   After these carts, laden with armour, there followed three thousand men which carried the ready money in seven hundred and fifty vessels, which weighed about three talents a-piece, and every one of them were carried by four men ; and there were other that carried great bowls of silver, cups and goblets fashioned like pitchers, and other pots to drink in, goodly to behold, as well for their bigness, as for their great and singular imbossed works about them. The third day, early in the morning, the trumpets began to sound and set forwards, sounding no march, nor sweet note to beautifie the triumph withall ; but they blew out the brave alarum they sound at an assault to give the soldiers courage for to fight.   After them followed six-score goodly fat oxen, having all their horns gilt, and garlands of flowers and nosegays about their heads, and there went by them certain young men, with aprons of needlework, girt about their middle, who led them to the sacrifice, and young boys with them also, that carried goodly basons of gold and silver, to cast and sprinkle the blood of the sacrifices about. And after these followed those that carried all coins of gold, devided by basons and vessels, and every one of them weighing three talents as they did before, that carried the great holy cup which Emylius had caused to be made of massive gold, set full of precious stones, weighing the weight of ten talents, to make an offering unto the gods. And next unto them went other that carried plate made and wrought after antique fashion, and notable cups of the ancient kings of Macedon ; as the cup called Antigonus, and another Seleucus ; and, to be short, all the whole cupboard of plate of gold and silver of King Perseus."

Another feature in the show was the procession of four hundred representatives of various cities of Greece, each bearing a golden crown of honour for presentation to the victorious general. Emilius was not only a successful soldier but a great admirer of art.

The triumph of Metellus, B.C. 146, was another great educational opportunity, as many of the choicest and most famous examples of Greek art, by Lysippus and other renowned artists and sculptors, were brought over to grace the festival. Pliny in his writings refers to the influence that such displays had upon his countrymen, in some cases apparently inciting to covetousness, while the language elsewhere suggests a worthier appreciation of these treasures. " Cæsar, when Dictator, consecrated, in the Temple of Venus Genitrix, six cabinets or caskets of rings and jewels ; and Marcellus, son to Octavia, dedicated one in the Temple Palatine of Apollo. Finally, this is to be observed, that the said victorie of Pompeius, which he atchieved over K. Mithridates, set men's teeth at Rome a watering after pearls and precious stones; like as the conquest obtained by L. Scipio and Cn. Manlius brought them into love with silver plate curiously enchased and embossed : also with rich hanging of cloth of gold, silver, and tissue; together with beds and tables of brass; even as the brasen statues and vessels of Corinthian brass, and the curious painted tables, came in request upon the victory that L. Mummius gained over Achæa."

Verres, when governor of Sicily, was accused of plundering the island of many choice works of art, as he was also said to have done in Achaia, Pontus, and other places that had the misfortune to find themselves under his domination. The Carthaginians, Persians, Macedonians, and Assyrians had in their victories all carried off such things as lawful prize of war, so that the Romans did not act without full precedent. Napoleon I. and his generals at a considerably later date stripped all the picture galleries of their numerous foes, and transported all manner of art-treasures to Paris; while the Louvre and the South Kensington Museum contain many choice examples of Chinese art that fell into their hands during an expedition that the soldiers of England and France made to Pekin.

The influence of war on art has nevertheless on the whole been distinctly more destructive than conservative. War does not create new objects of beauty; at the most it can but transfer their ownership, while *per contra* it presents unbounded facilities for their destruction. Up to the year 1687, for instance, the buildings and sculptures of the Acropolis were in almost perfect condition, when the Venetians must needs come and besiege the men of Athens; and the explosion of a magazine of gunpowder reduced in an instant to ruin what centuries of time had spared.[1]

As it would probably be considered by most of our readers to be as bad, artistically, to be a Goth or a Vandal as a Philistine, it is pleasant to put on record that these hordes, the savages that some would have us believe them to have been, were by no means all of them insensible to the claims of art. When Rome fell into the possession of Odoacer, in the year 476, he exerted himself to the utmost for the preservation of the artistic treasure of the city; and his successor, Theodoric, followed the same policy, and erected at Rome, Ravenna, and elsewhere many fine buildings. Later on, in 547, there is no doubt that Totila made a very clean sweep indeed of everything plunderable or capable of being smashed up.

The iconoclasts rose into power in 726. So enthusiastic were they for the suppression of all religious images and pictures, that during the century the sect was of influence, innumerable works of art were destroyed. The period of the Reformation in England was marked by a very similar zeal, which, however it may be defended

---

[1] The Parthenon was commenced B.C. 444, and finished B.C. 438.

from the theological point of view, wrought dire destruction of much that was of immense artistic interest.

The Crusades were a fruitful source of art development, as the Western nations then came in touch with another civilization. We find Eudes de Montreuil, a famous French architect of the thirteenth century, summoned to the Holy Land to superintend the erection of fortifications; but whatever the Saracens may have learnt from laborious and painful study of his energies in this direction, we may be well assured that they in turn opened his mind to a good many new ideas that bore fruit on his return. Crusaders and pilgrims visited in thousands the holy places, and returned home with the expansion of sympathy that is always very rightly credited to foreign travel.

On the capture of Majorca by the Pisans in the year 1115 the Moorish tiles and salvers [1] were held in such high esteem that they were built into the churches and palaces of Italy, not alone as trophies of victory, but from their decorative beauty; [2] while the Moors in Southern

---

[1] For a good book of reference the reader may turn to the "Descriptive Catalogue of the Hispano-Moresque, Persian, Damascus, and Rhodian Wares in the South Kensington Museum," by C. D. Fortnum, a book that gives a good historical notice, and the marks and monograms of the potters, and is freely illustrated both by chromo-lithographs and wood engravings. Jacquemart's "History of the Ceramic Art, a Descriptive and Philosophical Study of the Pottery of all Ages and of all Nations," containing 200 woodcuts and 1,000 marks and monograms, may also be consulted.

[2] "Majorca was valiantly defended for a whole year, but was taken about Easter, 1115, notwithstanding the energetic resistance of the Saracens, assisted by their numerous allies. The king was killed,

Spain have left behind them work of the highest interest and value.

One evil result of war upon art has been that, at the
call of patriotism and in the stress of national cala-
mity, no sacrifice that can be made is deemed too great.
Art, like everything else, must then give place. The
costliest plate is melted down to provide the sinews of
war, the choicest heirlooms are broken up if by their
destruction the cause can be at all supported or the evil
averted.[1] Hezekiah stripping the gold from the doors of
the temple, and from the pillars which he had overlaid,

---

his successor was made prisoner and conducted to Pisa, and spoils
and booty of immense value freighted the Pisan galleys in their
triumphant return to their native city. That the painted Moorish
pottery, an article of great value and supposed to have been almost
unknown at that time in Italy, formed part of these spoils, appears
probable from the fact of plates of apparently Moorish pattern and
origin being found incrusted in the walls of the most ancient
churches of Pisa, as well as in those of many other towns in Italy."
—Marryat, "Pottery and Porcelain."

"After having returned to the Conservatore the keys of the Campo
Santo, he was kind enough to walk and show me several specimens
of plates from Majorca, embedded in the walls of sundry churches of
the city, to which they form singular ornaments. It was a custom
at Pisa with the warriors returning from the Crusades and stopping
at Majorca, to bring home this peculiar earthenware by way at once
of testimony and trophy. They are accordingly only to be found in the
oldest buildings of the style that we in England should call Norman.
In San Sisto and Sta. Apollonica they are on the west front, and a
row of them is also to be seen running along the sides under the
cornice. In San Francesco are some near the top of the campanile ;
I afterwards observed others in the walls of two churches of about
the same date at Pavia."—Dawson Turner.

[1] " Clay, wood, iron, stone are materials which may well be
fashioned into beautiful forms ; but beware of silver, and of gold,
and of precious stones. The most fragile material often endures for

with the piteous cry to the great Sennacherib, "that which thou puttest upon me will I bear"; Louis Quatorze melting down the silver furniture of Versailles; Charles I. and his cavaliers turning their gold and silver into siege pieces, are but illustrations that at once rise to our minds out of multitudinous instances that might be brought forward.

Having dealt with the art of the great ancient monarchies, and endeavoured to show how, alike in peaceful commerce or in the fierce passions of sanguinary war, each was influencing all the others, and that in art as in all else it is most true that no man liveth unto himself, we turn now to a consideration of the noble art of Greece.

---

a long period of time, while the almost incorrosible silver and gold rarely escape the ruthless hand of the destroyer."—DRESSER.

"Beautiful though silver and gold are, and worthy, even though they were the commonest of things, to be fashioned into the most exquisite devices, their money value makes them a perilous material for works of art. How many of the choicest relics of antiquity are lost to us, because they tempted the thief to steal them, and then to hide his theft by melting them! How many unique designs in gold and silver have the vicissitudes of war reduced in fierce haste into money-changers' nuggets! Where are Benvenuto Cellini's vases, Lorenzo Ghiberti's cups, or the silver lamps of Ghirlandajo? Gone almost as completely as Aaron's golden pot of manna, of which, for another reason than that which kept St. Paul silent, ' we cannot now speak particularly.' Nor is it only because this is a world ' where thieves break through and steal' that the fine gold becomes dim and the silver perishes. This, too, is a world where ' love is strong as death'; and what has not love—love of family, love of brother, love of child, love of lover—prompted man and woman to do with the costliest things, when they could be exchanged or were bullion for the lives of those who were beloved?"—WILSON.

CHAPTER III.

THE early ornament of Greece shows strongly the influence of Egyptian and Asiatic art in its architectural decoration, jewellery, textile fabrics, and metal work; but, whereas in the older countries everything had been bound by stern convention and fettered by rules that had their source entirely outside the requirements and limitations of art, the Greeks opened to themselves and posterity an entirely new world wherein the human mind had free development. Even here, however, art was influenced by religion. Their creed was a deification of the human faculties and the passions and affections of mankind, and though this involved at times a weakness of moral fibre akin to that of common mortals, it also

placed before them a lofty ideal, and man, no longer a
cowering slave, looked upward to beneficent Zeus, and
claimed to be the offspring of God and the object of His
immediate care.

> " With Zeus begin we—let no mortal voice
> Leave Zeus unpraised. Zeus fills the haunts of men,
> The streets, the marts—Zeus fills the sea, the shores,
> The harbours—everywhere we live in Zeus.
> We are his offspring too ; friendly to man,
> He gives prognostics ; sets men to their toil
> By need of daily bread ; tells when the land
> Must be upturned by ploughshare or by spade—
> What time to plant the olive or the vine—
> What time to fling on earth the golden grain.
> For He it was who scattered o'er the sky
> The shining stars, and fixed them where they are—
> Provided constellations through the year,
> To mark the seasons in their changeless course.
> Wherefore men worship Him—the First—the Last—
> Their Father—Wonderful—their Help and Shield." [1]

This freedom from the old thraldom gave an impulse
that, in a comparatively short time, placed Greece in
the foremost rank—a position that she has never lost.
The architecture of her temples in its stately beauty has

---

[1] "As certain also of your own poets have said, For we are also His
offspring." In the " Phænomena " of Aratus will be found the beautiful lines we have quoted, and it was doubtless these that the scholarly
Paul had in his thoughts. We find them re-echoed in the lines of
Johnson :—

> " From Thee, great God, we spring, to Thee we tend,
> Path, motive, guide, original and end."

> " Father of all ! in every age,
> In every clime adored
> By saint, by savage and by sage,
> Jehovah, Jove, or Lord."—POPE.

never been surpassed, her sculpture has been an ideal for all future ages, her poets and philosophers have been the models and guides of all subsequent periods.

At the fall of Nineveh, B.C. 606, Greek art was in its infancy, though amongst the Ionians the arts were far in advance of the other states, owing to their greater proximity to Assyria and Persia. The earlier ideas of the Greeks in art matters, and in most other things as well, came from Egypt, and the primitive Greek statues show those foreign influences very distinctly. The bas-reliefs upon the monument from Xanthus in Lycia, now in the British Museum, are amongst the earliest remains of Greek art, and, like the Egyptian and Assyrian sculptures, the faces are in profile, while the eye is given as if in full view. Even in this very early work, almost agreeing with the destruction of Nineveh, we see abundant promise : the muscles have not that exaggerated development which we see in Assyrian art, and, while such care is not bestowed on fringes and such small details, the draperies hang in bolder and freer folds. The faces have the expressionless look that is common to all early art. The gradual progress from this archaic work to the glorious masterpieces of Phidias and Scopas can readily be traced, though it would take up far too much space to give the history in detail. The Greeks confined themselves almost entirely to the representation of humanity or to ideal figures of the gods and goddesses clothed in human form, though occasionally, as in the horses on the frieze of the Parthenon, they give lower forms of animal life with much truth and spirit. In the earliest Greek

sculptures the deities were in animal forms. The discoveries of Dr. Schliemann afford numerous illustrations
of this. Egyptian art has its cat-headed goddess, and
Anubis with the head of the jackal. Hindu art and
mythology has its Ganesa with the head of an elephant,
while the savage falls down before grotesque and horrible
monstrosities ; but the later Greek clothed his conception
of Deity in the form of man, His noblest work. Where
grosser ideas strove to give the idea of strength by the
semblance of the lion, or worshipped wisdom in the form
of a serpent, the Greeks realized that the true power was
no mere animal force, the true wisdom no cunning of
creeping thing.

The Greeks were familiar with previous civilizations,[1]
and the arts and institutions of earlier lands. These, as

---

[1] Thus Gladstone, in a paper on " Archaic Greece and the East,"
has some interesting remarks on particulars in the Homeric text
which appear to betray an Assyrian source. Thus—" 1. Homer
gives us the great encircling river Okeanos as the origin, not only of
rivers and fountains, but of gods and men. Compare a citation made
by Dr. Driver from the tablets concerning heaven and earth : —

'The august ocean was their generator,
    The singing deep was she that bare them all.'

2. Thalassa, the Greek name for the sea, is of Chaldean origin. 3.
Poseidon has a marked correspondence with the Hea of the Assyrian
Triad or Trinity, in certain respects. Neither of them was an ele-
mental god, but each was ruler of the sea. Poseidon was dark in
line ; and Hea was the creator of the black race. 4. Deification is
found on the tablets in the case of Izdubar. The only instance of
absolute and pure deification given by Homer is that of Leucothea,
and she belongs to the Phœnician or Eastern circle. 5. Babylonia
records the gigantic size and strength of primitive man, and so
Poseidon has relations with the giants in various forms. 6. The
Ishtar of the tablets appears to correspond with the Aphroditē of

they appropriated them, they recreated by their genius and refined by their taste, transfiguring all they touched; so that while the germ of the Doric order may be found possibly at Beni-Hassan, centuries before the earliest days of Greece or the Ionic in the bizarre capitals of Persepolis, the Greek etherealised all previous efforts, and so transmuted the works of other peoples that they became essentially their own. " Not merely myths are the stories of Cecrops and Danaus, and the introduction of the arts and learning of Egypt into Attica and Argos. The architecture of Greece is the architecture of Egypt, refined and glorified. Can we grasp and realize the truth of it? To structural principles which are those of the savage and the child, the Greek has brought a delicacy of percep-

---

Homer, the passage of whose worship into Greece we can trace by her association chiefly with Paphos, and next with Cythera or Cerigo. 7. Aïdoneus, the Greek Pluto, has among his other epithets in Homer that of πυλάρτης, the gate-fastener. The term receives little or no illustration from the Homeric text. But the Assyrian Under-World has no fewer than seven gates; and its leading idea is not that of receiving the dead, but of shutting in the dead. 8. The relation of sonship, and of a conformity of will attending it, between the god Merodach and his father is represented in a peculiar and most striking manner by the conformity of will between the Apollo of the Iliad and his father Zeus. 9. The Babylonian Triad of Anu, Bel, and Hea is the possible or probable source of the Homeric Triad of Zeus, Poseidon, and Aïdoneus. 10. Wherever there is any particular notice of stars in Homer it is always in Phœnician association, as if based upon accounts of the Chaldean astrology. 11. Heptaism, or the systematic and significant use of the number seven, is peculiarly Chaldean. The only marked use of this number in Homer is for the seven gates of Thebes. Now Thebes was the only one of the Achaian cities distinctly traceable in Homer to an eastern origin." Several other illustrations are given, but it is needless to add them to those already brought forward.

tion, has given a grace of line, has invented an appropriateness of detail, not only unequalled, but unapproached.
In the whole history of human mind and brain there is
nothing to be found more wonderful than this—this sudden attainment of a perfection which seems too marvellous
to be believed possible even while we gaze upon it.
Gifted as the race was in almost all things, it was gifted
most of all in art." [1]

The rise of the Doric, the Ionic, and the Corinthian
orders dominated not only the architecture, but the sculpture and the decorative details, since in the Doric we
have a noble and almost austere simplicity,—" the very
emblem of severe and simple majesty, of conscious, unen-
cumbered dignity, of compressed energy, of immovable
resolution," [2]—while in the Corinthian we have great
richness and sensuousness of character, and the Ionic
may be taken as a mean between these two opposites.

Noble Doric temples may be seen at Samos, Ægina,
Pæstum, and elsewhere, and in crowning beauty in the
glorious Parthenon.[3] It was formerly the custom to
speak of these orders as if each in itself was reduced to a

---

[1] Bishop, from the " Pictorial Architecture of Greece and Italy."
This and the companion volume, the " Pictorial Architecture of the
British Isles," should be on every student's bookshelf. They are
very inexpensive, and are freely illustrated with very reliable
examples.

[2] Holmden.

[3] " The finest edifice on the finest site in the world."—DR.
WORDSWORTH.

> " Earth proudly wears the Parthenon
> As the best gem upon her zone."—EMERSON.

rigid standard of uniformity;[1] but while all buildings of a common order agree in general type, no two are alike,

Fig. 39.

the Doric of the Pæstum temples, for instance, being distinctly different in detail from that of the Parthenon. The

---

[1] This bondage to lifeless rules is carried to absurd lengths. If we turn, for instance, to the "Mirror of Architecture" of Scamozzi, we find such passages as the following: "Here is shown how the columns follow each other, and how high each must be;" "The Doric must be twelve modules and fifty-three minutes and a half high;" and "The Tuscan arch must be three modules and fifty-two minutes wide." This "must be" of pedantry runs through everything.

cushion-like capital, the concave channels of the column, the triglyphs and metopes of the frieze are all very characteristic points.

In the Ionic order the feature that at once strikes the eye is the volute or spiral of the capital. See Fig. 39. The shaft, too, does not rise directly from the ground as in the Doric, but has a ring of mouldings at its base, and it is of more slender proportions. The Erechtheum at Athens is perhaps the best known example, and our illustration of the Ionic capital is taken from this source. Though found comparatively late in Greece itself, the Ionic order was fully established in Asia Minor in the sixth century B.C. The grand temple of Diana at Ephesus was Ionic, and this it is known was built by Crœsus, king of Lydia, who died B.C. 546, and destroyed by Herostratos, B.C. 356, and rebuilt during the reign of Alexander the Great. This later temple was discovered by Wood a mile from modern Ephesus, amongst cornfields, beneath level ground that did not present the slightest sign of any ruin, the remains being discovered some twenty feet below the ground level during excavations extending from 1869 to 1874. Many interesting remains from this temple, from its magnificence one of the seven wonders of the ancient world, may be seen in the British Museum.

The order known as Corinthian was so called from its reputed introduction by Callimachus of Corinth. Its capital, with volutes above and a ring of acanthus leaves below, must be well known to all our readers; but though it originated with the Greeks, it was not received by them with any great favour, while its mass of ornamentation

made it especially attractive to the pride and pomp of
Imperial Rome. It is a singular fact that no examples
of it are found at Corinth.[1]

The Greeks, like the Egyptians and Assyrians, made
a great use of colour, though the lapse of time has in

A

FIG. 40.

many cases removed all traces of it. Enough, however,
has been found to make the fact undeniable. To us the

---

[1] Mauch's treatise on the Greek and Roman orders, "Die Archi-
tektonischen Ordnungen der Greichen und Romer," containing 105
engraved plates, of details and measurements of the five orders, may
be consulted. Leeds on the "Classic Orders" is also a very useful
little manual. There are, of course, other good books that deal with
the subject ; a full list of these would run over many pages.

beautiful granite of Syenæ or the pure white Pentelic marble may seem sufficient, but the Egyptians and Greeks only saw in these materials substances of great durability and adaptability to art requirements, and amongst these requirements decoration by colour held a prominent place.

Certain ornamental forms are very characteristic of Greek work, such as the zigzag, wave scroll, the fret, the echinus, guilloche, patera, and anthemion. Most of these had already appeared in earlier work, and most of them have remained acceptable forms to the present day; we may therefore conclude that they owe their lasting value to some one or more fundamental principles. In the zigzag we have an arrangement of lines of the simplest nature, while the various forms of fret are ingenious variations of simple right-line forms. These fret forms (see Figs. 11 to 21) we find of world-wide service, the ancient Mexicans and Peruvians, the Chinese and Japanese, no less than the polished Greeks, freely introducing them. Figs. 11, 13, and 14 on Plate II. are Greek frets. Fig. 12 is from an Indian source; while the remaining examples on the plate are Chinese and Japanese. The wave scroll and the guilloche are based on a series of simple curved lines, while the patera and the anthemion both owe their charm to the beauty of radiating forms. In the echinus, the moulding marked A in Fig. 40, we get sharp alternation of light and shade, as well as strong contrast of form in the broad egg-like shapes and the thin spear-head forms between them.

The zigzag is found largely in Egyptian work, but is

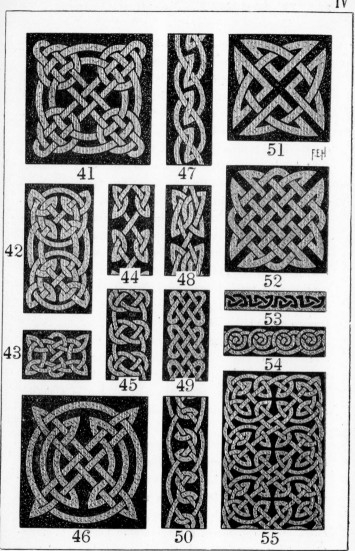

EXAMPLES OF CELTIC INTERLACING.

there ordinarily typical of water. A good example of this may be seen in Fig. 2, where we have a somewhat formal tank in which a lotus is supposed to be growing, though as a matter of fact it will be seen that the flowers and buds are not really issuing from the water at all. Both in Assyrian and Egyptian art we get exceedingly conventional representations of water, while the plants, fish, etc., in it are often very true to nature. The zigzag reappears in art from time to time : one finds it a good deal, for instance, in Early Italian work, and it is an especially characteristic moulding in Norman architecture. We may see it in the upper illustration (Fig. 99) of the various Norman mouldings. The scroll form is sometimes merely a series of spirals, and may then be considered a type of sea-waves ; but it is more often a continuous undulating line, having simple foliate forms thrown off on either side.

The echinus, or horse-chestnut, is also called the egg-and-tongue or egg-and-dart moulding—a variety of names that may be taken as conclusive of the fact that it bears no great resemblance to anything at all, but is a purely arbitrary form. It is the second moulding from the top in Fig. 40.

The guilloche, of which we have examples in Figs. 1, 5, 6, is a very characteristic Greek form ; but it is found on Egyptian work that dates two thousand years before the Christian era. It is also a very favourite ornament in Roman and Renaissance work, and, simple as it is in character, is capable of a considerable amount of variation. This repetition of simple elements is a very

FIG. 56.

FIG. 57.

FIG. 58.

FIG. 59.

FIG. 60.

marked feature in Greek work. It is a very common
principle in decorative work; and Nature, the designer's
great ultimate court of appeal, supplies numerous
examples. One of the most characteristic instances of
this repetition of simple parts is seen in the various forms

Fig. 61.

of snow crystals, of which Figs. 58 and 60 furnish us
with good illustrations. A greater richness is produced
by the alternation of one form with another in regular
sequence. We may see this very well in the snow crystals, Figs. 56, 57, 59, 61, 62.

The patera, or rosette, is a flower-like form, composed

of parts radiating from one centre. While we occasionally meet with it in Greek ornament, it is more especially
common in Assyrian and Roman work. The anthemion,
of which Fig. 63 is a good Greek example, and we may
see other illustrations of the form in Figs. 1, 39, 40, owes

Fig. 62.

much of its beauty to this principle of radiation from a
common starting-point. In the patera the forms all
spring from a central point, and, like the petals of the
wild rose, produce a multi-symmetrical form; while in the
case of the anthemion this springing point is at the base,
and the units range themselves on either side of a central

member, and form a bi-symmetrical figure. This anthemion type of form is met with in almost every style and
period of art. We have already, in Fig. 1, given a good
Assyrian example, and we have seen another, scarcely
less typical, scratched on an African calabash. The
anthemion is sometimes called the honeysuckle pattern.
It is an old dogma that the decorative form was suggested by this plant; but its more or less remote resemblance to the buds of the honeysuckle is accidental, not
incidental; and the charm, both in nature and in art, is
the inherent beauty of a mass of radiating and upspring-
ing forms, instinct with the suggestion of vitality and
growth.

Though no two Greek anthemions are absolutely alike,
the form, under slight variations of form and arrangement, is found so freely that one must confess to a
slight feeling of weariness of it. Probably all who are
at all conversant with the works of various designers will
bear us out when we say that in many cases a strong
tinge of monotony runs through the work of most men.
The first design of theirs that we see we admire immensely; the second strikes us perhaps as being almost
equally good, but rather like number one; and when we
have come across designs three, four, and five, we have
already a shrewd idea what six, seven, and eight will be
like. The study of Nature on the part of the designer is
a great corrective of this, as the man who feeds on his
own imagination comes quickly to the boundary line of
his powers, and loses all that infinity of variety that an
intelligent observation of Nature would afford. Both in

Egyptian and Greek art, we feel that though the work is good, and indeed often excellent, it palls somewhat upon one, just because the ground covered is too circumscribed. The Egyptians fully felt the beauty of natural forms, yet they give us little beyond the lotus, the papyrus, or the palm; while the Greeks scarcely utilise anything beyond the acanthus. It is perhaps not saying too much

Fig. 63.

if we suggest the probability of there being in the fertile delta of the Nile and the sunny land of Greece at least fifty other plants almost or quite equally available for the purposes of design. One feels the same monotony in the geometric designs of the Greeks. When we consider the infinity of design possible, the half-dozen frets and the three or four types of spirals and guilloches seem a very small contribution towards the possibilities of the case. It may no doubt strike some of our readers that this sort of talk is rank heresy; but it appears to us that all the art of the past is our heritage, and that we do not derive all the benefit from it that we should when we place it beyond criticism. Greek art is the noblest inheritance of the past; but, while feeling this to the full, we reserve to ourselves the right of private judgment. It may be said that Greek art is almost entirely conventional; but even in such a case, something of the wealth of Nature may be suggested to the mind by the variety of forms introduced.

No student of decoration can cross the threshold of the subject without finding himself brought face to face with the two great alternatives, naturalism or conventionalism of treatment. We may therefore at this point be pardoned a digression from the consideration of Greek art, while we consider principles that have influenced, in one direction or other, all art. We find Mohammedan art rigidly conventional, owing to religious obligations; while Greek art, equally conventional in treatment, is æsthetic in motive, has no other object than to give pleasure, and adopts this method to further this end. The Gothic of our own country in the thirteenth century is distinctly conventional, yet a century later we find it markedly naturalistic; and, if we look further afield for our illustrations, we have the distinction quite as keenly marked in the work of the Hindus, where the forms are purely arbitrary, as contrasted with the Japanese, who have gone further than any other people in the direct application of natural forms to the purposes of decoration. Is there any right or wrong in the matter ? Is there any canon or principle that we can invoke, and say that this or that is better or worse according to the measure of its approach to, or departure from, this law ?

To ourselves it appears that the pith of the whole matter lies between the terms application and adaptation. It is impossible to lay down one iron rule, or to formulate an ordinance as unyielding as the laws of the Medes and Persians ; but putting the matter briefly, we would say that to merely apply natural forms, while it is a homage to the beauty of Nature, is ordinarily a mistake. It is at best an imitative reproduction, and even then an imperfect one. One may admire roses very much, and yet not care to see them strewn in counterfeit presentment all over the walls of one's room ; one may appreciate to the full the grace of the lily, and yet not care to sit on it in the guise of a chair-covering ; and, in fact, the greater one's appreciation of the loveliness of Nature, the less will such attempts at its representation please. On the other hand, Nature is the great store-house of beauty and suggestion for the designer, and the man who wilfully shuts his eyes to it in petty complacency at his own imaginings and ideals, deprives himself of a power that would give life and strength to his work.[1] The *via media* of safety lies between these two extremes.

---

[1] " The pride which delights in self-contemplation, the indolence which rests in unquestioned forms, the ignorance that despises what is fairest amongst God's creatures, the dulness that denies what is

Where, as in wall-papers, things repeat mechanically and frequently, the forms should be distinctly conventionalised. It is an insult to the infinite variety of Nature to repeat at every few inches the same bunch of roses, or the same bird in the same position and engaged in the same act. Handwork, on the contrary, may justly be varied; and even if we still confine ourselves to our roses, we are able to produce a sufficient variation of grouping to prevent the tedious sense of sameness, and thus produce unity in variety and variety in unity. Machinery most readily produces identity of result, while the human hand and brain most readily produce variety of result; each, therefore, should be employed in the direction for which it is most fitted. Though we admire the long rows of Corinthian capitals, all exactly alike, in some noble temple, or the stately avenue of sphinxes in front of some grand ruin on the Nile, one cannot help feeling that individuality has been crushed out in their production, and we turn with a feeling of refreshment to the play of fancy, seen in all the varied details of some fine old Gothic pile, and breathe a freer air.

We owe the beauty of Nature the full tribute of our respectful appreciation, but we should never degrade her loveliness by putting it to unworthy service. The picture-painter throws his whole power into the attempt to reproduce natural truth ; but the designer, feeling the limitations of his materials, and the purpose to which

---

most marvellous in His working—a life of monotony for your own souls, and of misguiding for those of others, that is, if you think you can do better than Nature."—Ruskin.

his work must be applied, takes a different view, not because he appreciates Nature less, but because appreciating it so much he cannot bring himself to do it discredit by inadequate representation.

> "Art is the child of Nature; yes,
> Her darling child, in whom we trace
> The features of the mother's face,
> Her aspect and her attitude.
> All her majestic loveliness
> Chastened and softened and subdued
> Into a more attractive grace,
> And with a human sense imbued." [1]

We need scarcely say that any one attempting naturalistic work should have a good working knowledge of plant-structure, and even if he would hesitate to call himself a botanist, should be well acquainted with the leading laws of plant-growth. A wild rose spray, in all its picturesque beauty, is as much constructed according to law as the designer himself; the spiral growth of its foliage, and the beautiful foreshortening, therefore, of the parts that result from this rigid law, is as marked as any other law of Nature; and it is no more permissible to add a sixth to the ring of five fragrant petals in each of its beautiful flowers, than to consider it immaterial whether we put four, five, or six toes to the human foot.

"Ornament," Ruskin observes, "should be natural; that is to say, should in some degree express or adopt the beauty of natural objects. Observe, it does not hence follow that it should be an exact imitation of, or en-

---

[1] Longfellow, "Keramos".

deavour in anywise to supersede God's work. It may consist only in a part adoption of, and compliance with, the usual forms of natural things, without at all going to the point of imitation, and it is possible that the point of imitation may be closely reached by ornaments which, nevertheless, are entirely unfit for their place, and are the signs only of a degraded ambition and an ignorant dexterity. Bad decorators err as easily on the side of imitating Nature as of forgetting her, and the question of the exact degree in which imitation should be attempted under given circumstances is one of the most subtle and difficult in the whole range of criticism."

It is curious and characteristic that those who would desire to bespeak our goodwill, even for the lower forms of the Greek art that we have been considering, do so by trying to ally them with some suggestion of Nature, that the dentils are at least suggestive of teeth, that the egg-and-tongue moulding and the honeysuckle ornament were in some degree a tribute to natural forms, and hence have these propitiatory titles appended to them. How far they really resemble any natural form may be seen in the fact that what one calls egg-and-tongue another regards as the opening fruit of the horse-chestnut.

Sir Gardner Wilkinson, in his work on " Colour and Taste," writes : "The imitation of natural objects for merely ornamental purposes usually disagrees both with the materials used and the place where they are introduced. It is also an indication of poverty of invention, and a deficiency of taste for design. In a carpet, where roses and other flowers are figured, the very best rose is always unlike the reality, while the imagination is diverted from the general effect by the comparison of this imperfect copy with the natural flower. To obtain ideas for ornamental art, Nature should be carefully studied, and the beauties she presents should be fully understood, but she should not be directly copied in an unsuitable material." Wornum, in his "Analysis of Ornament," affirms: "You frustrate the very principle of Nature when you represent a natural form in a natural manner and yet apply it to uses with which it has in Nature no affinity whatever." Elsewhere he writes: "The details of all great styles are largely derived from Nature, but are for the most part conventionally treated, and theory and experience seem to show this to be the true system."

On turning to Owen Jones, another great authority on the subject, we read : "In all the best periods of art, all ornament was rather based upon an observation of the principles which regulate the arrangements of form in Nature than on an attempt to imitate the absolute forms of those works, and that wherever this limit was exceeded in any art it was one of the strongest symptoms of decline."

Jackson, in his "Lessons on Decorative Design," in the same way declares that "some people in their one-sided admiration of Nature, imagine that natural forms, being beautiful if copied, must necessarily be beautiful however applied. They regard Nature as a storehouse of ready-made ornament, instead of a book of reference for ideas and principles to be thought out with diligence, and applied with care. Ready-made ornaments are too often, like ready-made clothes, badly fitting and ill-suited to the subject."

Lewis Day, whose excellent text-books on ornament should be on the bookshelf of every student of the subject, sums up the whole matter very clearly and well in

Fig. 64.

the following words: "Experience proves that the fitting opportunity for realistic ornament very seldom occurs. It is for the most part contrary to the purpose or position of the object, ill-adapted to the material and the method of working it, and most especially it is calculated to draw undue attention to the object, or, which is worse,

to itself. A more subdued and reticent and altogether
simpler style of design is almost invariably found to be

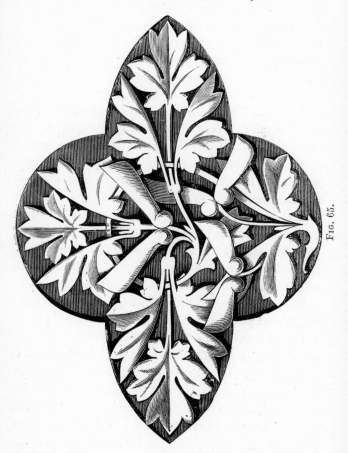

Fig. 65.

advisable, either in the shape of pure ornament or in some
adaptation of natural forms." This conventionalism may

be of varying degree. An ornamental treatment may be very suggestive of nature, and yet be purely decorative in feeling. Figs. 64 and 65, designs of our own, may be taken, we think, as very fair examples of this, as while the one is clearly based on the beautiful foliage of the hawthorn, the other no less evidently was inspired by the maple; they are not simply branches of these plants copied directly from nature, but are adapted to the decorative purpose of filling the panels, in the one case by branching from the spiral stem, and in the other by the symmetry and balance of the several parts. A natural treatment implies direct imitation of the plant in its form, mode of growth, and so forth; while an ornamental treatment does not necessarily, as we see in these examples, exclude natural forms in the details. Thus, on many of the Greek vases we see foliage strongly suggestive of the laurel, ivy, and other plants; but as these are almost invariably arranged in a positively straight line or a regularly waving one, they are still decorative and not merely imitative.

The term naturalistic is itself a happy one, and conjures up pleasant pictures to the mind; while on the other hand the word conventional is of somewhat ill-omen, and we associate with it something of the chilling influence of Mrs. Grundy. It suggests stiffness, formalism, and restraint, and one could heartily wish that some other equally expressive word that was free from these external suggestions could be substituted for it.[1]

---

[1] Shakespeare's question as to " What's in a name?" might be readily answered in the words " A good deal." In the political world,

It will possibly be noticed by our readers that we speak of nature as though it consisted of nothing but floral forms. We have not by any means forgotten the various animal forms that also appear so freely in decoration, but these we propose to deal with when we are considering Celtic work, since this is so distinctly zoomorphic in character that they will most naturally come before us for consideration then.

Greek art is many-sided and always excellent. We have already to some extent referred to architecture and sculpture, and their grandeur must be evident to all; but in the minor arts, the designing and execution of their coins, the beautiful work seen in gems and bronzes, and in the work of the potter, the wonderful art-feeling of the Greeks is fully as clearly seen. All these alike are worthy of careful study, though we shall run some little risk of deterring our readers if we call the pursuit, as an enthusiast some two centuries ago did, epigrammatonumismatobiblio-glyptoiconotoreumatoangeiography. With the opening portion of this, the study of Greek inscriptions, we have here no concern, but the numismatic portion we must deal with. Bibliography and iconography also are outside our present programme. The toreumatic section deals with metal objects, wrought or chased; while the closing "angeio" refers to the study of vases.

---

for instance, whatever view of parties our readers may hold, they will readily admit that the term Liberal conjures up on its own merits a pleasant picture of free-handed *bonhommie* that no doubt carries weight, though clearly both in matters political and decorative it is not what a thing is called, but what it is, that gives it its value.

The study of Greek coinage is of the greatest archæological value, as we have in coins a series of the most interesting illustrations of the successive phases of art, and by the aid of these one is enabled to accurately trace its progress from the most archaic examples, through its period of finest development, and thence to its decline and fall—a period of some seven hundred years. From these we see the conceptions of the gods worshipped, and are enabled to note in which localities each was held in especial esteem; we often find on them, too, representations of famous statues and buildings of antiquity,[1] of which we have now no other trace, and we also get a series of portraits of the sovereigns and other rulers of the various states. Geographically we derive an idea, too, of the extent, position, and comparative importance of the various colonies, and often get much local information from them; while to the artist and designer they are of the greatest value, as in them the whole spirit and genius of Greek art is admirably exemplified.

From about 700 to 400 B.C. the work is very archaic, though towards the close of this period great improvement is visible; while from 400 to about 280 B.C. the work is magnificent in its power and beauty. Thence onward to the opening of the Christian era the art was a declining one; the land was under foreign domination, and the

---

[1] The reader will find this phase of the subject worked out in Professor Donaldson's "Architectura Numismatica," the architectural medals of classic antiquity illustrated and explained by comparison with the monuments and the descriptions of ancient writers. The book is freely illustrated.

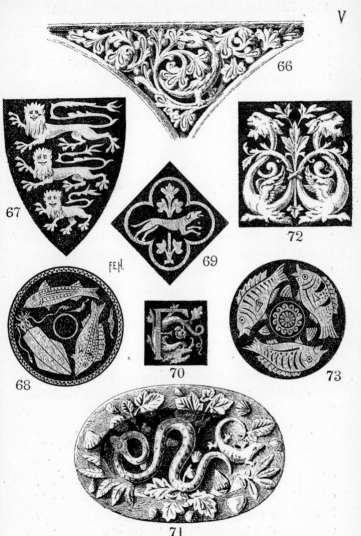

V

66

67

FE.H.

69

72

68

70

73

71

ANIMAL FORMS IN ORNAMENT.

103

grand art traditions of the former days had lost their power in the general decay of the national spirit under the yoke of all-conquering Rome.

On the coinage of Athens we get on the obverse the head of Athene, the tutelary goddess of the city, and on the reverse the owl, sacred to her, and the olive branch, in allusion to her gift of the olive-tree to the Greeks. The tetradrachms of Syracuse bear the heads of Pallas and Arethusa, those of Croton the figure of Herakles. On the coins of Ægina we find the sea-tortoise, emblem of Aphrodite; while the money of Metapontum bears an ear of corn in reference to the worship of Demeter. The coins of Ephesus often have a bee upon them, the symbol of the Ephesian goddess Artemis; while the coins of Rhodes generally bear the rayed head of Helios, the sun-god. Other coins, as we have already pointed out, are valuable from giving us representations of famous statues or buildings. Thus many of the coins of Ephesus have a representation of the famous temple of Artemis upon them; while the coinage of Cnidus has stamped upon it the Aphrodite of Praxiteles, one of the most renowned statues of the ancient world. The coins of Cnossus have on one side the Minotaur, and on the other the famous Labyrinth constructed by Dædalus for its abode. The designs are generally allusive to some legend associated with the state, or are the accepted symbols of it. At other times they are the records of victories won; while in some few cases it is not now possible to pronounce on the motive that influenced the selection of some particular device.

A very beautiful and common design is a biga or quadriga, the horses attached being either represented as tripping along or as in full gallop. The devices during the finest period—a space of one hundred and fifty years or more— are characterised by great vigour and freedom of action, perfect finish of execution, and great decorative richness ; in every way, in fact, showing a complete mastery of technical skill and of great artistic power. Many beauti- ful examples may be seen in the coin room in the British Museum, and those who think our encomiums excessive will, we doubt not, return from a visit to this gallery with a feeling somewhat akin to that of the Queen of Sheba as she realized how inadequately all the beauty that she at last saw with her own eyes had been pictured to her.

In Greek gems, again, we have a wide field of study and artistic development, and, as in the case of the coins, we find in them a rich store of mythological and symbolic lore. The designs may be either in intaglio, a term em- ployed when the device is sunk below the general surface, or in cameo, where it is in relief. They date from about the seventh century B.C. to the third century A.D., and are worked in steatite, sard, jasper, rock-crystal, and such-like materials. The engraving of gems is termed the glyptic art, and it is marvellous to note how in a space so small and with materials so intractable such beautiful work could be produced. Of these, again, there is a fine collection in our great national treasure- house.

Greek vases are to be met with in abundance. There

are thousands of examples in the British Museum,[1] thousands more in the museum at Naples, and countless others in the national and other large collections in Paris, Berlin, Athens, and elsewhere. They have been found in almost every site where excavation has been made, not in Greece only, but in Sicily, Etruria, and South Italy, and wherever a Greek colony was established, so that the study at all events is not likely to fail for want of material to work on. The painting on these vases is full of value and interest, and in them, as in all else that is Greek, we can readily trace the transition from archaic quaintness to the full tide of perfection, and thence to the ebb in the decadent examples of the closing chapters of Greek art.[2]

For some considerable period these vases were known

---

[1] The collection, already rich in illustrations of the earliest and purest styles of Greek art, received on the purchase by the nation of the Musée Blacas some 500 additional examples, and these of the later and more ornate period which had previously been imperfectly represented. There are also numerous excellent examples in the fine collection of all styles and ages of ceramic art in the Museum of Economic Geology in London. The material, clay, of which they are made, is of course their justification for being found in a geological collection.

[2] Those who care to pursue the subject thoroughly will find the following books very helpful :—

HAMILTON, SIR W.—Collection of Engravings from Ancient Vases, mostly of pure Greek workmanship, discovered in sepulchres in the Kingdom of the Two Sicilies, but chiefly in the neighbourhood of Naples, during the course of the years 1789–90, now in the possession of Sir W. Hamilton ; with remarks on each Vase by the Collector. 3 vols. large 4to. Naples.

MILLINGEN, J.—Ancient unedited Monuments. Painted Greek Vases, from collections in various countries, principally in Great Britain, illustrated and explained. 4to. London.

as Etruscan, as this state was where they were first discovered in any abundance. An enormous store of them
was found in Etruria in the year 1828, and it was not un-
naturally concluded that this must have been the seat of
manufacture.[1] Closer examination and study of them soon
revealed the fact that they were essentially Greek in
spirit, and that they were exported to the Etruscans
as an article of commerce. As a rule these vases have
been found in tombs,[2] being associated with the funeral
rites, and thereafter buried with the deceased.

The vase-painters never lost sight of the technical conditions of ceramic work, and while faithfully recognising
these limitations, produced designs which for decorative
beauty and fitness have never been surpassed. The subjects, where human figures are introduced, were chiefly
mythological,[3] or, not uncommonly, incidents of war or of

---

[1] It is very interesting to note that Wedgwood, whose beautiful
reproductions and adaptations of these classic forms are so well known
and so highly valued, when he established his manufactory on the
Staffordshire moorland, called the place Etruria, and Etruria the
district is to this day. The works were opened on June 13th, 1769,
and Wedgwood himself made the first start by "throwing" on the
wheel six vases. Three of these are still extant. They are of black
body, and have as subjects upon them scenes in the life of Herakles,
while on a thin band at the base are the words "Artes Etruriæ
renascuntur."

[2]   "Vases, and urns, and bas-reliefs,
        Memorials of forgotten griefs,
        Or records of heroic deeds,
        Of demi-gods and mighty chiefs."
                —Longfellow, " Keramos."

[3] Thus on one we get the contest of Herakles with the river-god
Acheloos, on another the birth of Athene from the head of Zeus, on
a third Herakles killing the centaur Nessos. Elsewhere we find

the chase, or other scenes of real life, and, naturally, a considerable section dealing with funereal rites and the sad associations of the tomb. In the best examples the designs are depicted in monochrome, being simple in character and of great dignity of treatment, while the vases themselves are pure in form. From the time of Alexander decay set in; the shapes of the vessels were less refined, they were often made of great size, and the figures were crowded together without due regard to the relation between the form of the vase and the design to be introduced on it. Polychromy and gilding also make their appearance, and the drawing becomes careless.

For convenience of study the fictile art of Greece may be divided into three very definite periods—the Archaic, extending from the earliest days of Greek civilization to about 440 B.C.; the period of finest work, from 440 to 336 B.C.; and the period of gradual decadence, from 336 to 100 B.C. The vases vary in form at different periods; hence not only the treatment of the subject, but the shape of the vessel upon which it is painted, assist us to determine its date.

The Greek alphabet changed a good deal from time to time by the addition or suppression of letters, and in the forms of the characters employed. As many of the vases have inscriptions on them, or the principal divinities or heroes have their names given, this affords another means of determining the age of the vase.

---

represented the exploits of Theseus, the pursuit of Daphne by Apollo, and many other mythological and legendary subjects.

In archaic work the designs are chiefly various simple geometrical forms, chequers, waved lines, patera forms, rough renderings of guilloches, and such like, arranged in concentric bands. Occasionally we find animal forms, but these are but sparingly introduced, and are ordinarily very rude in draughtsmanship: representations of the human figure very rarely occur, and if seen at all are of most inartistic character. After these came the style that is now generally termed the Asiatic, as it is believed that it was developed under Assyrian inspiration. In this a great use is made of zones or bands of animals encircling the vessel, and a little later on the human figure appears, and often with considerable power of drawing and expression of action. In the early Greek vases the subjects ordinarily deal with war and the chase. Later on these still occur, and also representations of various myths met with in classic literature; later still, scenes where death and mourning occur are common, and there is also a preference for sentimental and effeminate subjects.

During the finest period of Greek ceramic art the figures are ordinarily in red on a black ground. The drawing is severe and pure, and the designs very simple and good in composition. Many of the works of this period are signed by the artists who produced them: thus in the British Museum we see on various vases the names of Pamphaios, Euxitheos, Polygnotus, Meidias, Douris, Epictetos, and many others.

We occasionally find, as in all periods and styles of ceramic work, Greek pottery in the form of men or of animals; but this ordinarily arises from that love of the grotesque that seems inherent in humanity, and to which we shall presently have to refer at some little length. The artistic element in these is generally not a strong feature.

Bronze, an alloy of copper with a small quantity of tin, or more rarely of lead or silver, was largely used by the ancients, the Egyptians, Assyrians, Phœnicians, Romans, and others; but it was reserved for the Etruscans and Greeks to develop its art possibilities to the full. It was used for statuary, the prows of the war galleys, ornaments of the temples, mirrors, vases, candelabra, and many other purposes. Most of the examples now extant have been found either in tombs in Etruria[1] or have come from Pompeii and Herculaneum; but purely Greek examples are extremely rare, and it is impossible to define their date in the way that can quite readily be done with the temples or the vases and coins and statuary in marble.

Homer notices that " the Egyptians excel in the manufacture of arms, rich vases, and other objects inlaid and ornamented with metal"; and Herodotus tells us that " the Egyptians drank out of bronze goblets." The copper was found in Egypt, while the tin was brought by the Phœnicians from India, Spain, and Britain. Herodotus

---

[1] The Etruscans made bronze statues before the foundation of Rome, 750 B.C., and on the foundation of the infant city we are told that Romulus commissioned from Etruria a statue of himself; and his successor, Numa Pompilius, according to Pliny, established a guild of workers in bronze, so that they might be independent of foreign aid, not only in their statuary, but in all the needs of daily life, door sockets, tools, weapons, and so forth.

describes the grand metal doors of the temple of Belus at Babylon; while the description of the various bronze articles used in the temple of Solomon, a thousand years before the Christian era, gives us an excellent idea of the value of the work and the progress that the art had by that time attained to. Nebuchadnezzar, B.C. 596, on his capture of the Holy Land, broke up the pillars, the molten sea, and other metal of the temple, and had the pieces conveyed to Babylon; so that it is very possible that many of the articles from Nineveh that we may see in the British Museum are made from the bronze of the Jewish temple, and that Cornish tin is one of the constituents of the material.

The island of Delos was very famous for its bronze founding, and that of Ægina was scarcely less so. The fame of both these rivals was however afterwards eclipsed by that of Corinth. Pliny affirms that the material employed " consisted of gold, silver, and copper, and was considered more precious than silver, and little less valuable than gold "; and in the Syriac version of the Scriptures it is stated that Hiram made the various vessels of Solomon's temple of Corinthian brass.

Rhodes, in the height of its prosperity, was adorned, we are told, with over 3,000 statues[1] of bronze, one of these, the Colossus, being one of the wonders of antiquity. It was erected 290 B.C., but was overthrown about 224

---

[1] The wealth and dignity of a state or city were to some degree indicated in this way amongst this art-loving people; Athens, Delphos, and other cities, like Rhodes, were adorned with some thousands of statues.

B.C. by an earthquake, and lay in ruins upon the ground for nine centuries.

The Etruscans amongst the early Latin races were especially distinguished for their love of art and the successful prosecution of it. Their territory had a considerable coast-line, and in the early ages of the world it was the land, with its impassable forests and marshes, rugged mountains and fierce beasts of prey, that divided nations, while the sea, even in those early days of navigation, brought them together. Thanks to this commercial intercourse with Egypt and Phœnicia, the men of Etruria were very familiar with the art of the then known world, and they themselves had a great reputation for working in bronze and for their skill in terra-cotta. They were skilful architects, as their city walls and massive tombs testify, and the Etruscan gem engraving and jewellery was of the highest artistic merit. The animals and other forms introduced often show a strongly marked Assyrian or Persian influence, but after a while this Asiatic bias gives place to the rising art power of Greece. They lacked the inspiration of the Greeks, and were to a great extent copyists, but they at least had the power to appreciate what was excellent. Their territory was close to that of Rome, and the rising state, jealous of the influence and power of Etruria, did not rest until after prolonged and considerable resistance it lay at her feet, and was absorbed under the Roman sway.

The Romans, though a great people, were not an artistic race. To the Greeks it was given in an especial degree to develop all that was grand and beautiful in literature and in art, while to the Romans was assigned the task of jurisprudence and the reign of law and order, and each has exercised an immense influence on the world. In unbroken advance Rome became mistress from the shores of the Caspian to the storm-beaten coasts of the Atlantic, and included in her mighty empire cities as distant as Alexandria and York. Hundreds of cities were the garrisons of her troops, and her wealth gave even to remote provincial towns no mean imitation of the baths, amphitheatres, and other features of Imperial Rome. The strong and far-reaching arm of her government gave a universal repose, and the remains of magnificent aqueducts and roads testify to the well-directed energy of her rulers.

With prosperity and domination came luxury: at first the just pride in grand public buildings, and noble and beautiful things for all; and then, after a virile career of twelve centuries, general enervation, followed by irremediable decay and ruin. The Romans derived their art in the first place from Etruria,[1] and afterwards from Greece. They did little or nothing artistic themselves, but depended almost entirely upon the foreigner for all art refinements. From 510 to 167 B.C. may be termed the Etruscan period. Later on the conquest of Greece brought a change of ideas and a new art influence. The celebrated Wolf of the Capitol is a piece of Etruscan work of archaic style, but Pliny and others mention works of Etruscan origin to which they give high commendation. The

---

[1] See Inghirami's "Monumenti Etruschi o di Etruscho nome."

Etruscans made a great use of the arch,[1] and the Romans seized upon this feature, and made it very characteristically their own. Very good examples of this may be seen in the triumphal arches, such as that decreed to Titus on the capture of Judæa, or that of Constantine, and again in the Colosseum, and the aqueducts. In the case of the monumental arches and the Colosseum, the main structure is based upon the arch, the columns that are added to the designs carrying no weight, but being in each instance a merely decorative feature. This is a marked change from Greek procedure, for if we dislodge the columns of a Greek temple, the whole edifice comes at once to the ground, while we may strip away all the columns from the Colosseum, and we have but removed a surface veneer that is no sense really constructive.

The splendour of the city of Rome must be dated from the days of Augustus (30 B.C. to 14 A.D.). He was able with justice to boast that the city which he had found of brick he had left of marble. Vespasian, Titus, and Trajan too had a passion for architecture, and the public works with which Hadrian adorned every province of his empire were executed not only by his orders, but under his immediate inspection. In the prosecution of these works the emperors were eagerly imitated by their principal subjects; for the opulent senators of Rome deemed it an honour, and almost an obligation, to contribute to the

---

[1] Brought by them from Asia Minor on their migration, and originally derived from Assyria. It is a very marked feature in the temple façades of Nineveh and Babylon.

splendour of their age and country. The provinces were embellished by the same liberal spirit of public magnificence, and were filled with amphitheatres, temples, baths, aqueducts, and whatever else was conducive to the health, the pleasure, or the devotion of the meanest citizen.

The Romans inherited the arts of the earlier peoples, and of the nations that one by one fell beneath their sway, adapting from them whatever could administer to their luxury and magnificence. In their early days unceasing struggle for dominion left little time or opportunity for this luxury; but by the time of Augustus the Romans were masters of the world, and the sterner and simpler life of the earlier ages gave place to an era of indulgence in all kinds of pleasures, and the great capital of the world absorbed to itself all that could tend to its gratification, artistic, gastronomical, and so forth, while the abounding wealth enabled every taste to be satisfied to the full.[1]

The Greek orders were considerably modified by the Roman architects, and the Doric and Ionic, being too severe in style, were soon abandoned. Vitruvius and other ancient writers make mention of an order which they term Tuscan, but no authentic examples of it have been found; but so far as their description of it goes, it

---

[1] Martial, Seneca, and other writers give us vivid pictures of the luxury and ostentation of the latter days in Rome; the former's description of the man Charinus, for example. It is too long to quote; but one item, the fact of the wearing of sixty rings on his hand at the same time, is enough. As geologists from a bone can recreate some antediluvian Saurian, so from this one item we can reconstruct Charinus and his fellows.

would appear to have been little more than a spurious and debased Doric.

Roman Ionic may be seen in the Temple of Concord, the Temple of Fortuna Virilis, the Colosseum, and Theatre of Marcellus, besides numerous smaller remains. A considerable variation of form is seen, and many of the versions are not unpleasing, though they lack the refined taste of Greek work. One marked difference between Greek and Roman work is that the mouldings in the former are of much more subtle curve than the latter; in the Roman, in fact, they are always made portions of circles.

While the Corinthian order took but little hold in Greece, the Romans adopted it most freely, and made many modifications of it, almost all in the direction of still greater richness. One of these variations, in which the volutes at the angles are enlarged almost to the size of the spirals in an Ionic capital, was termed the Composite, but there is very slender justification for bestowing a special name upon it. It is only one variation the more, and at most a little more marked than some of the others. Perhaps the best examples of the Corinthian are seen in the Temple of Jupiter Stator and the Pantheon; while the so-called Composite is exemplified in the Arch of Titus, the Arch of Septimus Severus, and the Thermæ of Diocletian.

Palladio, Scamozzi, Vignola, and other writers have endeavoured to prescribe for each of these so-called " five orders " a positive and unchangeable standard, and for each portion of entablature and column have given certain fixed measurements; but actual study of the ancient examples will show that no two of them are alike, and that the same general name covers very marked differences when we try and formulate a definition. To establish a fixed and uniform canon is a fatal mistake, as it at once reduces all to a dead level, thereby giving an unjust idea of the ancient practice, and in modern procedure substituting the letter of bondage for the spirit of liberty.

While with the Greeks the aim was dignified simplicity, with the Romans the object was florid enrichment and magnificence. Roman art was not really original, it simply exuberantly elaborated elements already to hand;[1] and while most of the architects and artists were Greeks, they had come to Rome, the capital of the world, to seek employment or at the special call of the Emperor, and their interest and mission was not to please themselves, but to meet the wishes of their employers.[2]

---

[1] As, for instance, the use of a gigantic column to commemorate a victorious campaign of the Emperor Trajan, the shaft not being plain or simply fluted, but sculptured throughout its length with a spiral band of sculpture, illustrating incidents in the war. A very good cast of it may be seen in the South Kensington Museum. See Pollen's book, "The Trajan Column as reproduced in the South Kensington Museum." See also the folio volume of Bellorius, entitled "Colonna Trajana," or the book "De Columna Trajani" of Fabretti.

[2] Any one desiring to work up Roman art thoroughly will find any or all of the following books very useful:—Visconti's folio volume on the buildings of ancient Rome, entitled "Raccolta delle più insigni Fabbriche di Roma Antica e sue adjacenze. Misurate Nuovamente e dichiarate dall' Architetto Giuseppe Valadier, illustrate con osservazioni antiquarie da Filippo Aurelio Visconti, ed incise da Vincenzo Feoli." The four volumes of plates and nine of text of Canina, on

One marked feature in Roman ornament is the very free use of the scroll. We have seen it already in Fig. 9, and Fig. 74 is another illustration of it. In Greek work the scroll is often simply a curved line, but in Roman examples this curved line is a stem from which foliage is freely given off. The acanthus leaf is another element of constant recurrence in Roman decoration : we find it not only on the capitals, but also forming rosettes of foliage ; and the scroll line, already referred to, is generally enriched with masses of acanthus that often from their richness almost entirely cover and conceal the stem. In our present example (Fig. 74) the illustration is taken from a mosaic, and therefore a simpler type of foliage was necessary. The acanthus foliations are not all of the same character, as in some examples we find the sub-divisions of the leaf much more cut up into lobes than in others.

Both Greeks and Romans introduced mythical crea-tures, such as the chimæra, sphinx, griffin, and triton, in

---

" Ancient Architecture, explained by its Monuments : Greek, Roman, etc. L'Architettura antica descritta e demostrata coi Monumenti." The two folio volumes of Taylor and Cressy on " The Architectural Antiquities of Rome." Piranesi's magnificent twenty-nine volumes on Greek and Roman antiquities, and Albertolli's work on the Friezes from the Forum of Trajan and others in Rome and else-where—" Fregi trovati negli scavi del Foro Trajano, con altri esistenti in Roma ed in diverse altre città ; disegnati e misurati sul luogo da Ferdinando Albertolli." To these may be added Lübke's " History of Art," and the excellent " History of Architecture " of Ferguson. Vaux, " Handbook to the Antiquities of the British Museum." Müller, " Archäologie der Kunst." Pistolesi's eight folio volumes of " Il Vaticano." Desgodetz, " Edifices Antiques de Rome."

ornament, but such forms are far more characteristic of Roman work.

In the Baths of Titus, and elsewhere in the excavated portions of ancient Rome, we get numerous examples of decoration; but our great storehouse of information on this head is found in the ruins of Pompeii, a comparatively unimportant provincial town, and therefore to some extent wanting possibly in some of the refinements of

Fig. 74.

life in the capital, but nevertheless a perfect treasure-house to the historian, archæologist, and all who would desire to realize the daily life, amusements, and occupations of the Roman people.

After remaining quiescent for hundreds of years, Vesuvius, in the year 79 A.D., burst into tremendous volcanic energy, overwhelming with sudden destruction Herculaneum, Pompeii, and other smaller towns and hamlets. Herculaneum, from its closer proximity to the burning mountain, was buried beneath successive lava streams, that from their hardness and great depth, being seventy to a hundred feet in thickness, have made excavation most difficult; whereas Pompeii was covered by showers of ashes and stones that form a comparatively loose and friable mass that is rarely more than ten or fifteen feet in depth, and can therefore be easily removed.

For over sixteen centuries Pompeii remained thus buried, as the excavations did not commence till the year 1755. It is remarkable that so long a time should have elapsed, as Dominico Fontana, an eminent architect and engineer, in the year 1592, in bringing the water of the river Sarno to the town of Torre dell' Annunziata, tunnelled through a portion of the ground upon which Pompeii was standing, and several times found portions of the basements of buildings. Beyond a passing curiosity at the discovery, no interest in the matter seems to have been excited, and Pompeii slept on undisturbed for another century.

Pompeii was a Greek colony long before its subjugation by the Romans, and even in the later days of its incorporation in the empire the taste was still more or less Greek, and the artistic work done to meet the wishes of its wealthy inhabitants was the work of Greek artists and artizans. The result was naturally somewhat hybrid, as the artistic feeling had to subordinate itself to the whims of a wealthy patron whose art knowledge was possibly small.

The greater number of the Pompeian houses are decorated by means of horizontal bands of colour, the lowest being ordinarily the darkest. This has generally a more or less conventional bordering, and we see much the same arrangement in a lighter key of colour as an upper frieze. The large intermediate space is generally set out in bold panelling, and in the centres of these panels are figure-subjects, sometimes groups, but more commonly single figures. These are very gracefully and powerfully drawn. In one instance we have the picture of a lady artist, palette in hand, copying on a slab before her a statue that stands in the corner of her studio. In another the artist is a man who is engaged on the portrait of a distinguished sitter, while his colour-grinder is preparing him his pigments. Two friends come in, and, standing behind the easel, exchange comments on the progress of the work. Elsewhere we find a chariot-race of Cupids, a domestic supper party, Diana surprised by Actæon, a group of dancing fauns, the parting of Achilles and Briseis, a battle of Amazons, the sacrifice of Iphigenia, Perseus and Andromeda, a winged Cupid milking a goat, and many other subjects, mythological, historic, social, and fanciful. Occasionally we find landscape subjects, and the introduction of buildings in the scene is a marked characteristic: the perspective of these is generally somewhat deficient and exaggerated. Occasionally the subjects are treated grotesquely, and we sometimes have pictures of still life, fish, game, and fruit.

The magnificent folio of Zahn, giving the best examples of the ornaments and mural paintings of Pompeii, should be seen by every student. It was published in Berlin, so all references are in German; but the illustrations are beautifully drawn and coloured, and stand in very little need of any explanation at all. For reference its full title is—" Die schönsten Ornamente und merkwürdigsten Gemälde aus Pompeii, Herkulanum, und Stabiæ, nebst einigen Grundrissen und Ansichten, nach den an Ort und Stelle gemachten Originalzeichnungen, von Wilhelm Zahn." Another book that may very well be consulted is the "Pompeiana" of Gell and Gandy, four volumes devoted to the topography, edifices, and ornaments of Pompeii; or the student may turn to a book published at Naples in 1808, entitled, "Gli Ornati delle Pareti ed I Pavimenti delle Stanze dell Antica Pompei incise in Rame," atlas folio, containing sixty-seven fine large engravings of the ornaments, ceilings, wall decorations, and mosaic pavements of the Pompeian houses; or the folio volume of Raoul Rochette, " Choix de Peintures de Pompeii."

In the more conventional decoration that is freely met with, the anthemion form is largely introduced, though ordinarily treated in a peculiarly thin and poor fashion ; but a good deal of the conventional floral ornament is very good, and dashed in in a very masterly way. A great use is made of arabesques, where various animal and floral forms, vases, weapons, masks, musical instruments, and so forth, are strung together into one composition with more or less happy effect. The Baths of Titus [1] in Rome still afford us abundant examples of the taste of the day, both pictorial and decorative, and in each direction they are almost identical in style with those

---

[1] It was during the reign of Titus that Pompeii was destroyed.

ANIMAL FORMS IN DECORATION.

found at Pompeii. It is scarcely likely that the artists who worked for Titus would seek employment in a small provincial town, but the painters of the arabesques at Rome and at Pompeii were at all events contemporaries. The Baths of Titus were discovered in the sixteenth century, and Rafaelle, struck with the decorations, largely introduced them and others of the like spirit in ornamental work in the Vatican. This arabesque treatment thereupon grew very popular, and was a good deal employed in panels, pottery,[1] and elsewhere.

The term Arabesque is not a particularly happy one. It implies that such decoration is Arab in character—an inference that is entirely untrue, as the religion of Mohammed forbids the representation of any natural object, whether animal or floral, so that such arabesques as those of Pompeii are entirely impossible in the art of the Arabs.

One of the most characteristic forms of Roman decoration is mosaic. Wherever between the Tyne and the Euphrates a Roman settlement, or even an isolated villa, is unearthed, there we may almost invariably find examples of this work; and whether they are discovered in the city of London or the city of Carthage, in York or Alexandria, they are all of very similar style, and have a strong family likeness. If then we would desire to get

---

[1] "Maestro Giorgio shines
     With madre-perl and golden lines
     Of arabesques, and interweaves
     His birds and fruits and flowers and leaves."
                    —LONGFELLOW, "Keramos."

an idea of what a Roman mosaic at Ephesus, Utica, or
Halicarnassus was like, we may readily do so by an
inspection of those discovered at Brading, Horkstow,
Cirencester, Silchester, Littlecote, Bignor, and many
other localities in England. Many good illustrations of
these latter will be found in Morgan's "Romano-British
Mosaic Pavements," where a history of their discovery
and an interpretation of the designs is duly set forth, and
the more important examples figured in colours. Sometimes these mosaics take the form of mural decoration,
but it is as pavements that we most freely encounter
them. The use of mosaic is derived from the earliest
periods, and may be traced through the practice of Egypt
and Assyria to Greece, and thence swept into the all-gath-
ering net of Rome. Christian Byzantium, on the fall of
pagan Rome, made a great use of it, and its introduction
in ecclesiastical and other buildings has continued to the
present day.

We read incidentally in the Book of Esther, in the
description of a feast in the palace at Shushan (Susa) of
King Ahasuerus, of a pavement of red, blue, white, and
black marble, or according to the reading in the margin,
of porphyry, and marble, and alabaster, and stone of blue
colour. The Egyptians some three thousand years ago
practised a curious kind of mosaic, wherein the pattern
was produced by a number of very small rods of opaque-
coloured glass arranged in rows perpendicularly to the
surface of the design, so that if any number of sections
were made horizontally through the glass, each would
have exactly the same pattern. Winckelman mentions a

specimen of this minute Egyptian work where, in a space one inch long and the third of an inch in breadth, a bird resembling a duck is given. He adds that the most delicate pencil of the miniature painter could not have traced with greater clearness the circle of the eye-ball or the feathers on the neck.[1] In the reign of Alexander the Great mosaic pavements were common throughout Greece, not only of a geometric character, but also of more elaborate design.

The early pavements were composed of small pieces of natural stone or marble cemented on an underlying bed into geometric patterns, figure subjects, floral borders, but later on a greater variety of colour was more easily obtained by using coloured clays, and this in time gave place to glass. Until the end of the third century we find little or no mention of the use of mosaic as a wall decoration. The ordinary arrangement was to cut up the floor space into very definite geometrical forms, emphasized by borders of geometric character, such as chequers, guilloches, plaits, or frets, and then to place in the centres of these spaces mythological figures, historic incidents, scenes of the chase, symbolic figures of the seasons, and so forth. Marine subjects often occur; thus, in an example from Halicarnassus in the British Museum,

---

[1] Another famous example is that known as the "Doves of the Capitol." It was found in the villa of Hadrian at Tivoli, and secured for the Capitoline Museum by Clement XIII. One gets some idea of its extreme minuteness of workmanship on learning that in one square inch of it one hundred and sixty distinct pieces of marble have been counted. This, of course, was equivalent to a picture, and not by any means to be trodden under foot.

we see Amphitrite amidst dolphins and other fish, and on either side of her a triton. In one from Carthage we see a fish-basket turned over, and strewn around are numerous fish and other sea creatures; amongst them we can identify sea-perch, mullet, prawns, wrass, eels, and lobsters. In a hunting scene we find the following animals introduced: wild boar, stag, ostrich, fox, and panther; while in another we see peacocks, guinea-fowls, and several other kinds of birds. The tesseræ used were generally cubes of about three-quarters of an inch side. From the writings of Pliny it would appear that this mosaic-work first became prevalent in Rome about 100 B.C., though it had been gradually growing into favour for some considerable time. He gives the name of several eminent workers in mosaic, and writes of it as a thing well established.[1]

Amongst wall mosaics one of the most famous and best known is that representing the battle between Alexander and Darius at Issus. It is about twenty feet long and ten feet high, and was discovered at Pompeii in the year 1831, in the building that, on its excavation, was entitled the House of the Fawn. In composition, general attitude, foreshortening, treatment of drapery, and all else that goes to the making of a picture, it is excellent.

As the conquests in Asia introduced a taste for ornamental display that vitiated the old Greek refinement and

---

[1] The student may advantageously refer to the "Universal Art Inventory." Part I.—Mosaics and Stained Glass. Part II.—Goldsmiths' Work, Enamels, Ivories. Part III.—Bronze, Iron, and other Metal-work. Part IV.—Wood-work and Sculpture.

substituted richness and excess of decoration, so in like manner the simplicity of early Rome developed ultimately into boundless luxury and indiscriminate extravagance. Vitruvius exclaims, "What our forefathers accomplished by art we attempt to affect by gaudy colouring." Pliny complains that "a man now cares nothing for art, provided he has his walls covered with purple." "During the first four ages," says Gibbon, "the Romans, in the laborious school of poverty, had acquired the virtues of war and government; by the vigorous exertion of these virtues, and by the assistance of fortune, they had obtained in the course of the three succeeding centuries an absolute empire over many countries of Europe, Asia, and Africa. The last three centuries had been consumed in apparent prosperity and internal decline." Philosophers and satirists inveighed against the unbounded luxury that was so conspicuous in every direction; but all such warning was unheeded, and the nation hastened to its fall.

> " Thou stranger which for Rome in Rome here seekest,
>   And nought of Rome in Rome perceiv'st at all,
>   These same old walls, old arches, which thou seest,
>   Old palaces, is that which Rome men call.
>   Behold what wreck, what ruin, and what waste,
>   And how that she which with her mighty powre
>   Tam'd all the world, hath tam'd herself at last,
>   The prey of Time, which all things doth devoure.
>   Rome now of Rome is th' only funerall,
>   And only Rome, of Rome hath victory;
>   Ne ought save Tyber, hast'ning to his fall
>   Remains of all: O World's inconstancy !
>   That which is firm, doth flit and fall away ;
>   And that is flitting, doth abide and stay." [1]

---

[1] Spenser's "Ruines of Rome."

On the transfer of the seat of government to Byzantium, A.D. 328, and the introduction of Christianity, entirely new influences arose. Amongst these influences the greater proximity to the schools of art of the East, with their great love for colour, and the change of creed powerfully affected the arts, and we may well make the consideration of the new state of things that sprang up a fresh departure.

CHAPTER IV.

On the general break-up of the Roman or Western
Empire we find the artistic and intellectual influences
shifting their centres from Rome to Constantinopolis, the
city of Constantine, the modern Constantinople, the
ancient Byzantium. With the inroads of the men of the
north upon Rome—a thing that in the purer days of
Roman life would have been impossible, but for which
Roman luxury and enervation and the division of the
empire [1] had now paved the way—chaos for a while ruled

---

[1] " History is little more than the history of capital cities. ' Paris

supreme, the old classic forms of art sank into abeyance, and from them ultimately arose forms that were no longer Roman, though largely suggested by them, and hence termed Romanesque. Architecture, and the arts generally, had broken from the old moorings, and were drifting hither and thither without rudder or compass. From this confusion, while men were feeling their way, arose a variety of young and vigorous offshoots, and it is very difficult, and, in the small space at our disposal, impossible, to follow these through their various modifications. On the introduction of Christianity into Italy many of the old courts of law or basilicas were used as churches, and the form and arrangement of these being found very suitable for the purpose, these were copied in the new buildings ; hence, in what was termed Lombardic, the basilican type of construction, with its old classic forms, was a good deal in evidence. The noble basilica of St. John de Lateran, together with those of St. Laurentius, St. Agnes, St. Peter, and St. Paul at Rome, were some of the first-fruits of the zeal of Constantine, the first Christian emperor.

Very similar results were working out at Byzantium, though the causes were different. In Rome the old state of things perished in flame and bloodshed, while in Con-

---

is France.' Blot out from English annals all that was originated or consummated in London, and what have you left ? Rome was the ultimate focus of vital force in the ancient world. No people ever successfully organized and maintained itself with a plurality of capitals. A second capital rent the Roman empire in twain. Babylon culminated on the ruins of Nineveh."—CONANT.

stantinople the introduction of Christianity caused a
mental reaction against everything associated with the old
pagan beliefs, and made the Corinthian capital of Jupiter's
temple almost as abhorrent as Jupiter himself. At the
same time art came much more under Oriental influence,
and to the new capital flocked men who brought with
them new canons of art. Byzantine work was itself influenced by, and in turn influenced, Persic and Saracenic :
and though on the fall of Byzantium, on its capture by
the Turks, the new religion produced new modifications,
Byzantine art has in Russia, the great seat of the Greek
Church, survived to the present day. Byzantine art
made its appearance in Ravenna [1] in the first half of the
sixth century, and later on in Venice. The Romanesque,
or basilican, or Lombardic, call it which we will, travelling mainly north and south, affecting the buildings in
Sicily, and markedly seen at Hildesheim and Bonn, had
several points of contact with the Byzantine, travelling
mainly east and west, through Ravenna and Venice to
the South of France, to Angoulême and Perigeux. From
the blending that arose from contact sprang Norman and

---

[1] The Goths on the conquest of Italy established their capital, not
in Rome, but at Ravenna. Theodoric, a great lover of the arts,
embraced the new religion and erected several churches. The city
is of immense interest, from its very ancient buildings and the
mosaics within them dating mostly from the fifth and sixth centuries. The magnificent basilica of San Vitale, a circular church,
built in the reign of Justinian, is very rich in mosaic-work. Other
famous churches are the basilica of S. Giovanni Evangelista, built in
the year 414; S. Giovanni Battista, 438; Sta Maria in Cosmedin, S.
Appollinare, S. Francesco, and SS. Nazario e Celso, the mausoleum
of Galla Placidia, daughter of Theodosius the Great.

Gothic art, and we may in Paris, Caen, Canterbury, Lincoln, or Durham, see capitals that can be distinctly traced back to the acanthus form developed by the Greeks four centuries before the Christian era.[1]

One of the most characteristic of Byzantine buildings is the cathedral of Santa Sophia—the Heavenly and Eternal Wisdom—at Constantinople, for centuries the noblest shrine of Christian worship. Constantine transferred, about 328 A.D., his capital to Constantinople, and built, amongst many stately edifices, a cathedral dedicated to the Eternal Wisdom; but this building and another that succeeded it each perished by fire, and the structure we now see was erected in the reign of Justinian, being commenced about the year 532 A.D., and finished in the short period of six years. The architect was Anthemius, a Greek. St. Mark's, Venice, is another very characteristic Byzantine building. This also was executed under Greek influence.

All students of the subject should take an opportunity of studying the noble and richly illustrated work of Salzenburg on Santa Sophia. Other works on this period of art that may be profitably consulted are the following: Knight's "Saracenic and Norman Architecture"; Quast's book on Ravenna; Texier and Pullan's fine work on Byzantine architecture; Bunsen's "Basilicas of Christian Rome"; Heideloff's book on Byzantine architectural

---

[1] Reference may here be made to the work of Hubsch, "Monuments de l'architecture Chretienne depuis Constantine jusqu'a Charlemagne," a finely illustrated book that shows the widely extending influence of the new ideas.

details, capitals, panels, and the like; Osten's book on "Les Monuments de la Lombardie"; Wyatt's Mosaics; Ruskin's "Stones of Venice"; Verneilh's "L'Architecture Byzantine en France"; and Kreutz's book, "La Basilica di San Marco in Venezia."

The acanthus is still freely found in Byzantine work, but it assumes a quite different character, the forms being much more angular than those of Classic date. While the flowing curves of the earlier form are to a great extent lost, the new treatment is full of vigour, and is perhaps quite as pleasing. The great feature, however, of Byzantine art is its essentially symbolic character. During the first and second centuries of the Christian era these symbols were only secondarily of decorative service, the chief motive for their introduction being as exhortations to faith, and as teachers of religious dogma. Where a form is primarily introduced from the meaning it conveys it may have little or no beauty, and while the mind is instructed there may be very little decorative charm. It is palpably a mere chance if there is. As time went on, and the fear of paganism declined, the scroll form, the anthemion, and some few other classic features were admitted, and, decoratively, the style developed into one of much greater interest. All forms employed were very conventional in character, even the animal forms and human figures that were so freely introduced were, in their proportions and angularity of treatment, very unlike nature. The later Byzantine designs, where the symbolism is less obtrusive, are often very beautiful.

In architecture great use is made of the dome,[1] a symbol of the vault of heaven, and the cross, circle, and other symbolic types constantly recur; but into the symbolic significance of the various forms introduced we need not here enter, as we have already, in another volume of this series, gone fully into the history, principles, and practice of symbolism as exemplified in Christian art, and to that volume we would, rather than here repeat ourselves, refer the student. The subject is one of immense interest and value.

The influence of Byzantine art was very great throughout most of Europe for more than five hundred years, while its power over the conquering Arabs was equally marked, as we may see in the buildings erected in Cairo, Alexandria, Jerusalem, and Sicily. A good deal of Persian work is also very Byzantine in feeling, though in this case probably the influence was mutual, as many Persian workmen were employed in Byzantium, and the result, in homely phrase, was "give and take."

Whatever the objection on religious grounds to the use of pagan forms, no such difficulty could arise in the case of colour; hence one very strong feature in Byzantine art is its lavish use of this potent element in decoration. The influence of the sunny East was here exercised with very marked effect, and in addition to this the luxury of the Court and the gorgeous ritual of the Church led to the introduction of the most costly materials, marble of the rarest and most varied beauty, an abundant use of gold,

---

[1] We may still see this feature very markedly in the Russian churches.

silver, and precious stones, richly embroidered hangings, and whatever else tended to the glorification of the State or the State creed.

Magnificent mosaics and richly tesselated pavements were one very characteristic feature in this wealth of ornament. Though we have seen in classic work a great use of mosaic, the art did not attain to its full splendour until the period now under consideration; and though many excellent early examples may be seen, its chief development was after the spread of Christianity. The Byzantine mosaics were ordinarily of glass, and the backgrounds of the subjects nearly always of gold. The original use of mosaic as a pavement naturally suggested the employment of variously coloured stones, materials that after all did not give a very extended or varied scale of colour; but the principal use of mosaic in this early Christian art was for mural decoration, and in this position, out of harm's way, the brilliant tints obtainable in glass were at the service of the artist. The designs are almost always figure subjects, though in subordinate positions we may get conventional foliage, geometric or other decorative treatments.[1] The figures have the stiff-

---

[1] Of the geometric type, Digby Wyatt's book on "Geometric Mosaics" affords many characteristic examples. It contains some twenty plates of illustrations printed in gold and colours. It is a book to be seen by any one desirous of understanding the character and possibilities of this geometric work. In Tyrwhitt's excellent book on the "Art Teaching of the Primitive Church" will be found a very interesting chapter on the mosaics of Rome, Ravenna, etc., where the whole subject is treated with an elaboration that is here impossible.

ness and elongated proportions that are so characteristic of Byzantine work, but they are ordinarily very noble in their dignity. The domes and apses are covered with figures of angels and archangels, saints and prophets, confessors and martyrs, the central figure being the Saviour of the world. The eternal glory of Christ and of His followers is alone represented, sorrow and sighing are for ever gone. "I am He that liveth and was dead, and behold I am alive for evermore." The effect of these mosaics, their brilliancy partly subdued by the dim light and the dust and stain of time, is very grand.

For nearly a thousand years, from the fourth century after Christ to the time of Giotto, mosaic was almost exclusively employed for wall decoration, and for four centuries was absolutely so employed. Hence they are of the greatest possible interest and value : links in the long chain of art that we could not possibly spare. On the re-introduction of fresco-painting, the more laborious art gave way to the new-comer, though it has never entirely died out. Successive popes have employed mosaic in the decoration of St. Peter's at Rome, and many of the celebrated and perishing works of the great masters, Rafaelle, Da Vinci, and others, have been translated, after, in some cases, twenty years of labour, into a material that no length of time will have power to affect, and which, so long as the fabric endures within which it is placed, may be justly deemed imperishable.

Amongst modern illustrations of its revived use we may instance the frieze that runs round the Albert Hall at South Kensington, where an area of over five thousand square feet is treated in mosaic. The tesseræ are in this case ceramic, and are of only three colours, the whole of the composition, figures, animals, etc., being worked in buff, and defined from the chocolate-coloured background by outlines of black. All details of features, folds of drapery, and the like are also indicated by black lines. In the south court of the South Kensington Museum may be seen the figures of men eminent in various arts [1] worked in mosaic as a wall decoration. Other examples may be seen in the Albert Memorial Chapel at Windsor, the Albert Memorial Monument in Hyde Park,[2] and elsewhere. It is also proposed to employ mosaic very largely in the decoration of St. Paul's Cathedral.

"Venice," to quote the words of Sismondi, "witnessed the long agony and the termination of the Roman Empire; in the west, the birth of the French power, when Clovis conquered Gaul; the rise and fall of the Ostrogoths in Italy; of the Visigoths in Spain; of the Lombards, who succeeded to the first; of the Saracens, who dispossessed the second. Venice saw the Empire of the Kalifs rise, threaten to invade the world, and decay. Long the ally of the Byzantine emperors, she by turns succoured and oppressed them. She saw the Eastern

---

[1] A series extending from Phidias to Mulready, through, amongst several others, these intermediate links—Apelles, Cimabue, Fra Angelico, Ghiberti, Donatello, Della Robbia, Durer, Holbein, Titian, Palissy, Grinling Gibbons, Wren, and Hogarth.

[2] Reference may here be made, if the student so please, to the account of this memorial written by Doyne Bell, where the various groups of sculpture, the mosaics, the metal-work, and all else, architectural or decorative, is duly described and illustrated.

empire fall, and the ferocious Mussulmans rise on its
ruins." The Venetians, originally fugitives before Alaric
and his Goths, in the year 452 sought shelter in the
islands of the lagoon; but ere long they rose to greatness,
and, as merchant princes, carried on extensive commerce
with the then known world. In the magnificence of their
operations and all that contributed to power, they rivalled
ancient Tyre. We read that in 1420 their mercantile
navy consisted of over three thousand sail, and the piazza
of St. Mark was the great market-place of Christendom.[1]

> "Once did she hold the gorgeous East in fee,
> And was the safeguard of the West; the worth
> Of Venice did not fall below her birth,
> Venice, the eldest child of Liberty,—
> She was a maiden city, bright and free:
> No guile seduced, no force could violate;
> And when she took unto herself a mate,
> She must espouse the everlasting sea." [2]

The cathedral of St. Mark was commenced in the year
977, and for more than five hundred years the wealth of
Venice was freely lavished upon its adornment. The floor
is inlaid with jasper, porphyry, alabaster, and precious
marbles, the walls are encrusted with magnificent
mosaics. The wealth of the world flowed through
Venice, and Venetian princes gathered from everywhere

---

[1] "There," says Coryate, who saw it more than two hundred years
ago, "you may see many Polonians, Slavonians, Persians, Grecians,
Turks, Jews, Christians, of all the famousest regions of Christendom,
and each nation distinguished from another by their proper and
peculiar habits—a singular show, and by many degrees the worthiest
of all the European countries."

[2] Wordsworth.

offerings of priceless value, as the argosies of the Queen of the Adriatic transported from Alexandria and all the havens of the East to this sandbank of the lagoon precious stores of all kinds for the progress of the work.

Ruskin, with his subtle and poetic insight, thus describes St. Mark: "There rises a vision out of the earth, and all the great square seems to have opened from it in a kind of awe, that we may see it far away—a multitude of pillars and white domes, clustered into a long, low pyramid of coloured light; a treasure heap it seems, partly of gold and partly of opal and mother-of-pearl, hollowed beneath into five great vaulted porches, ceiled with fair mosaic, and beset with sculpture of alabaster, clear as amber and delicate as ivory, sculpture fantastic and involved, of palm leaves and lilies, and grapes and pomegranates, and birds clinging and fluttering among the branches, all twined together into an endless network of buds and plumes; and in the midst of it the solemn forms of angels, sceptred and robed to the feet, and leaning to each other across the gates, their figures indistinct among the gleaming of the golden ground through the leaves beside them, interrupted and dim, like the morning light as it faded back among the branches of Eden, when first its gates were angel-guarded long ago. And round the walls of the porches there are set pillars of variegated stones, jasper and porphyry, and deep green serpentine spotted with flakes of snow; their capitals rich with interwoven tracery, rooted knots of herbage, and drifting leaves of acanthus and vine, and mystical signs, all beginning and ending in the Cross; and above them, in the

broad archivolts, a continuous chain of language and of
life—angels and the signs of heaven and the labours of
men, each in its appointed season upon the earth ; and
above these another range of glittering pinnacles mixed

Fig. 84.

with white arches, edged with scarlet flowers, a confusion
of delight, amidst which the breasts of the Greek horses
are seen blazing in their breadth of golden strength, and
the St. Mark's Lion, lifted on a blue field covered with

stars, until at last, as if in ecstasy, the crests of the
arches break into a golden foam, and toss themselves far
into the blue sky in flashes and wreaths of sculptured
spray, as if the breakers on the Lido shore had been
frost-bound before they fell, and the sea nymphs had inlaid them with coral and amethyst."

It is somewhat of a shock, after this glowing imagery,
to find another authority describing the interior of the
church as " dark, heavy, barbarous, nay, poor, in spite of
all the porphyry and oriental marbles and mosaics that
would enrich the walls, the vaults and pavements "; while
Fergusson can only go as far as to say that " the all-
hallowing touch of age and association disarm the critic,
and force him to worship when his reason tells him he
ought to blame." In truth, a building of this kind is so
entirely outside every-day experience that it comes on the
eye and mind somewhat as a shock; but when one is able
to put aside these prosaic experiences for awhile and to
project the mind back, and to endeavour, feebly of course
at best, to try and realize the feelings of the builders,
such work grows wonderfully upon the imagination and
the sympathies. St. Mark's, the Parthenon, the Temple
of Karnak, the Taj Mahal, cannot be seen at all in any
real sense until personal feelings and prejudices have
been banished, nor can a building that bears upon its
front the history of centuries be adequately judged by
the tourist between luncheon-time and *table d'hôte.* Some
people, we know, think that they have seen Stonehenge
when they have assisted at a pic-nic amongst its mysterious circles, and sought the shelter of one of its massive

trilithons while they discussed cold fowl and salad; but the eye sees no more than the mind will allow it to see, and bodily vision must be supplemented by mental to be of any real value.

Lombardic work, rude and archaic as it is, is full of dignity and power. The subjects introduced are often Biblical or legendary, at other times deal with war or

Fig. 85.

incidents of the chase. These are often mixed up with grotesque animals or convolutions of acanthus or other foliage, while elsewhere the dragons and other monsters are themselves knotted together and interlaced with great ingenuity and complexity of treatment. With ourselves the development of the Romanesque became the Norman or round arch Gothic style, and this in turn gave place to the pointed Gothic of the thirteenth, fourteenth, and fifteenth centuries. This again was superseded by the vagaries of the Elizabethan and Jacobean era, to be in turn supplanted by the work of the Renaissance, until we finally arrive at the present day, when we find experiments of all kinds; so that in Piccadilly we have a place of entertainment simulating an Egyptian temple, nearly opposite to a restaurant that is a pretty close copy of one of the Venetian Gothic buildings, while the Government Offices at Whitehall are Renaissance in style, and the British Museum is an Ionic temple.

The interlacing either of mere bands or lines, as in Figs. 41, 42, 43, 44, 45, 46, 47, 48, 49, 50, 51, 52, 53, 54, 55, or of grotesque animal forms, as in Fig. 85, is a very characteristic feature in Pictish and Celtic work, but we find it also a good deal in Byzantine and Romanesque examples, the symbolic serpent and dragon being often thus treated. We may see it again in Early Italian [1] and in Arab and in Anglo-Saxon decoration, and even in the art of savage tribes. This general use arises doubtless from the innate love of mankind for searching out mystery, for conquering difficulty, for unravelling entanglement; while the intricacy of the pattern, the alter-

---

[1] It has been suggested that the great use of interlacing patterns in Italy may have taken its rise from the influence of Irish monks journeying from "the Island of Saints" to Rome; but we may clearly see the beginning of this love of interlacing in the mosaic pavements of classic Rome, while no specimens of Celtic interlacing can be found of earlier date than the fifth century. If, therefore, there has been any borrowing—a by no means necessary supposition—it would appear to have been in the reverse direction.

FIG. 86.

nate rise and fall of the interlacing as the forms cross and recross, may be taken as a symbol of the woven warp and woof of fate and human life.

In Fig. 84, a key of the Renaissance period, this interlacing of the cipher is almost the sole decorative feature; while the Celtic and Anglo-Saxon examples (Figs. 86, 94), with the exception of a few bosses or studs, owe their decorative effect entirely to this very characteristic treatment.

Celtic ornament, whether we find it on metal-work, on the wayside cross, or in the magnificently illuminated MSS. of the period, is of almost identical nature, so that a piece of ornament from any one of these sources could be at once transferred to either of the other two without any sense of incongruity. It has three marked elements of design in it. These are not characteristic of special localities or periods, but all occur together, and very often on the same piece of work. These are—firstly, designs based on the spiral line; secondly, fret or key patterns, differing from Greek and most other types of fret in having their lines thrown obliquely instead of parallel with the sides of the panels that enclose them; thirdly, interlacing, either of pure line or of serpentine, draconic or other animal forms.[1] The form to be decorated is invariably marked off into panels or other quite definite spaces that are separated from each other by a

---

[1] " In one of the pages in the Gospels of St. Chad, which we have taken the trouble to copy, there are not fewer than one hundred and twenty of the most fantastic animals."—OWEN JONES.

ANIMAL FORMS IN ORNAMENT.

distinct band or plain margin, and the ornament in each of these spaces is complete in itself, and is frequently not repeated in what one may term the opposite or balancing space in any composition, each panel being not only self-contained, but individual and special.

On the deaths of the somewhat numerous Celtic saints, their books, crosier, bell, the chalice they used, and other belongings became treasured relics, and were enshrined with great reverence, as they were held to be of potent efficacy as pledges of victory in the day of battle, to heal the sick, to sustain the dying, and in multitudinous other emergencies where a little spiritual help would be very acceptable. In the museum of the Royal Irish Academy in Dublin are preserved several copies of the Gospels that belonged to notable Irish saints, each of these being enshrined in a costly and elaborately ornamented casket. Fig. 86 is the shrine or outer covering containing a bell that belonged to St. Patrick. This also is in the Dublin collection. The bell itself is referred to as a relic in a MS. dating from the year 552, but the bell-cover illustrated was made about the year 1100. To meet a possible objection we may point out that the bell itself is not of modern circular form, but taperingly quadrangular.[1] Another fine bell-shrine, enclosing the bell of St. Culan, may be seen in the British Museum.

Brooches and other articles of personal adornment are

---

[1] A common Swiss cow-bell on our table as we write is the very thing, made out of a sheet of metal roughly bent up into this shape and then rivetted down the sides to keep it together. Such were the bells of the early Celtic Church.

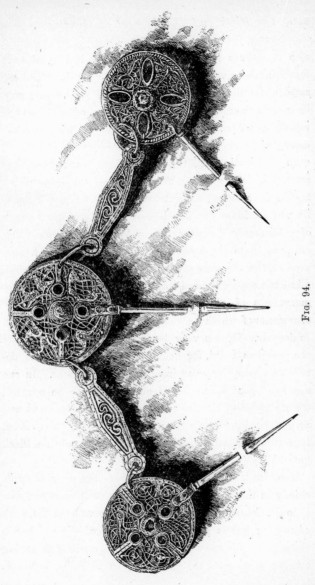

FIG. 94.

also sometimes found. The pins shown in Fig. 94 were found in the river Witham, and are very beautiful examples of Celtic art and workmanship. These also may be seen in the national collection. Many of these, as the magnificent Tara brooch, are richly adorned with coloured enamels.

In the illuminated MSS. of Celtic handiwork the designs are wonderfully striking, alike in their faultless precision and in their variety and intricacy. " In delicacy of handling, and minute but faultless execution, the whole range of palæography," writes Digby Wyatt, " offers nothing comparable to these early Irish manuscripts, and those produced in the same style in England. When in Dublin I had the opportunity of studying very carefully the most marvellous of all—'The Book of Kells,' some of the ornaments of which I attempted to copy, but broke down in despair. Of this very book Mr. Westwood examined the pages, as I did, for hours together, without ever detecting a false line or an irregular interlacement. In one space of about a quarter of an inch square he counted, with a magnifying glass, no less than one hundred and fifty-eight interlacements of a slender ribbon pattern, formed of white lines, edged by black ones, upon a black ground."

The Book of Kells is a copy of the four Gospels, chiefly in the Latin Vulgate. While some have ascribed it to St. Columba, others believe it to have been the work of angels; but it seems very doubtful whether either of these guesses is correct. It derives its name from having originally belonged to the monastery of Kells in Meath.

St. Columba, under whose direction the book was very possibly executed, was born in the year 521. He was a great missionary in the western isles and north of Scotland, and was so continuously employed until his decease in the year 597 that it is impossible that he could have written either this book, which is itself the task of a long life, or numerous others that have been accredited to him.

Of Saxon art we have but few remains, either in architecture, manuscripts, or elsewhere. The execution is crude, and the forms, either of intention or inability, are often grotesque. At Sompting Church, Sussex, one of the capitals has a rude resemblance to Corinthian, while another has curved volutes that are very suggestive of Ionic. The period, however, was not by any means an artistic one. The churches were often built of wood and thatched with reeds. Bede in his "Historia Ecclesiastica" tells us that when St. Augustine came to Britain, A.D. 597, he found many of the Roman temples still standing. These had in turn been utilized by the Saxons for their pagan worship, and those which were substantially built St. Augustine consecrated and converted to Christian service. It was not until the seventh century that the art of building in stone was revived. Bishop Hiscop collected together masons, makers of glass, and other valuable helpers in France, and these instructed the Saxons in many useful arts. We are expressly told by an old chronicler that the numerous ecclesiastical buildings that sprung up from the seventh to the tenth centuries were built "after the Roman manner," debased copies of work itself debased, but a fact sufficient to account for the Sompting capitals and such-like suggestions of classic influence.

The examples that are extant of Norman art are almost entirely architectural in their origin, and such as we find in wall-paintings, the capitals, and occasionally the shafts, of columns, and the archivolts of arches. A considerable use of human figures and other animal forms is made in the decoration of fonts, tympana, etc. These are often very grotesque in character—a result that, as in the Saxon work referred to, is frequently not by any means intended. Rude as they are in execution, they ordinarily convey some spiritual lesson if one can only interpret it. The Agnus [Dei is often introduced in what appears to be a very incongruous way with other animals—wild boars, stags, and so forth ; but these boars are symbolic of the wicked compared in the Bible to a wild boar of the wood rooting up and destroying right and left, while the stags are typical of the righteous that strive after holiness as the hart panteth after the water-brooks. The Agnus Dei is represented as fighting with the dragon on a capital at St. Lawrence Church, York, and may be seen again on the arch mouldings of doorways at Barton-le-Street, Bishop Wilton, Brayton, Dalmeny, and elsewhere. One great difficulty in dealing with the early sculptures is to identify the different animals at all, apart from any question of their symbolic significance, as the representations of them are often very unlike the real creatures.

The use of animal forms seems especially characteristic of certain periods, and these periods are ordinarily, though by no means invariably, when the art-power is not fully equal to the art-intention. The child will endeavour to draw a man or a horse on its slate rather than a rose or a lily, and is by no means dissatisfied with attempts that strike the elders as being atrociously bad. In art matters we can tolerate work of very varying degrees of merit of execution. Hence we accept thankfully the magnificent horses on the Parthenon frieze, the delightfully rendered birds and fish of the Japanese, or the impossibly powerful dragons of the Chinese, with all their wealth of scaly horror. Failing these, we can enjoy the most archaic and bizarre results so long as they are a genuine testimony to the delight felt by the artist in the creatures that he attempts to portray. Hence from this sympathy with the wild creatures around him, the Esquimaux carves from the tusk of the walrus the walrus itself, the reindeer or the seal; while the North American Indian models his pipe-bowl into the form of the beaver and the alligator, or daubs with rude art his tent with representations of the moose-deer, the grizzly bear, and the deadly rattle-snake.

Though all departments of organic nature have from time to time been laid under contribution in the service of design, the animal kingdom has nevertheless been far less employed than the vegetable. Several reasons suggest themselves to the mind why this should be so. The very fact of animals being far higher in the scale of creation than acanthus leaves in itself unfits them for many positions where some decorative treatment is required, for the eye that is not offended by seeing a symmetrical grouping of foliage would feel the incongruity of placing animals, creatures having volition, under like rigid conditions. Another potent reason doubtless is that while mediocrity can carve out Tudor roses or lotus buds by the score or the thousand, it cannot grapple adequately with higher forms.

The repetition that is so marked a feature in all work produced under the influence of machinery is also greatly against the use of these higher forms. Incongruity again is felt when in a wall-paper or damask, for example, fifty butterflies, all spaced out at equal distances, are all soaring upward at the same angle ; or fifty stags, all tripping with the same measured gait, advance with a perfection of discipline that suggests the monotonous drill of the barrack-yard rather than the glorious freedom of the ferny glades of the forest, or the wide expanse of purple moorland.

Animal forms in the ornament of the past will ordinarily be found to owe their introduction either to their connection with some mythological incident, as in much of the art of ancient times; or to some symbolic meaning that has been attributed to them, as in many examples to be met with in early Christian art, such as Fig. 116, the eagle symbol of St. John, from old stained glass in the South Kensington Museum; or to the requirements of heraldry,[1] as illustrated by numerous examples in

---

[1] We have in another volume of the series dealt with the history, principles, and practice of heraldry at considerable fulness, and would therefore refer our readers to numerous examples that are there duly set forth.

mediæval or modern work, of which Figs. 67, 115, 118, may be taken as illustrations. As the language of heraldry, at least in the earlier times, is frequently as symbolic as that of religion, the two might very reasonably be here classed together as one influence, the symbolic, though practically it is convenient to subdivide it into two classes—the religious symbolism, that advances truth and dwells on the glory of God; the heraldic, that deals rather with earthly glory and ministers to the pride of man.

When animal forms are found in the work of those peoples whose art level is somewhat low, they are generally as naturalistic as imperfect means and powers permit, and in most cases probably owe their introduction to pleasure and interest found in the creatures. Later on the forms become symbolic and more or less conventional, and the choice is guided by the inner life rather than by the outward form. Hence it is rather the cunning of the fox in this latter case that influences the selection than the delight in its lithe suppleness of bodily form, the courage of the lion, the greed and rapacity of the wolf, the gluttony of the pig, the vigilance of the cock, rather than an appreciation of the mere outward appearance of these creatures that has led to their introduction. Our readers will readily recall many other such examples in illustration of the feeling that has thus influenced the choice. Where we fail to grasp the idea involved, it will in many cases arise from our inability to enter into the state of mind of some far-distant people, remote either in time or locality, or else that the special historical or legendary associations connected with the forms are unknown to us. Thus a Maori getting hold of an English sovereign bearing the device of a man on horseback killing some strange monster, while he admired the vigour of action, could not penetrate into the motive of adoption; for to him, we may assume, the legend of St. George and the dragon would be wholly unknown.

Reasoning from this, if we find certain devices—say, for example, on early Greek coinage—that, rude as they are, clearly point to some religious belief, are the attributes of some deity, commemorate some event in the national history, or are the recognised badge of some state or colony, we may not unreasonably assume that other devices, to us meaningless, possess no less some inner significance, could we but pierce beneath the surface.

Though the number of mythical forms introduced in art is very great, and naturally so, when we consider the extent of the field and the great variety of beliefs extending throughout the mythologies of Mexico and Peru in the New World, the more refined imaginings of the classic nations of antiquity, or the quaint beliefs of the Eastern nations, as exemplified in the paintings and sculptures of India, China, and Japan, those that we find most freely recurring in art examples are comparatively few in number. In some cases the forms introduced are too seldom employed to have received a distinguishing name, and in many cases are probably, as in some of the forms seen at Pompeii, but the individual fancies of some one mind; but in many other cases the particular form has been

Fig. 95.

freely adopted and frankly accepted. Various examples
of these mythical forms will be found in Figs. 66, 70,
72, 76, 90, 91, 127. Of this class the sphinx, sea-horse
sea-lion, phœnix, cockatrice, griffin, dragon, chimæra,
mermaid, wyvern, centaur, unicorn, hydra, harpy, basilisk, or salamander, may be accepted as types; for though
none of these creatures have, or ever had, any real
existence, being wholly the creations of fancy, they
have received a certain precision of treatment that
makes any of them as clearly recognisable as any strictly
natural form. We may, in passing, point out the curious
fact that the wit of man seems to have almost wholly
failed to create a really original form. Perhaps the
dragon of the Chinese, as we may see in Fig. 95, is as
nearly purely fanciful as any; but practically these
various monstrous forms are not creations at all: they
are merely combinations and adaptations of natural
forms, types familiar enough to us in themselves. Thus
a mermaid is but a human being terminating in the
body and tail of a fish; the centaur is partly human,
partly equine; the harpy is the union of the head of
a woman with the body and feet of a bird. The illustrations on Plate X. are curious Norman examples of
various monstrous forms.

The bull, ram, stag, lion, horse, dog, goat, boar, wolf,
fox, and many other quadrupeds are found in art. It
would be impossible and, in any case, needless to dwell
at any length upon each of these creatures. We will content ourselves, therefore, with giving some few details of
the bull, the first in our catalogue. This animal is fre-

-quently introduced in early art. Amongst the Egyptians the bull Apis was worshipped as a god, as the earthly type, manifestation, and representative of great Osiris. This sacred animal therefore naturally occurs throughout the art of this ancient people.[1] Fore parts of bulls joined together at the centre of the body form the commonest type of the capitals of the columns found in the palaces of Persepolis and Susa, and the animal figures again very largely in the Assyrian remains. It is, however, always human-headed, and bears therefore probably considerable analogy to the Egyptian sphinx, the union of material strength with intellectual power. The sphinx is always represented as recumbent, while the Assyrian figures of like character are invariably standing, and are ordinarily in pairs, one on either side of a doorway.

In classic art, representations of the bull are freely found. It is a very common device on ancient coinage; we see it on that of Chalcedon in Bythinia, on that of Sybaris, Samos, and many other places. A considerable variety of treatment may be found. On the coins of Gelas and of Neapolis the bull is human-headed; on those of

---

[1] Thirty tombs of these bulls, who lived one after the other for a space of some six hundred years, have been discovered at Memphis, the chief seat of Apis worship. It will be remembered how this Apis cult that had been so familiar to the children of Israel while in bondage in Egypt fascinated them and turned them aside over and over again from the worship of Jehovah, as for example :—

> "When their borrowed gold composed
> The calf in Oreb ; and the rebel king
> Doubled that sin in Bethel and in Dan,
> Likening his Maker to the grazing ox."

Phocis we get the animal's head alone, and given in front view; on those of Thurium and Tauromenium the bull is represented as charging; while in the coins of Eretria the animal is in repose. The coins of Metapontum, a Greek colony in Sicily, have on the obverse the river god Archelous, a river of that part of Greece from which the colony sprang. The deity is represented in human form, leaning on a reed, and having the head of a bull. The figure of a bull was often used to symbolise a stream. Homer, in narrating the combat between the river god Scamander and Achilles, says of the former that he roared like a bull—an idea afterwards employed by other poets. In the fable of the conflict of Hercules with the river-deity Archelous, the latter is represented as actually changing himself into a bull, the deep roar of the bull being no doubt suggested by the sound of the torrent, while the impetuosity of the attack not inaptly symbolises the rush of the stream as it carries all before it. On the coins of Camarina, a Syracusan colony, we find the same idea treated with great beauty and refinement, the centre of the coin being filled with a youthful human head, full face, having the budding horns of a bull just rising from the hair, while the whole is surrounded by the wave scroll, the well-known symbol for water.

A not unfrequent treatment on early coinage is the conflict between a lion and a bull. We may see an illustration of this in Fig. 80, from a beautiful coin of Acanthus in Macedonia. Various theories have been broached in explanation of this device. By some it is held to symbolise the triumph of the ruler or the state over external or domestic foes—a not improbable motive for its adoption. By others the lion is held to typify the sun, and the bull, as the symbol of a river, to represent the unwholesome vapours and exhalations of earth; being thus, like the dragon device on our modern English sovereigns, one symbolic rendering the more of the great struggle between the good and the evil that in one form or another—as in Fig. 79, again a lion and dragon in conflict—is so often the subject of art. In the Etruscan gallery of the British Museum may be seen an embossed relief representing a frieze of lions, bulls, and winged ibexes. It is a very early example of Etruscan art. The capture of the Cretan bull by Hercules, and afterwards of the cattle of Geryon, figure with the other famous labours of the demi-god; and the slaying of the Minotaur, a monster having a human body and bull's head, by Theseus is another favourite subject in classic art.

Europa, beloved of Zeus, who transformed himself into a white bull, was by him borne over the sea to Crete. There she gave birth to three sons, who each became the founder of an illustrious line. The people of Crete, proud of their descent from so noble an ancestry, represented this incident in many ways. Sometimes the bull alone figures upon their coins, at others he is bearing the fair Europa to their shores. The abduction of Europa was a very favourite subject, not only with the Cretans, but throughout the whole realm of classic art. The goddess Silene is sometimes represented as riding in a chariot drawn by bulls.

What are termed bucrania — sculptured ornaments

M

representing ox-skulls wreathed with flowers—were employed to adorn the frieze of the entablature in the Ionic and Corinthian orders of architecture. As the allusion was to the sacrificial rites that took place within the temple it is evident that they cannot be legitimately employed in the decoration of modern churches, though they are sometimes introduced when the features of classic architecture are slavishly adhered to, without due thought of their significance.

The ram's head (Fig. 117) appears on a coin of Delphis, while the greyhound (Fig. 114) is from a coin of Segesta, and the boar (Fig. 108) is a device found on the money of Salapia.

We not unfrequently find in art examples of animals terminating in scroll-work. It is a common feature in classic decoration, as, for example, the horse from Pompeii (Fig. 76). We therefore find it freely again in Renaissance work, as in Fig. 113, a piece of wood-carving, where the central mask is elaborately foliated. Other good examples are Fig. 72, from a piece of pottery in the South Kensington Museum; Fig. 70, where the dolphin is certainly a very considerable departure from nature; and in the panel, Fig. 93, where the suggestion of animal forms is present, but so disguised as to be scarcely recognisable. Though a characteristic piece of Renaissance design, we would venture to say that the ribbons coming out of the eyes of the mask, the absurdly floral bird forms in the upper part of the composition, and the creatures below, with one leg ending in a paw and the other in a leaf, make altogether a most unsatisfactory result.

The lions of England (Fig. 67) and the isolated lion (Fig. 118), from a tile, are good examples of heraldic treatment, as is also the chained hart (Fig. 115), from Westminster Hall. Fig. 75 is a curious little stag panel from a Roman mosaic.

The elephant, though naturally a creature rather to be looked for in the art of the East than in that of these Western regions, must not on that account be overlooked, since it figures so very freely in the art of India and of other Oriental nations with whom we are brought in contact. The elephant is occasionally seen in Japanese art, but it is only as a Buddhism emblem, and is copied more or less imperfectly from Indian work, as the elephant not being found in Japan, the artists have ordinarily had no opportunity of studying the beast from the life.

The wonderful sagacity of the elephant is the subject of too many stories to need enforcing here, and we are not therefore surprised to find that Ganesa, the god of wisdom, one of the most important members of the Hindu mythology, has the head of an elephant. All sacrifices and religious ceremonies are commenced by an invocation to him.[1] Figs. 88, 89 are illustrations of the use of the

---

[1] The original bestowal of the elephant's head would appear, however, to have been very much of the nature of a chance. We read that Ganesa, the eldest son of Siva and Parvati, was so unfortunate as to get embroiled with Vishnu, one of the three superior gods, and that Siva was so incensed that he cut his son's head off. His mother, Parvati, greatly grieved at the loss of her child, was so terribly afflicted and practised such austerities, that Siva, at the earnest request of the other deities, would have restored him to life again had it not unfortunately happened that the severed head could not be found.

elephant in Oriental art ; they are from illustrations in the South Kensington Museum. The first of these is a small portion of a long band or frieze made up of nothing but these elephant forms, all in some way varying from each other. Fig. 89 would appear to be a representation of an elephant seeking amidst the welcome foliage, cool beneath his feet and sheltering overhead, a refuge from the heat, or, it may be, from the plague of insect life that doubtless finds some vulnerable points even in the mighty elephant.

We find the elephant again very freely in Siamese work, on coinage and elsewhere, as it is one of the national emblems of Siam. China again affords illustrations of its use. In the great cemetery at Nankin, the resting-place of the bones of the Emperors of the Ming dynasty, we find, for example, two avenues of colossal stone figures of animals, such as elephants, lions, camels, bears, and others, which were deemed emblematic of the monarch there interred.

A lamp found at Pompeii had two elephants' heads projecting from its sides ; and in the bronze room devoted to Greek and Roman antiquities in the British Museum may be seen a figure of Africa, on her left side a lion, on her right an elephant's tusk—a sufficient indication that the animal was known to Western artists. It was the custom of victorious generals on their return to Rome to bring

In this emergency, the case being urgent, there was nothing for it but to appropriate the first head that came to hand, and this happened to be an elephant's. All the deities, to appease and console Parvati on this very partial restoration of her son, consented that on all occasions he should be first invoked.

with them, as part of the spoils, any curious animals of the countries that had been the scene of their victories; and we know from the ancient writers that elephants were amongst the creatures so introduced to the citizens of Rome.

An elephant carved by Bishop Bruère, an Oriental traveller, may be seen on a misericord in Exeter Cathedral. This is earlier even than the famous picture in one of the Cottonian MSS. of the first elephant brought to England, an event that happened A.D. 1255. Those of our readers who are familiar with the Albert Memorial in Kensington Gardens will readily recall the four groups representing the four quarters of the world, that, together with the band of sculpture running round the podium, form so noble a base to the monument. The four animals that form the centres of the groups of typical figures are the camel, bull, elephant, and bison.

Various bird-forms are very freely introduced into decorative art, such as the eagle, dove, owl, pelican, swan, swallow, stork, and peacock. Examples of this decorative use of birds may be seen in several of the illustrations on Plate XI., all from Japanese sources. Fig. 82 is from the quaint bordering of the Bayeux tapestry.[1] Figs. 78 and

---

[1] The Bayeux tapestry has, by permanent photography, been reproduced of the same size as the original work. As its cost, coloured in fac-simile, is £75, those of our readers who are not maniacs or millionaires will probably elect to see it in the libraries at South Kensington or the British Museum. The centre of the strip is occupied by the representation of the various incidents that relate to the landing of William the Conqueror, while above and below run continuous borders or strips that are filled with various grotesque forms that have no connection with the historical scenes.

83 are two very good examples from the mural paintings of Pompeii, powerfully drawn, and of excellent decorative feeling. The cock (Fig. 77) is from a Greek coin, while the quaint but happy treatment seen in Fig. 110 is from a Gothic flooring tile. Fig. 92 is a very good Egyptian drawing of a group of pelicans. Any one who has noticed these birds preening their feathers, or resting in the stolid, contemplative way that they do, will at once recognise the sketch as being most happily suggestive. Amongst the very archaic Greek sculptures from Xanthos in the British Museum may be seen a frieze of cocks and hens of admirably life-like execution.

The decoration of the Natural History Museum at South Kensington is very happily based on divers of the specimens, zoological or botanical, therein contained. Figs. 96 and 97 are two of the panels. The special circumstances of the case justify a very naturalistic treatment. The whole series well repays careful observation and study.

Fishes and other marine forms are very commonly found in ornaments. Of these the dolphin, regarded by the ancients as the king of fishes, as the lion was of beasts, or the eagle of birds, is of most frequent occurrence. It is also a symbol of maritime supremacy. It may be seen in Figs. 90, 109. The ancient colony of Phocea bore on its coinage a seal, and that of Coressus a cuttle-fish. Other good examples are the coins shown in Fig. 111, and Figs. 68 and 73, two pateræ of Greek work in the British Museum. Fish forms, except as heraldic devices, very sparingly appear in mediæval art; Fig. 87, a capital of the Norman period, is, however, an illustration. The Japanese draw fish admirably. Some examples will be seen in Plate XI. The lithe forms and simple contours

Fig. 96.

and the graceful and pleasing motions are easily produced by the somewhat dashing sweep of the brush that is so characteristic of the work of this artistic race.

Serpents, lizards, butterflies, and many other forms are found in art. The Palissy ware, of which Fig. 71 is an example, makes great use of various animal forms, such as snakes, lizards, toads, and the like; and in various

Fig. 97.

museums we may see examples of Old English pottery, where a frog or toad is placed within the cup or mug. This of course is not intended to be decorative. It was supposed to be humorous, the point of the joke being the disgust and surprise of the drinker on finding, as he emptied the vessel, this creature apparently ready to jump down his throat.

In literature we find repeated references to this use of animal forms in art. Thus Herodotus describes a linen corslet that Amasis, king of Egypt, sent to the Lacedæmonians, as having a vast number of animals interwoven in its fabric. In the " Odyssey " we read that in the robe of Ulysses—

> " In the rich woof a hound, mosaic drawn,
> Bore on full stretch, and siezed a dappled fawn ;
> Deep in the neck his fangs indent their hold :
> They pant and struggle in the moving gold."

Quintus Curtius again, in describing the dress of Darius, says that " the waist part of the royal tunic was woven in white, and upon his mantle of cloth of gold were figured two golden hawks, as if pecking at one another with their beaks." Many other most interesting references might be given ; it will suffice to instance but one more, and that from Chaucer, who describes in one of his poems the dress of a maiden, who sat—

> " In a robe ryght ryall bowne
> Of a red syclatowne
> Be hur fader syde ;
> A coronell on hur hedd set,
> Hur clothys with bestes and byrdes wer bete
> All abowte for pryde."

Those who care to pursue this side of our subject further may find abundance of references in the old chronicles, heraldic treatises, and church and cathedral inventories.

Tempting as the whole subject is, we must nevertheless forbear, and return, after this lengthy but legitimate digression on the general use of animal forms in
art, to the point whence we started—Norman decoration.

On the accession of William the Norman to the throne,
the new style of building and decoration rapidly took
root and spread, and entirely supplanted the older type
of work; and though it had in due time to give place to
Gothic, many excellent examples of it yet remain to us.
Out of the sum total of our English cathedrals, no less
than twenty-two retain portions of Norman work. The
general character of Norman was plainness and massive
solidity, the great opportunities for decorative work being
either in the string courses, the capitals, or most notably
in the magnificent doorways that are so marked a feature
of this period. Most of these doorways have the head of
the arch filled in solidly, the space between the square
opening and the semicircular mouldings being called the
tympanum. This is generally filled with sculpture of a
religious and symbolic character. The central figure is
often that of our Lord, in allusion doubtless to His own
words, "I am the door; by Me if any man enter in, he
shall be saved." Fig. 98 gives a good idea of the valuable opening for sculptured decoration that this tympanum
space afforded. Even when centuries of modifications
have passed over these early buildings and entirely
changed them, the noble doorways of the twelfth-century
work have frequently been preserved. The arches are
semicircular, and great richness of effect is produced by
successive bands of moulding. Sometimes these occupy

only the semicircular part, and are then replaced by shafts, and at others they go right down to the ground on either side. These bands of mouldings are entirely independent of each other, so that the greater or less richness of the doorways of the various buildings de-

Fig. 98.

pends to a great extent upon the more or less number of these.

Of these mouldings by far the commonest is the zigzag or chevron (Fig. 99). In early work it is as shown, but later on the narrow mouldings are cut into rows of circular beads, and the broader intermediate parts are carved into deep hollows. The billet (Fig. 100) is another characteristic moulding, as is also the cable, a form like a twisted

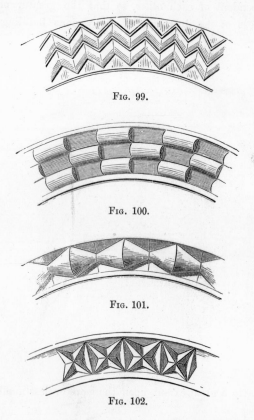

Fig. 99.

Fig. 100.

Fig. 101.

Fig. 102.

rope, and the nail-head. Other common forms are shown in Figs. 101, 102, 103, 104. Fig. 105 is what is termed the beak-head. The capitals are very simple in form, and their shafts are either plain or cut into zigzags, cables, and other enrichments. Good Norman work may be seen in the cathedrals of Winchester, Canterbury, Durham, Ely, Peterborough, Lincoln, and Worcester; Waltham Abbey, Malmesbury Abbey, Romsey Abbey; the Tower of London; St. Bartholomew's, Smithfield; St. Mary's, Marl-

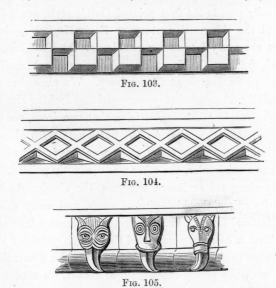

Fig. 103.

Fig. 104.

Fig. 105.

borough, in Wiltshire; at Iffley Church, in Oxfordshire; South Ockenden, in Essex; Castle Rising, in Norfolk; St. Peter's, Northampton; Shoreham Church, in Sussex; Barfreston, Kent; Brinsop, in Herefordshire; Wootton, in Gloucestershire; Stourbridge, in Cambridgeshire; Christchurch, Hampshire; St. Mary's Church, Porchester; Ketton, in Rutlandshire; and many other localities. Through a period of transition which has been termed semi-Norman, which is contemporary with Henry II. and Richard I., and which was distinguished by the arches in many cases becoming pointed and of greater span, the shafts lighter, a greater use of a rude type of foliage, and the mouldings of less massive character, we gradually pass to the first pointed Gothic style, generally termed the thirteenth-century or Early English period. There are many interesting remains of the Transitional period, perhaps the finest example being the beautiful chapel of St. Joseph at Glastonbury. We remember in the small and somewhat poverty-stricken-looking church of Ogbourne, in Wiltshire, noticing that two doors, one on the south and the other on the north side, were almost identical in the zigzags and other mouldings ; but while one was semicircular, the other was distinctly pointed.

The elongated or lancet windows, the slender shafts, the lofty spires, the high-pitched roofs, and many other architectural features mark a striking difference between the thirteenth-century work and that which preceded it ; but as our present business is rather with the decoration than with the purely constructional details, we need not here dwell upon these. Perhaps the most striking ornamental feature is that the zigzags, cables, billets, beak-heads, etc., utterly vanish, and their place is taken by the moulding known as the dog-tooth, a form that is found only in Early English Gothic, but which is there found in profusion. The simple mouldings round arches, windows, doorways, and so forth, are few in number, but they consist of rounds alternating with deeply cut hollows, so that they throw a very strong light and shade, and are very effective. The foliage introduced has great boldness of effect, and is freely used in the capitals, spandrels, bosses, and so forth. It is very deeply under-cut, as in Fig. 106, and is generally treated with great flexibility and beauty of curve. The ornament, whether painted or

Fig. 106.

carved, is often based on the scroll. The form of foliage employed is a conventional one, somewhat resembling a trefoil. The spandrel shown in Fig. 66 is a very characteristic example. When used in the capitals, as in Fig. 107, it always grows boldly from the base-mould-ing or necking. It is not, as we shall find to be the case in the next century, wreathed horizontally round the capital, but suggests the idea of upward and vigorous growth. The shafts of the columns in windows, porches, pulpits, fonts, and elsewhere, stand boldly out from the general surface, so that the hand could be passed right round them ; and these shafts are often made of various marbles.

A great use of arcading is very characteristic of Early English. One may see this very well at Westminster,

Fig. 107.

Wells, Peterborough, and Salisbury, and in fact in any good example of the period. These arcades are filled with statues of prophets, apostles, martyrs, virgins, confessors, kings, and bishops. The figures are often very dignified and beautiful in treatment, and have a very fine effect. Fine as the architecture is, the sculpture is fully worthy of it, when we bear in mind the limitations under which it was produced. The Greeks had, beneath their sunny skies, and in the public games, countless opportunities of acquiring a knowledge of the human form, which were not available to the men of the north. The material, too, in which the mediæval sculptors worked, had not the hardness of the Greek marble, and the fingers of Time have left their mark upon it. In cities, too, the corroding influence of the sulphur resulting from the continuous combustion of coal is a great foe to all external work, and the rains and frosts of each recurring winter have exerted their influence for evil. The iconoclastic zeal of the puritan and of the excursionist have not been expended, either, without result; and all these untoward influences must be taken into consideration, when we ask our readers to admire with us some possibly featureless or headless statue. Some of the Gothic work is an offence to all good taste, but it rarely deliberately defiles itself and becomes a shame to its makers, as some old and some modern work does, while it is often delightfully quaint, and at times rises to a grandeur and dignity worthy of the highest regard and the most careful study. Some of the figures, for example, of kings, confessors and saints, in the great west portals of Rheims, or occupying the multitudinous niches in Wells, are as perfect in grace and conception as the mind can imagine. Beautiful examples of Early English work may be seen in Westminster Abbey, Lincoln Cathedral, York Cathedral, Romsey Abbey, Salisbury Cathedral; Higham Ferrers Church, in Northamptonshire; Selby, Yorkshire; the Lady Chapel at Hereford; the transepts at Canterbury, the abbeys of Rivaulx, Fountains, Netley and Tintern, and at Beverley Minster.

In many situations, as in spandrels or the heads of

N

doorways, that would otherwise look bare, a considerable use is made of circles containing trefoils or quatrefoils, but in rich examples of the style these spaces are filled with diapers. These are almost always based on the square, and these squares are usually filled by foliate forms in fours or eights that radiate from the centre and fill up the figure. These squares are ordinarily placed close together like those of a chessboard, but we occasionally find them separated by a band, more or less broad, of plain surface. Diapers were also largely used in the Decorated or fourteenth-century Gothic, and in the Perpendicular or fifteenth-century period. During these two latter it is often a painted instead of a carved enrichment, and probably was so in the thirteenth century, though no examples of this application of it are now forthcoming. We must bear in mind that grey and dingy as many of our cathedrals and churches look now, they were in mediæval times richly adorned with colour. We must not therefore divide diapers into two classes, the painted and the carved. There is no such division: in most cases probably they were both at once.

The term diaper is applied to any small repeat of geometric character that evenly covers a space, and such treatment may of course be found not only in architectural work but in illumination, textile fabrics and the like; and as a matter of fact we do throughout the Middle Ages find these diaper arrangements a very popular form of decoration, and often referred to as such. Thus Chaucer, in his " Knight's Tale," describes how—

> " The gret Emetrius, the king of Jude,
>   Upon a stede bay, trapped in stele
>   Covered with cloth of gold diapred wele,
>   Came riding like the god of armes, Mars ; "

and elsewhere of a seat that was—

> " With damaske whyte and azure blewe
>   Well dyaperd with lylles newe."

The Church inventories have frequent reference to various vestments, with diapered patterns upon them. It has been suggested that the word is derived from Yprès in Flanders, a town of considerable repute for its manufacture of various fabrics,[1] many of which would no doubt be covered with diaper designs; but unfortunately for this derivation the town of Yprès did not rise to this manufacturing eminence till some considerable time after the word diaper was in common use. The Byzantine Greeks had the term diaspron, a word derived from the verb to separate, thus signifying a pattern that is isolated from the ground-work; and we find an equivalent term in Latin.

As time passed on,[2] the style known as the thirteenth-century Gothic, like all things else in this world of change, altered its character, and after a lengthened period of

---

[1] This theory would the more easily take root as many such names do take their origin from the places with which the material or whatever it may be is connected. Thus muslin derived its name from Mosul, a great seat of its manufacture, and damask from Damascus.

[2] Any or all of the following books may advantageously be consulted on these successive periods :—

" Britton's Cathedral Antiquities of Great Britain," with upwards of 300 engravings by Blore, Le Keux, and others. 5 vols. Giving

gradual transition entirely lost its original features, and merged into the fourteenth-century or decorated Gothic. In this latter the windows were no longer of the simple character of the preceding century, but by degrees became more and more filled with tracery, at first of a strictly geometrical character, but afterwards of the most freely flowing forms. The dog-tooth entirely disappeared, being supplanted by an ornament almost as popular, known as the ball-flower. This was of globular form, and had

---

numerous examples from the Cathedrals of Bristol, Canterbury, Exeter, Gloucester, Hereford, Lichfield, Norwich, Oxford, Peterborough, Salisbury, Wells, Winchester, Worcester, and York.

"Brandon's Analysis of Gothic Architecture," illustrated by upwards of 700 examples of Doorways, Windows, etc. 158 plates.

Colling's "Examples of Mediæval Foliage and Coloured Decoration," taken from Buildings of the Twelfth to the Fifteenth Century, and giving about 150 illustrations.

Colling's "Gothic Ornaments," being a Series of Examples of Enriched Details and Accessories of the Architecture of Great Britain, taken from the Structures of the Thirteenth, Fourteenth and Fifteenth Centuries. 209 plates. Also, by the same author, two volumes entitled "Details of Gothic Architecture," measured and drawn from existing examples of the Twelfth, Thirteenth, Fourteenth and Fifteenth Centuries. 200 plates.

Rickman's excellent book, modestly termed "An Attempt to Discriminate the Styles of Architecture in England, from the Conquest to the Reformation, with a Sketch of the Grecian and Roman Orders."

Another good book to see is Waring's "Illustrations of Architecture and Sculpture," upwards of 400 figures, comprising Choice Examples of Mediæval Sculpture, Metal Work, Architectural Ornament, etc.

In conclusion we may mention Labarte's "Handbook of the Arts of the Middle Ages and the Renaissance as applied to the Decoration of Furniture, Arms, Jewels, etc." A book containing a large number of good illustrations.

VIII

ANIMAL FORMS IN ORNAMENT.

three or four leaf-like portions that turn back sufficiently to enable a ball inside to be seen, the outer part being a sort of enclosing husk to the fruit-like form within. Examples of it are abundant in work of this period. They are often placed in hollow mouldings by themselves, and the intervals between them made about equal to the spheres. At other times we find them further apart, and represented as growing from a spiral line. Another very favourite form is a four-leaved flower of very square character that is placed at intervals in hollow mouldings, and associated with this are often other leaves, or human heads, these latter being generally of grotesque character. The capitals are very seldom two alike, and the foliage wreaths the bells of the capitals horizontally, instead of growing upwards from the necking mouldings. In Early English work the foliated scrolls or other ornaments always appear, as in Fig. 106, to spring from the mould- ing itself, and to be an inherent part of it, so that if we removed them it could only be by making a visible fracture, whereas the decorated ornaments suggest the idea that they are merely adherent, and that five minutes' vigorous chiselling would entirely remove them, and leave the rest of the work unaffected by their absence.

The foliage is no longer of the conventional type that is so characteristic of the thirteenth century. In the period now under consideration this is exchanged for an excess of naturalism, and the capitals and string courses become wreathed with all the treasures of the hedgerow—the richly cut leaves of the buttercup, the sprays of the wild rose, the sturdy growth of the acorn-laden oak, the beauti-

ful leaves of the maple or the hawthorn or the bryony,
the spiny foliage of the thistle, and many others. The
lines of Scott, in his description of the cloister garden,
recur to our minds, where he dwells on how the—

> " Spreading herbs and flowrets bright
> Glistened with the dew of night,
> Nor herb nor flowret glistened there
> But was carved in the cloister arches as fair."

At first sight one might say that this love of nature
must be a decided step in advance, but on reflection we
do not feel it to be so. The grand simplicity and sugges-
tiveness of the earlier work is gone, and all the elaboration
and intricate detail of the later carving fail to do justice
to the grace of nature. Beautiful as it is in intention
and in appreciation of natural forms, the delicacy and
grace of the wild denizens of the hedge-bank and the
forest cannot be adequately expressed in stone-work, nor
would it be desirable, on other grounds, that they should
be. Hence it would appear that we have arrived at this
unhappy state of things : that we blame the old carvers
because their work does not express the lightness of
nature, while we add that if it did we should censure
them no less, because then the sense of solidity and
support so essential in a capital or other architectural
feature would be lost, since a constructional detail must
be not only actually strong enough for its work, but must
give that sense of strength to the eye. But the moral
clearly is that in any case in such a position the direct
imitation of the natural forms is a mistake, and the blame
is not that the carver made his maple leaves too light or

too solid, but that he put maple leaves there at all, since he was bound in doing so to transfix himself on one horn or the other of the dilemma.

The diapers of the fourteenth century are of more elaborate type than those they succeeded, being based not only on the square, but on the equilateral triangle, hexagon, and other geometrical forms.

Paving tiles are largely employed throughout the Gothic period. They appear to have come into use about the end of the twelfth century, and they continued in use for over four hundred years. The designs on the thirteenth-century tiles bear the very characteristic form of foliage that we have already seen in the capitals and elsewhere ; a very good example of these may be seen in the pavement of the Chapter House, Westminster Abbey. In like manner the tiles of the fourteenth century bear the impress of the prevailing taste, and are often composed of designs based on the oak, ivy, vine, and other foliage. Apart from such patterns a great variety of designs may be seen. Religious monograms are not uncommon, and at other times tiles bearing a single letter may be seen, and these were arranged in orderly sequence to spell out any required inscription. A great use is also made of animal forms (Figs. 69, 110, 118), and of various heraldic devices and badges, crosses, and other religious symbols, figures of mounted knights, of kings and queens and bishops, geometrical patterns, and so forth. In many cases the pattern on the tile is complete in itself, but in some instances each tile only bears a portion of the whole device, and it requires four, nine, sixteen, or more, to be arranged together before the figure is complete. The tiles are ordinarily red and yellow, but other colours are also introduced. The red and yellow are easily produced by natural clays, while other tints call for the intervention of the chemist; thus green, for example, was produced by the addition of oxide of copper.

Fig. 119.

Various methods of manufacture were adopted. In some cases we find the pattern in relief, the whole tile being of one uniform colour. It was soon found that such tiles were very ill-adapted for pavements, as they readily chipped. This not only mutilated the pattern, but was otherwise unsightly, as the chipping removed the glazed

surface, and the part laid bare was of a different colour.
Such tiles were therefore soon relegated to the walls,
where, as portions of a general scheme of mural decoration,
they were distinctly effective, and also out of harm's way.
Tiles also are met with where the pattern, instead of being
raised, is sunk; but these too were open to objections in

Fig. 120.

much the same way as the others, seeing that in these
also there was an inequality of surface that laid them
open to breakage. By far the commonest and the most
practicable kind is that wherein the pattern is inlaid.
The pattern was impressed by stamp or mould upon the
soft ordinary clay, and then this sunken portion was

filled in with white clay, and then the whole being covered over with a yellow glaze, the result was that the ordinary clay, on firing in the kiln, turned red, and the pattern upon it being yellow a good sharp contrast of colour was obtained, and the whole tile, ground-work and device, was one level surface. There were no sharp edges to be worn away, and the tile being in two colours instead of one, was much more effective. As the patterns were stamped upon the raw clay by a mould, it will be seen that identity of pattern was at once attainable. In addition to these, some few examples are found where the pattern was produced by painting the design with thin white clay upon the ground, and then glazing and firing it; but the process was not a particularly good one, and took no great hold. These were chiefly made in Spain and Flanders, and did not appear till about the sixteenth century.[1]

The Gothic carvers delighted both in nature and in the grotesque, some of their designs being of the most homely character. In one of the capitals, for instance, at Wells. Cathedral, we find amongst the foliage an old woman

[1] The following extract from memoranda of expenses incurred by Henry VIII. in his building operations is of interest in this. association :—

" To Jo Norton for XXVI C. Paving Tiles of yellow and green for the New Hall at iij*s.* viij*d.* the hundred vj*l.* xvi*d.*"

" Item, of MMMM Flemyshe pavynge tiles of greene and youllow at v*s.* the hundythe."

"Pavynge tiles anneled for the kynges new hall at xxvi*s.* viii*d.* the M."

" VI thousand and fourscore of pavynge tiles delivered at Hampton Court, for to pave the kinges new hall at xxvj*s.* viij*d.* the thousand."

freeing her foot from a thorn. There are some other capitals in the same cathedral all equally homely in tone, and passing almost imperceptibly from the picturesque to the ludicrous; a good example of the former may be seen in a woodman proceeding to his labours. Over his shoulder he carries his axe and provision wallet, while his costume, heavy boots, and thick gloves all give character and truth to the figure. Animals are also sometimes introduced: the bird upon her nest, the coiled snake, the squirrel cracking his nuts amongst the hazel leaves.

In estimating the ludicrous or grotesque, we must be careful to discriminate between what is deliberately intended and that which merely results from the inability of the designer to compass that one step which we are told alone separates the sublime from the ridiculous. We are of course all of us well aware from our own experience of life that a person is sometimes never so funny as when he has not the slightest intention of being so. The love of the grotesque is a very marked art feature, especially amongst some races, and our readers will readily discriminate between the intentionally and the unintentionally humorous by a reference to Plate IX: The man, a Peruvian, who devised the owl-like jar (Fig. 132) was seized with a quaint idea, and meant it to amuse us; while the old cottage woman, from whose needlework we become possessed of the peacock and pigeon (Figs. 128, 129) had not the slightest intention of being comic, and her work is grotesque without meaning to be so. She might possibly say that from the necessity of working in squares on the material it would be impossible to produce a better peacock than the one evolved by her, to which one could only reply, that granting it to be so, it would be well another time to change either the material or the design. Much the same comment might be made upon the headless men, from a piece of basket-work (Fig. 134) of North American Indian handiwork, in the British Museum.

Where everything has to be worked in squares, and the outlines all look like flights of steps, a fatal bar is placed in the way of an adequate representation of the grace and delicacy of nature. This may be very well noticed in carpets and lace curtains. A clever and practised designer for this class of goods will produce an approximation to nature under this limitation that is often surprising; but the struggle is, after all, too unequal, and the result can only be tolerated when the squares are so small that at a little distance the eye fails to perceive them. In such a case a frank recognition of the inadequacy of the means to reproduce the flowing lines and delicate curves of nature, and the consequent recourse to a conventionalised treatment, is far preferable to striving after a result that is, at best, but a caricature.

Some designers, with perverted ingenuity and restless search after novelty, have even cramped themselves with these staircase outlines when the method of production, as in stamping and printing, made them entirely unnecessary.

In the examples shown in Figs. 119, 120, the two results, the intentional and the accidental grotesque, may be discriminated. They are both of the same period and of like honest intention. In Fig. 119 the animals seizing upon each other are grotesque of deliberate intention, and as it pleased the sculptor so to have them ; while in Fig. 120 the three horsemen raise a smile as we note the riders actually imbedded in their horses, and mark the especially attenuated proportions of the lowest of them. Here the sculptor had no intention at all of being funny, and was doubtless heartily vexed when he saw how unfortunately he had judged his spaces.

Another good example of the accidental grotesque arises from the anachronisms that are so freely seen in a good deal of thoroughly well-intentioned work. As an illustration of this we may refer to the Schreyer monument at St. Sebald's, Nuremburg, the work of the famous Adam Krafft.[1] The memorial is in three divisions : in the right-hand compartment we see Christ falling beneath the weight of His cross, while urged forward by blows and taunts ; in the central panel His dead body is carried to the sepulchre ; while the third or left-hand recess represents the Resurrection. The whole of the costumes, weapons, and accessories are those of the sculptor's own

---

[1] " In the church of sainted Lawrence stands a pix of sculpture
rare,
Like the foamy sheaf of fountains, rising through the painted
air."

Thus sings Longfellow in his poem on Nuremburg. The pix in question is carved in white stone and is some sixty feet high or more. The painted air is caused by the sunlight streaming through the richly stained glass of the church. This noble pix or tabernacle for the sacramental vessels is also the work of Adam Krafft.

time and country, and the fortified walls of Jerusalem
are recognisable as those of Nuremburg. The small
figures kneeling in the foreground represent various
members of the Schreyer family and the highly respect-
able burghers connected with them by marriage—a fact
which may be readily recognised by the bearings on the
various shields.

The love of the marvellous is deeply engrained in
human nature. We may see abundant proof of this in
such classic myths as that of the Sirens, in the monstrous
forms carved or depicted in the temples of Mexico, on the
canoes of the South Sea Islander, in the popularity of such
books as the Arabian Nights Tales, or the adventures
of Gulliver, down to the fearful joy of the youngsters
in the nursery in the sanguinary giant whose food was
the blood of Englishmen—

> " Far away in the twilight time
> Of every people, in every clime,
> Dragons and griffins and monsters dire,
> Born of water or air or fire,
> Crawl and wriggle and foam with rage
> Through dark tradition and ballad age ; "—

and they certainly crawl and wriggle no less through
the whole domain of art. Of these monsters dire the
fell harpies, the death-dealing basilisk, the monstrous
roc, the deadly cockatrice, the kraken, the firedrake,
the ghastly wehr-wolves, are but a few examples that
at once occur to one's thoughts.

The grotesque in art may take several distinctly
different forms. It may, for instance, be the morbidly

horrible and blood-curdling, or it may be the broad joke, or any point between these two extremes. It may also be a teacher; thus in that most popular mediæval subject—the Dance of Death—the ghastly theme is generally treated in the most grotesque way, and yet with high moral aim.

Though the thing it expressed had been in use some few hundreds of years before, the term grotesque was first employed in art towards the end of the fifteenth

Fig. 121.

century, when the "grottos" or baths of ancient Rome were brought again to daylight and the quaint and whimsical designs they contained attracted the attention of the artists of the day. The lamp, Fig. 121, is of Roman work; and on the walls of Pompeii many examples of the grotesque may be seen. In one example that we recall, a parrot is gravely standing in a chariot and driving his steeds, two grasshoppers.

In Fig. 122 we have a satirical design of mediæval date, where the saintly Reynard preaches a discourse against gluttony to his congregation of trustful geese, but concludes by carrying one off for his dinner. As is common in much early work, the story is told in the one composition in more than one of its phases. These

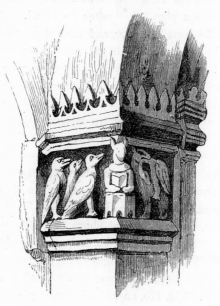

satires on the ecclesiastics are of very common occurrence in Gothic art.

The ease with which clay can be worked has made pottery in all ages the vehicle of the whimsical.[1] The

---

[1] For various examples of this, plus a great deal of still more interesting matter, the reader may very advantageously turn to any of the following works: Birch's " History of Ancient Pottery," Egyptian,

highly artistic and refined Greeks could not altogether resist the temptation; while in the two Peruvian illustrations (Figs. 131, 132) it is rampant. In collections of ceramic ware vessels of brown glazed earthenware, called "Sussex pigs," may often be found. They are made in the form of a pig, and have a removable head that can be used as a cup, in order that at every filling—such is rustic humour—each drinker may be said to imbibe a hogshead at a draught! One of these is shown in Fig. 123; when full it is of course sat up on end. Another of these earthenware monstrosities is placed alongside it—a jug, also with a removable head, in the form of a bear. We have also seen an owl-pot that is employable under the like conditions. Fig. 124, technically known as a "Toby fill-pot," is another of the grotesque vagaries of the potter's art.

The illuminators were not above this little weakness, and often somewhere in the borderings or initial letters of their most magnificent pages or in the representation of some sacred scene give some quaint detail that moves to risibility. Fig. 125, an initial letter, is compounded, it will be seen, of two human figures, minstrels. A reference

Assyrian, Greek, Etruscan and Roman.——Waring's " Ceramic Art in Remote Ages," with Essays on the Symbols of the Circle, The Cross and Circle, The Circle and Ray of Ornament, The Fylfot and the Serpent, showing their relation to the Primitive Forms of Solar and Nature Worship. 55 plates.——Jewitt's book, " The Ceramic Art of Great Britain, from Prehistoric times down to the present time," being a History of the Ancient and Modern Pottery and Porcelain Works of the Kingdom, and of their productions of every class, illustrated with nearly two thousand engravings.

to the magnificent work of Professor Westwood on Celtic MSS. will indicate to what a very marked extent this

Fig. 123.

love of the grotesque influenced these early illuminators, as letter after letter is built up of strange monsters, their legs, bodies, necks, beaks, tongues, tails, crests, all knotted together in the most marvellous way. A fish dashing horizontally at another catches it open-mouthed in the middle of the body, and gives it such a curling-up that the result is a capital E. Another fish that is

Fig. 124.

plunging downward catches by the tail one that is rising, hence a very good V; while there is no difficulty whatever in curving the lithe form of a dragon into an excellent S. In the noble thirteenth-century MS. in the British Museum, known as the Image du Monde,

the stern satirist chastises the follies and vices of the
world; and in one of the beautiful initial letters we
find the centre taken up by the representation of a
monk who has found his way to the cellar, or has maybe
gone there in the course of his duty, but who at all

Fig. 125.

events, while he holds the jug to the tap of the barrel
with one hand, raises a capacious bowl to his mouth
with the other. Here again, as in so many other cases
during mediæval days, an opportunity is deliberately
made to fling a satire at the ecclesiastics.

The grotesque is a very marked feature of Chinese work, while with the Japanese, with all their graphic power, it frequently seems entirely irresistible, as they often appear to find pure nature scarcely sufficiently

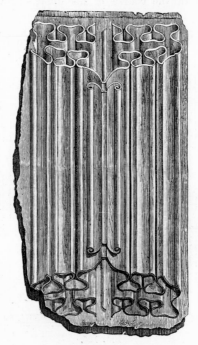

Fig. 126.

piquant, but deal in the most exaggerated action and the most bizarre forms.

In the third period of Gothic, that of the fifteenth century, or, as it is often called, the Perpendicular, the

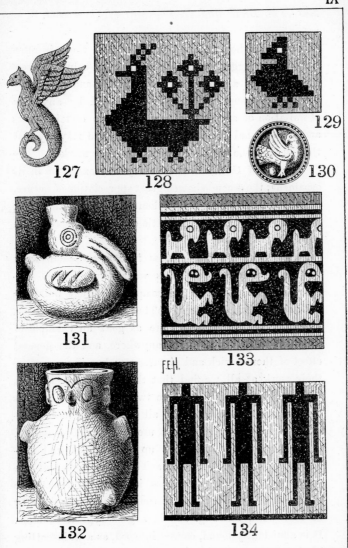

IX

EXAMPLES OF THE GROTESQUE IN DECORATION.

foliate forms become very arbitrary, and there is often little or no suggestion of nature in them, being, in most cases, such as a man could most readily and effectively produce by gouge and chisel, unfettered by any idea of imitation of any natural form. Within certain limits and exceptional examples allowed for, one may say that the fall from the previous work was very marked. The first period of Gothic was in every way excellent in its ornament; the second showed great appreciation of nature, but failed from having a mistaken though high ambition ; the third failed from having little or no such appreciation at all.

There is a great sameness in Perpendicular work wherever we see it, and this want of variety is conspicuous, not only when we compare different buildings with each other, but when we study any special example. The Houses of Parliament are as good an example of this period as one may see anywhere, and the general effect of them is rich and picturesque ; but if we analyse their work at all, we find that the thought expended in one bay, say roughly a space twelve feet wide, suffices for a whole façade, and that all the rest is mere repetition of this strip. A great use is made of panelling, the whole surface being cut up and divided and subdivided by these horizontal and vertical lines, and one very popular filling for these is what is termed the napkin ornament. Of this, of course, many varieties may be met with, but Fig. 126 is a good typical example. It is abundantly found, carved in wood, as a wainscotting in the more stately halls and dwelling-houses of this

period. Any one referring to the "Baronial Halls of
England," by S. C. Hall, will see any number of illus-

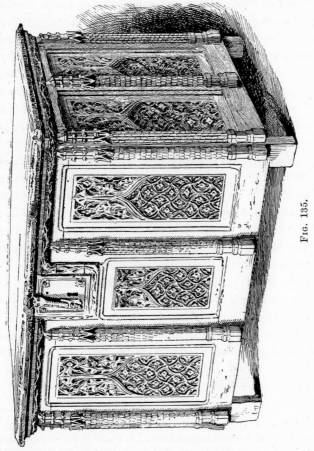

Fig. 135.

trations of its recurrence. Its use would seem to any
one not overawed by precedent and ancient authority

to be very absurd, as there seems no special charm
in surrounding one's self with carvings that suggest nothing so much as a monotonous array of brown towels.
As a general principle in the decline of taste everything
is frittered and cut up into so-called ornament, and
no beauty is seen in the noble breadth and simplicity
that is ordinarily characteristic of earlier work. Thus
Henry VII.'s Chapel is what an old writer calls all
" cut-work and crinkle-crankle." [1] Ornament needs a
foil and a resting-place for the eye ; when everything is
equally covered, all repose is lost.

Angelic forms are very often introduced in Perpendicular buildings. They may be seen, for instance, supporting
brackets in Henry VII.'s Chapel at Westminster ; often
in capitals, as at Stoke-in-Teignhead Church, Devonshire ;
at the ends of the hammer beams of the roof, as at
Trunch or Wymondham Churches, in Norfolk. These
are but a few illustrative examples ; their use is so
persistent that the slightest personal investigation will
readily supply a much longer list. These angels are
almost invariably bearing shields.

The use of heraldic devices, carved, painted, in the
stained glass, on the hangings, in the designs of the
flooring tiles, everywhere in fact where it was possible
to introduce it, is a very marked feature of the work

---

[1] A very elaborate and reliable monograph on this typical
specimen of Perpendicular work will be found in the folio volume
of Cottingham, giving plans, elevations, sections and detail, both
exterior and interior, of the chapel. These illustrations extend over
seventy-two large plates.

of this period. Another very characteristic point is the
great use of architectural forms merely as ornaments and

Fig. 136.

apart from all constructive necessity. Thus in the coffer
shown in Fig. 135 we find shafts and pinnacles, and in

the panel given in Fig. 136 the whole of the filling in simulates window-tracery. We have even seen a cupboard or dressoir surmounted by a sloping roof with rows of minute fictitious dormer windows in it.

The mouldings in Perpendicular work are much shallower than in the preceding periods, and all the ornaments are far less deeply cut; but a very great use is made of gold and colour, and the rich polychromatic effect produced by its use everywhere, in the mural painting, the brilliant tinctures of the herald, the magnificent stained glass, is a very marked feature.

It is convenient to speak of these various periods of Gothic as the styles of the thirteenth, fourteenth, or fifteenth century; but these dates are, after all, only approximate, and the student must not be deceived into believing that all went with the regularity of clockwork, and that at the close of each century, as the clock struck twelve, a new era opened. Norman work was in vogue for some hundred and thirty years, and lasted during the reigns of William I., William II., Henry I., and Stephen. During the reign of Henry II. the old forms were giving place to the new; and by the time Richard I. came to the throne, in 1189, the so-called Early English had developed, and held its ground during the reigns of John and Henry III. Edward I.'s reign was again a period of architectural transition, and after a duration of about a century Early English was abandoned in favour of the Decorated style. This, though it had two very distinct phases, the geometric and the florid sub-styles, only lasted some seventy or eighty years, and may be taken as synchronous with Edward II. and Edward III. Matters then again, during the reign of Richard II., 1377 to 1399, were in a transitional state; and finally the Perpendicular was evolved, and held its ground for something like one hundred and seventy years, right through the reigns of Henry IV., Henry V., Henry VI., Edward IV., Edward V., Richard III., Henry VII., and Henry VIII.

While it is naturally easier, in dealing with old Gothic work, to make reference to the architectural stone carving, as this is the most enduring and most readily accessible, we must remember that a great use was also made of wood-work, such as church stalls, screens, and noble roofs, that metal-work also was freely employed in memorial brasses, hinges, supports for lights, and many other services, that the art of the herald, the illuminator, and the painter was on all sides called into employment, and that stained glass, the most glorious development perhaps of decorative art, was everywhere adding its beauty to the whole.

When our readers have mastered the intricacies of this very considerable study, we may further remind them that we have dealt, after all, only with Gothic as we find it in England. Even the Gothic of Scotland has its distinct individuality; and when we cross the Channel, the very beautiful Gothic of France abounds in details that differ from those in English buildings. German Gothic, again, has a very marked character of its own, and so has Italian. All differ from each other; and any one who has studied the subject should be able, on seeing anywhere a fairly characteristic piece of work, say a cast in a museum, to declare both the country of its origin and the approximate date of its execution. A piece of thirteenth-century work from Chartres Cathedral, and of fifteenth-century work, say from the Hôtel de Ville of Ghent, are as different from each as it is possible to conceive, and yet each have equally good and full claim to be included in the comprehensive title of Gothic.

Stained-glass windows are of two markedly distinct kinds : the first and earliest is called mosaic; where the design is composed of pieces of variously coloured glass cut to the shapes required by the pattern and fastened together by lines of lead, any features or other details being outlined in brown colour ; while the second is the enamel method, in which the glass used is white, and the picture is painted upon it with enamel colours. In practice both methods may be combined together.

In the thirteenth century the windows often have a line of geometrical panels running up the centre, and these are filled with figure subjects, while the rest of the space is filled with geometrical patterns or foliated scrolls. The pieces of glass employed to form the designs are small, and consequently the lead lines are numerous, but the effect is very rich and beautiful. In the Decorated period the pieces are considerably larger, and instead of the geometric forms and rich mosaic of colour we often find single figures occupying a whole window, and placed on a plain field of colour, generally red or blue. The flat character of the design of the earlier glass has vanished, and light and shade effects on the draperies and other details are given. We occasionally get the whole window *en grisaille*, everything being expressed in a delicate silvery grey. In the Perpendicular work the figures are often more richly habited, are placed under very elaborate canopies, and a very great use is made of heraldic devices.

CHAPTER V.

GOTHIC art, after some three hundred years of healthy
life, passed away; why it died out so utterly has been
variously accounted for. Some theorists tell us that the
break-up of the old order of things at the Reformation
was the main cause, that the dissolution of the monas-
teries and the confiscation of their estates at once put an
end to the erection of new buildings, or the maintenance
in their pristine splendour of the older foundations, and
that, apart from the diversion of funds, the new ideas
were hostile to the art that was associated with the
ancient creed;—that, in fact, the men of this new period

could not erect such buildings if they would, for they had not the means; that they would not build them if they could, as they had no longer the desire to do so. Others tell us that the general spread of learning and literature, which had long before made itself felt in Italy, and that had speedily dethroned Gothic in that country in favour of classic models, in due course influenced England. Others, again, tell us that Gothic died of its own weakness, that the life in it was extinct, that a mechanical precision, an exaggerated splendour of gold and colour on petty details frittered out of all grandeur and dignity,[1] and the complacency in such *tours-de-force* as the fan-vaultings finally destroyed its vitality.

Those who imagine that the first two of these explanations—the difficulty of providing funds, and the disinclination to persevere with work so intimately associated with the discarded beliefs—were the cause of its downfall, can at all events point, in support of this theory, to the fact that we do find the style continued for some considerable time afterwards, when these conditions do not affect it, in the noble halls and manor-houses where individual resources allowed of their erection, and where their entirely civil character called for no appeal to religious prejudices.

---

[1] " The process could be carried no further; complication had reached its limit. The richness of the expiring Gothic differed from the richness of all previous styles. It was not real ornament, not artistic, or deriving its value from the amount of thought embodied. It was only a sham richness produced by endless repetition of the same features."—GARBETT.

Had it been that the style perished from faults inherent in itself, we should naturally have expected that what succeeded it would be a return to pristine simplicity of work and a purer style, whereas the facts are that in Elizabethan and Jacobean work it is bathos rather than a new birth that takes its place. It was not till these in turn had held their ground for some time that the field was so evidently vacant that the importation of entirely new ideas became an art necessity.

The real truth would appear to be that while some weight must be attached to these reasons, the greatest cause doubtless arose from the fact that during the Tudor period Englishmen were travelling abroad much more freely than they had done previously, and thus came under continental influences. Foreigners,[1] too, were passing and repassing between England and France and Germany, and a new leaven was working in many ways. Men were learning to think for themselves, not only in religious matters, but, consequently to this, in many others. The mediæval period was at an end; feudal domination was gone for ever; the renascence of the finest literature of

---

[1] "The first introduction of the Revival into England dates from the year 1518, when Torrigiano was employed by Henry VIII. to design a monument in memory of Henry VII., which still exists in Westminster Abbey, and which is almost a pure example of the Italian school at that period. In the same style and of about the same date is the monument of the Countess of Richmond at Westminster. Torrigiano designed this also, and very shortly afterwards went to Spain, leaving, however, behind him several Italians attached to the service of Henry, by whom a taste for this same style could not but be propagated."—WARING.

the classic authors burst as a flood of light upon the land,[1] and in the first glow of the new enthusiasm it was held that tyranny and superstition had vanished before the rising beams, and that henceforth the great examples of ancient civic virtue and eloquence, poetry and art, were to regenerate the world.

The first steps in the new direction were necessarily tentative ; much that was good in the old work was retained, while with it was blended more or less successfully an entirely new series of forms. Into any analysis of Elizabethan work, from the point of view of the architect, we are not here called upon to enter. It suffices to say that while some of the examples strike us as sufficiently bizarre both in stone and timber construction, many of the mansions of the nobility had much that was pleasing and picturesque in effect ;[2] but when we limit our view, as our title naturally suggests that we should do, to the decoration of these sumptuous homes, there remains but little that can be heartily commended.

The classic orders are freely introduced, though both

---

[1] Dante, in the thirteenth century, modelled his noble verse on the style of Virgil, and was a profound scholar in all classical learning. In the following century Boccaccio and Petrarch, best known to us by their own works, laboured incessantly in the preservation and restoration to the world of the writings of the authors of Greece and Rome. The ancient Roman laws were revived and adopted by learned commentators and jurists. Men of wealth and culture accumulated in their libraries ancient texts.

[2] Good examples may be seen in Holland House, Kensington; Longford, Wilts ; Wollaton Hall, Notts ; Audley End, Essex; Crewe Hall, Cheshire ; Hatfield, Hardwick, Burleigh, Bramshill, Penshurst, Knowle, and many others.

in proportions and in details great liberties are taken, and the columns, pilasters, and piers are continually broken by broad bands of square blocks. These blocks ordinarily have their vertical surfaces cut into diamond-shaped projections or facets: a most characteristic feature of Elizabethan work. The ceilings of the principal rooms are very elaborately panelled or covered with flowing scroll-work, and the effect is often extremely grand. Very little foliage is seen, but an enormous use is made of strap-work and cartouche forms, often of very ingenious and complex design, but even at their best not very satisfactory. During the reign of Queen Elizabeth England was bound both politically and by strong religious sympathy with Holland, and there was consequently a considerable Dutch influence on art. In the time of Henry VIII. the Italian influence was supreme, while amidst the inroad of foreigners Englishmen too were endeavouring to hold their ground. It can scarcely be wondered, then, that a strange medley should result. The student in quest of full information may very advantageously consult the following works : Shaw's "Details of Elizabethan Architecture," Richardson's "Architectural Remains," and his "Studies from Old English Mansions," the excellent book of S. C. Hall on "The Baronial Halls of England," Clayton's "Ancient Timber Homes in England," Britton's "Architectural Antiquities of Great Britain," and Nash's "Mansions of England of the Olden Time."

The Renaissance period has three marked styles, known respectively, from their dates, as the Trecento, Quattrocento, and the Cinquecento. It will be seen that these periods approximately correspond in time with our English Gothic,[1] and it was only at the close of this Gothic period that the art of Italy affected that of our own country. It is natural that a student should suppose that Renaissance was subsequent to Gothic; but this misconception arises from taking too narrow a view of the subject, in limiting the observation to our insular art. Though it was not till well into the fifteenth century that the art reached its full maturity and beauty, as a matter of fact Italian art was building itself on classic models all through the centuries that with us were exclusively devoted to Gothic in one or other of its forms. "The material monuments of the ancient Romans, scattered thickly over the soil of Italy, were so substantial and majestic that it was impossible to live under their shadow and forget them. Fragments of exquisite beauty, in stone, bronze, and marble, were to be had for the trouble of turning up the soil that scarcely covered them. Hence the Gothic style was at once slow to take root in Italy, and destined to bloom brilliantly but for a short season. Almost concurrently with the introduction of the pointed arch, early in the thirteenth century, a protest was commenced in favour of the ancients and their arts by that great reviver of antique sculpture, Niccola Pisano."[2] This

---

[1] The student must add a century to each of these periods to bring them into line with English ideas. The Italians call all the years, for instance, that have fourteen hundred in them, such as 1405, 1433 or 1490, the fourteenth century, while we call it the fifteenth.

[2] Digby Wyatt.

change from Gothic to Classic gradually, through various types of transition, spread throughout almost every European country, under certain modifications of temperament, climate, and other affecting causes, and this foothold it has more or less retained to the present day.

Amongst the great names associated with the Renaissance may be mentioned Niccola Pisano, Giotto, Orcagna, Luca della Robbia, Lorenzo Ghiberti, Raffaelle, Benvenuto Cellini, Palissy, Palladio, Holbein, Inigo Jones, and Sir Christopher Wren,[1] and to these might readily be added many others who in one direction or another, in one country or another, or one period or another, took part in this great art movement.

As in the earlier ages symbolic Egyptian art gradually developed, as we have seen, into Greek æsthetic art, so the art that up till this period, in its various stages and modifications of Byzantine, Romanesque, Gothic, had been largely symbolic, was now supplanted by a new set of ideas, or rather the new-birth of very old ones, in which the prime aim and consideration was beauty, the artists of the Renaissance being entirely in sympathy with the sentiment expressed by Ralph Waldo Emerson—

---

[1] Some of his more notable buildings are the Cathedral of St. Paul, Chelsea College, Greenwich Hospital, the Monument to commemorate the Great Fire of London, and Temple Bar. He also built some fifty parochial churches in London—St. Mary-le-Bow, St. Bride's, St. Vedast's, Christ Church in Newgate Street, St. Clement Dane's. A scarce old book, originally published in the year 1715-71, and entitled "Vitruvius Britannicus," illustrates the work of the leading Englishmen, Inigo Jones, Wren, Sir J. Vanbrugh, and others, very thoroughly. It was began by Campbell, and continued by Woolfe and Gandon ; its five folio volumes containing five hundred plates.

"If eyes were made for seeing,
Then Beauty is its own excuse for being."

Art and religion parted company, and though, as in the great cathedrals of St. Peter at Rome, or St. Paul's in London, or the numerous churches built by Wren, Renais_sance architecture is the medium employed, they differ but little really from the great Italian palaces, or the Louvre, and other buildings erected under the same inspiration. By our knowledge of their use and association of ideas we entirely accept them as buildings devoted to sacred purposes, but there is little or nothing especially ecclesi-astical in them. So much rectangular fenestration, rus-tication of stone-work, more or less classic columns, balustrading, and so forth, in one case is a palace, in another a cathedral.

From the fact of the Renaissance having arisen in Italy, it is often called Italian as an alternative title, but it is evident that this is a somewhat awkward limitation of the matter. Each nation that has adopted the style has in some degree modified it (thus the French is marked by the great use of the lofty Mansard roof), and even in Italy we can trace considerable differences of procedure. In the Florentine buildings, for instance, we have great breadth of treatment, strongly marked recesses, an equally strongly marked cornice surmounting the whole, very little use of ornament, a noble Doric simplicity. Of this the Strozzi Palace may be taken as an excellent type. This was commenced in the year 1489. Another characteristic example is the Pandolfini Palace, commenced in 1520. In the Venetian examples

we have, instead of this severity of treatment, a great use
of ornament, arches, domes, columns, introduced at the
great risk of belittling and frittering away the whole;
and as we have compared the Florentine in its massive
grandeur to the Doric, so the art of Venice of this period
in its self-display and luxury may be compared to the
Corinthian. The Roman school varied again from either
of these, and may, in fact, be considered as intermediate,
some buildings inclining towards one extreme, others to
the other, and therefore less easily defined as a whole. In
the Florentine very little use is made of columns; in the
Venetian several series of these are sometimes super-
imposed in one building; while in Roman work there is
ordinarily one line alone, and this often rises from near
the ground, and is continued right up the edifice, irrespective of the number of storeys that the building may
have. Hence, therefore, the arch is but little used in
Florence, greatly used in Venice, and occupies an intermediate position in Roman work.

The conspicuous feature of Trecento ornament is a great
use of interlacing and of delicate scroll-work. These
scroll forms bear foliage of a more or less conventional
character. The works of Giotto and of Niccola Pisano are
the most beautiful illustrations of its capabilities, and
its best examples will be found in Florence and Assisi.
In the Quattrocento the names of Lorenzo Ghiberti, Pietro
Perugino, Francia, and Luini are perhaps the most famous
amongst many others scarcely less so. Ghiberti is best
known by the noble gates of the Baptistery of San Giovanni
at Florence. In this period of art the forms employed

are very naturalistic; and though their arrangement in
bands, panels, or festoons is conventional, the flowers, fruit,
birds, and other accessories are in detail entirely derived

Fig. 137.

Fig. 138.

from nature. In the Ghiberti gates, for instance, we find
the squirrel sitting amongst the nut foliage, clusters of
pomegranate fruits and leaves, pears, and many other

natural forms that are at once recognisable. The cartouche also appears very freely, and for the first time
in modern art grotesque arabesques, similar to those
found in ancient Rome and Pompeii, are introduced.

In the Cinquecento we get the most perfect art development of the re-birth of Classicalism. Amongst its
greatest masters were such giants in art as Michael
Angelo and Raffaelle. Rome, Venice, and Verona are
full of choice examples. The anthemion, fret, guilloche,
and other classic forms are freely introduced, but the
most marked feature of the period is the arabesque scroll-
work. This combines together griffins, sphinx forms,
birds, dolphins, shells, vases, instruments of music,
acanthus leaves, fruit, and any rendering, in fact, naturalistic or conventional, of any forms whatever in the
animal or vegetable kingdoms. These scrolls are ordinarily arranged on either side of a central upright
line, and are either absolutely identical on either side
or have a general similarity and balance of masses. The
Loggie of the Vatican, the work of Raffaelle and his
scholars, is the finest illustration. The classic forms
were more severe in character than those we find in
the resuscitation. As the taste for this style of work
travelled northward, its freedom from classic restrictions
became more marked, and in the hands of the northern
races, with their greater love for whimsical design, invention ran riot. Both Pliny and Vitruvius made their
protest even against the ancient arabesques on the
ground of false and incongruous taste, and it is evident
on reflection that the mere antiquity of a thing does

not necessarily make it a model for imitation. Many beautiful pieces of carved work of this period[1] may be seen in the South Kensington Museum on tombs, monuments, and the like, and the fine collection of Italian Majolica should also not be overlooked. Arms, armour, jewellery, and bookbinding afford many excellent illustrations. When these arabesques were painted in mural decoration the colour was ordinarily admirably applied, the favourite tints being orange, purple, and green, strengthened and accentuated occasionally by touches of primary colour. These tints are excellently blended and harmonised. The Trecento and Quattrocento were stepping-stones, tentative attempts, in which incongruous elements were admitted through want of knowledge; but in the Cinquecento the various discoveries of antique work bore fruit, and the result was more truly a renascence of the ancient art. Figs. 137, 138, are very pleasing modern designs of arabesque character.

Renaissance decoration requires on the part of the designer considerable knowledge, both with the kingdoms of nature and with the arts of antiquity, and calls besides for a perfect intimacy with the anatomy of the human figure and a general mastery and power of drawing, plus a feeling for grace and a play of fancy that does not fall to the lot of all designers. The student should cultivate the beauties as carefully as he should avoid the

---

[1] See Robinson's " Italian Sculpture of the Middle Ages and Period of the Revival of Art." A descriptive and illustrated catalogue of the leading works in the above section of the South Kensington Museum.

extravagances of this style of design, and the abundant liberty of choice open to him entails a corresponding responsibility in its correct use.

The literature of the subject is very extensive. The following are but a few of the books that deal with one or other phase of it, but they are all works that the

Fig. 139.

student may advantageously consult. The "Collection of Antique Ornaments" of Antonelli; the "Recueil d'Ornaments de la Renaissance" of Bernard; the "History of Art by its Monuments," by D'Agincourt; "Collection of Ornaments of the Renaissance Period," by Clerget; "Les Monuments de la France," by De Laborde;

X

140   141

142   143

FEH

144   145

THE GROTESQUE IN ORNAMENT.

"La Renaissance," by Lacroix; "Les Arts au Moyen Age," by Sommerard; "The Vatican Described and Illustrated," by Pistolesi; "The Tombs and Monuments of Italy," of Bettoni, and "The Buildings and Monuments of Venice," by Cicognara; the "Edifices of Modern Rome," by Letarouilly. Gruner's "Specimens of Ornamental Art," selected from the best models of the classical epochs, eighty beautiful plates, comprising the most beautiful specimens of paintings, carvings, friezes, ceilings, ornaments, and decorations, of the thirteenth, fourteenth, fifteenth, and sixteenth centuries, executed in the palaces and churches of Rome, Verona, Mantua, Milan, etc., by Jacoba della Turrita, Bramante, Luini, Giulio Romano, Rafaelle d'Urbino, etc.; and by the same author, "Fresco Decorations and Stuccoes" of the churches and palaces in Italy during the fifteenth and sixteenth centuries, fifty-six large and elaborate engravings, after the original paintings of Raphael, Giulio Romano, Giovanni da Undine, Baldassare Peruzzi, Sebastiano del Piombo, Correggio, Moretta, Ambrogio da Fossana, Bramantio, Bernardino, Luini, Pinturicchio. "Das Ornament der Italienischen Kunst des XV. Jahrhunderts;" this is a splendid collection of the choicest examples of the ornament of the Early Italian Renaissance, selected by Professor Nicolai, of the Royal Academy of Arts, Dresden, and contains one hundred folio plates. The two volumes of Schoy's "L'Art Architectural, Decoratif, Industriel et Somptuaire, de l'Epoque Louis XVI.," a fine collection of illustrations of ceilings, panels, borders, friezes, and every variety of ornament, repro-

·duced from the works of Lasinio, Albertolli, Adam, La
Londe, De la Fosse, Neufforge, Cauvet, Piranesi, and
other masters, the whole forming three hundred large
plates of ornament. The excellent book of Violet le Duc,
"Dictionnaire du Mobilier Français de l'Epogue Carlo-
vingienne à la Renaissance," six volumes, containing
nearly two thousand four hundred steel and chromo-
lithographic plates and woodcuts. This embraces furniture, pottery, jewellery, musical instruments, costumes,
vestments, arms, armour, etc. Berty's "La Renaissance
Monumentale en France, Specimens de Composition et
d'Ornamentation Architectonique, depuis le Regne de
Charles VIII. jusqu'a celui de Louis XIV.," containing
·one hundred fine plates. Daly's "Motifs Historiques
d'Architecture, de Sculpture et d'Ornement pour la
Composition et la Décoration: Commencement de la
Renaissance a la fin de Louis XVI." This gives two
hundred and four plates, exhibiting examples of doorways, windows, panels, balustrades, cornices, vases,
fountains, and every variety of sculptural detail, in
two volumes folio. Oakeshott's forty folio plates of
"Ornament of the Italian Renaissance," comprising
examples of panels, pilasters, spandrils, corbels, trusses,
brackets, balusters, pedestals, columns, capitals, cornices
and architraves, iron gates, palustrading, grilles, bronze
candelabra and brackets, intarsia and niello work. The
book by Kinross, "Details from Italian Buildings, chiefly
Renaissance," consisting of a selection of fifty folio
plates. The work of Von Schutz on "Die Renaisance in
Italien," containing three hundred and thirty-two folio

plates of examples of Italian art; the subjects are
selected from Rome, Florence, Venice, Naples, Genoa,
Sienna, Pisa, Bologna, Ferrara, Brescia, Parma, Vicenza,
Pavia, Milan, Bergamo, and other cities of Italy. "Renaissance Architecture in Lombardy," by Tito Vespasiano
Nobile Paravicini, with fifty-nine plates of details. "Palladio's Architecture, in Four Books, containing a Short
Treatise of the Five Orders and the most necessary Observations concerning all sorts of Buildings, as also the
different Construction of Private and Public Houses,
Market Places, Temples, etc.," revised by Giacomi Leoni,
two hundred and thirty fine plates, two volumes folio.
Rouyer's "L'Art Architectural en France de François I.
jusqu'a Louis XVI.," containing two hundred plates of
architectural and decorative details, including wall and
ceiling decorations, chimney-pieces, iron-work, panels, etc.

In France the Classical revival was not accepted until
long after it had established itself in the land of its birth.
The style came into favour in the reign of Francis I.
(1515–1547), but it was for a considerable period a compromise between the Gothic and the Classic. Many
beautiful buildings of this blending period may be seen
in France, notably the chateaux of Chambord and Blois,
and there are other good examples in Angers, Orleans,
Rouen, and Caen. Later on the style became purer, though
subject to great fluctuations, and a considerable use is
made of sculpture. By the sixteenth century the liberty
of the designer had developed into a license that brought
about the decadence of the style, and sanguinary wars
abroad and revolution at home completed the debasement

of all art work. Under the influence of Louis XIV. an
attempt at revival was made, but ostentation and vulgar
display were more conspicuous than taste or refinement.
A great use was made of gilded stucco work to the exclusion of colour, and scroll and shell forms were very
freely introduced. The Louis Quatorze was succeeded by
the Louis Quinze, dating from about the year 1715 to
1774. It differs from the preceding work in being somewhat thinner in character, but more especially in its almost
complete abandonment of symmetry, and at last the whole
becomes a mere mass of aimless forms without any plan or
definite arrangement. This state of bizarre chaos is known
as the Rococo,[1] and it may be taken as marking the lowest
ebb of ornamental art. Two Italians, Bernini and Borromini, exercised a most unfortunate influence on French
art at this period. They became "the mode," and used
the position tyrannously. "From his fervid imagination
and rare facility as a draughtsman and designer, Borromini soon obtained ample employment, and in his
capricious vagaries every tendency to extravagance that
Bernini's style possessed Borromini contrived to caricature. Until near his death in 1667, he continued
sedulously occupied in subverting all known principles of
order and symmetry, not only to his own enrichment, but
to the admiration of the leaders of fashion of the day.
The anomalies he introduced into design, the dispro-
portionate mouldings, broken, contrasted, and re-entering
curves, interrupted and crooked lines and surfaces be-

---

[1] So called from rocaille coquille, rock and shell work.

came the mode of the day, and all Europe was speedily busy in devising similar enormities. In France the fever raged."[1] During the reign of Louis XVI. there was to some extent a revival of ornament, the forms introduced being of the graceful though thin and liny type that in our country we find in the work of the brothers Adam. After the great Revolution severe simplicity was the mode; but when the empire succeeded the Republic, the best artists were employed by Napoleon I. in the development of a more ornate style of work. It is, however, needless and hopeless to attempt to follow these various and rapid changes, since taste, after all, had less to do with them than the whims of fashion and the influence of political feeling.

Italian architecture and ornament finally and completely took root in England in the early part of the seventeenth century during the reign of James I. This was largely owing to the work of one distinguished man, Inigo Jones, who after a couple of visits to Italy and a careful study of the works of Palladio and other great authorities, erected many noble buildings that led to a general appreciation and adoption of this style of art. The banqueting house at Whitehall is the work of Inigo Jones, and an excellent illustration of his genius. Sir Christopher Wren and his pupil Hawksmoor, Gibbs, Stuart, Chambers, and other notable Englishmen were all workers in the same field of art.

Stuart, and a fellow-architect, Revett, less known to

---

[1] Digby Wyatt.

fame, were the joint authors of a well-known work "The Antiquities of Athens," a publication that exercised an immense influence. The book originally appeared in the year 1762, and its four imperial folio volumes were adorned with three hundred and eighty-four excellent illustrations of Hellenic art. Up till that time Roman and Italian models had been the sole source of Renaissance inspiration, and the insight into Greek work that this book afforded was a revelation. Unfortunately, Hellenic forms at once became the fashion, and Greek temples pure and simple became the vogue, until the incongruous absurdity that often resulted became so patent that the error of judgment rectified itself, and zeal without discretion gave place to wiser counsels.

Much good decorative work was done by Chippendale, Cipriani, Robert and John Adam, Sheraton, Grinling Gibbons, Wedgwood, and many others. The first of these, Chippendale, was a great designer of furniture, such as wardrobes, cabinets, mirror frames, and the like. He published a book of designs in 1754. This is now very scarce; it is entitled somewhat awkwardly, "The Gentleman and Cabinet-maker's Director." It is of folio size, and contains one hundred and sixty plates. When a third edition of the book appeared in 1763, two hundred plates were given; but this edition contains really over one hundred plates that did not appear in the first and second editions, as he cancelled more than sixty plates that were in these earlier copies and substituted others in his later and happier style. The brothers Adam built many houses in the Adelphi, Hanover Square, Portland

Place, and other parts of London, and all the accessories, such as door frames, the designs upon the ceilings,[1] and other decorative details are very pure and good in style. Many of their original drawings are carefully preserved in the Soane Museum. The forms are based on classical types, capitals, mouldings, shell flutings, light garlands and wreaths all carefully and tastefully introduced. One Charles compiled a volume of the decorative designs of Robert Adam from the drawings in the Soane Museum; and another writer, Akerman, has made a happy selection of some twenty-six folio plates of the work of R. and J. Adam. The brothers Adam themselves issued a book in three volumes of their designs, but this is now only to be met with very rarely, and the reproduction of Akerman gives the cream of it, and is therefore a public benefaction. Sheraton more especially designed furniture. Sheraton also, like Chippendale and the Adams, published a series of designs. This work he termed "The Cabinet-maker and Ulpholsterer's Drawing Book." As new ideas flowed in, he also published "An Accompanyment" and "An Appendix" thereto. All are now exceedingly scarce, as they have gone through two very trying periods,

---

[1] Decorative rather than pictorial design is the more suitable for the decoration of a ceiling. In the Sistine Chapel, for instance, the main subjects are all so placed that to see them correctly it is necessary to face the altar, and from all other points of view they are seen sideways or upside down. This in a decorative composition would be immaterial, as the designer, foreseeing the difficulty, would so arrange his scheme as to make his work equally effective from all standpoints. Noble pictorial work is not done justice to under such limitations, and such work should be placed on the walls, where it can be studied without difficulty, rather than overhead on a ceiling.

—the first being when the work of this period went out of fashion and nobody wanted either it or any illustrations of it, and the second being when this same fickle fashion set strongly in that direction again, and all the old lumber-rooms and book-shelves were diligently searched and lucky finds run up to fabulous prices. The cabinets, mantelpieces, and other available articles of this period were often decorated by the insertion of decorative or pictorial panels by Angelica Kauffmann, [Cipriani, and other designers, or by the plaques of Wedgwood. Grinling Gibbons, born in the year 1648, was introduced by Evelyn to the king, and was largely employed at Windsor and Whitehall in carving in marble and wood. His fame rests so greatly upon his exquisite carvings in lime, pear, and other white woods, that his work in other materials is almost forgotten.[1] At Windsor, Gibbons carved the pedestal in marble for the equestrian statue of the king in the principal court. Another notable work of his is the

---

[1] In the accounts still preserved for work done at Whitehall we find the following items : " The said Grinlin Gibbons and Arnold Quellin, for making and carving the great altar-piece of white marble, veined, wrought according to a design and contract, they finding all materials and workmanship, with two marble columns under the throne, fluted, with capitals and bases, £1,875 1s. 8d." This was afterwards removed to Hampton Court, as the following entry will show : " To Grinling Gibbons, master-carver, for taking down the marble altar-piece, with the columns, ornaments, and figures thereto belonging, in the late King James II.'s Chapel at Whitehall, and loading the same into barges, and delivery thereof at Hampton Court, according to contract, £130. More to him for carving cornishes, mouldings, and other picture-frames, for architrave, frese, subbase, and other carver's work by him done in and about the said buildings, £520 7s. 4d."

white marble font in St. James's Church, Piccadilly. It is supported by the Tree of Life, and has sculptured upon it the Temptation in Eden, the baptism of the Saviour by John, and other scriptural subjects. He is also known to have worked in ivory.

Fine specimens of the wood carving of Grinling Gibbons may be seen in the choir of St. Paul's Cathedral, the reredos of the Church of St. Nicholas, Abchurch Lane, in St. James's Church, Piccadilly, and other churches; but the finest examples of his skill are at Petworth House in Sussex, and at Chatsworth. In the library at Trinity College, Cambridge, are various coats of arms embedded by Gibbons in masses of fruits and flowers; and at Lyme Hall, near Disley, are some fine examples of his work. Amongst the accounts of work done at Windsor, we find frequent reference to the carvings of Gibbons, as for example: "Grinling Gibbons, carver, for carving work done and laid upon twenty-eight seats and stalls, carved with fruit, flowers, palms, laurels, pelicans, pigeons; five foot of cornice that has two members, enriched with leaves between each seat; twenty foot of framing to every seat, according to contract, £518. More to him for carving the six vases with the thistle, roses, and two boys, laurels, palms, etc., in the front and upon the top of the King's Seat, with drapery, fruit, etc., etc.; several other ornaments of carving about the altar pews, and other places in and about the King's Chapel, he finding timber and workmanship, according to contract, £498 0s. 5d.—£1016 0s. 5d." "Grinling Gibbons, carver, for an extraordinary fine piece of carved work, made and carved by him for his Matie, and sent by his Matie as a present to the Duke of Florence, £150. And more to him for his pension after the rate of £100 per annum, according to his Mat's warrant, and due to him for half a year ended at Midsummer 1682, £200." This latter piece of carving is still preserved at Modena. His foliage, birds, flowers, and other details are in groups, festoons, pendants, garlands, panels, or other arrangements that suit the position, but are themselves entirely naturalistic in character. Much of his work, owing to the ravages of insects, has entirely decayed.

Wedgwood, the potter, in his noble reproductions from the antique, or the production of work inspired by classic influence, notably contributed to the English Renaissance. The spirit in which he worked may be excellently seen in the remarks with which he concluded a trade catalogue that he issued in 1777: " A competition for cheapness, and not for excellence of workmanship, is the most frequent and certain cause of the rapid decay and entire destruction of arts and manufactures. The desire of selling much in a little time, without respect to the taste or quality of the goods, leads manufacturers and merchants to ruin the reputation of the articles which they make and deal in ; and whilst those who buy, for the sake of a fallacious saving, prefer mediocrity to excellence, it will be impossible for them either to improve or keep up the quality of their works. All works of art must bear a price in proportion to the skill, the taste, the time, the expense, and the risk attending the invention and execution of them. Those pieces that for these reasons bear the highest price, and which those who are not accustomed to consider the real difficulty and expense of making fine things are apt to call dear, are, when justly estimated, the cheapest articles that can be purchased, and such are generally attended with much less profit to the artist than those that everybody calls cheap. Beautiful forms and compositions are not to be made by chance; and they never were made, nor can be made in any kind at a small expense; but the proprietors of this manufactory have the satisfaction of knowing, by a careful comparison, that the prices of many of their ornaments are much lower, and all of them as low as those of any other ornamental works in Europe of equal quality and risk, notwithstanding the high price of labour in England; and they are determined rather to give up the making of any article than to degrade it."

Wedgwood died on Saturday, Jan. 3rd, 1796. On the following Saturday the *Staffordshire Advertiser* contained an eulogium upon him, of which we gladly quote a few passages, as they indicate the esteem in which he was held by his contemporaries and neighbours. "We feel," the writer says, "more than common regret in recording the death of Josiah Wedgwood, Esq., F.R.S., potter to the Queen, etc., at Etruria in the Potteries, and we would wish to say something that might embalm his memory in the hearts of Englishmen. . . . Possessed of great public spirit and unremitting perseverance, with a mind fraught with general intelligence, and particularly with philosophical and chemical knowledge united to a most refined taste, he raised the manufactures of earthenware from the obscure state in which he found them to the degree of utility, elegance, and splendour by which they are now distinguished in every part of the world. . . . What honours have not been raised to men who have been most successful in planning and executing systems of devastation and war—and their monuments are emblazoned with all the proud trophies of human slaughter— but a far higher eulogium belongs to the man whose death we now lament; for the name of Josiah Wedgwood the heart of the widow, the poor, and the afflicted will feel emotions of gratitude and pleasure; and the community at large, who have received benefit by his existence, will for ever respect his memory."

The student who desires to follow the career of Wedgwood and his association with Flaxman in the production of these beautiful works of art will find in Meteyard's "Life of Josiah Wedgwood" the fullest details, and an abundance of excellent illustrations of the various vases, plaques, cameos, and other productions of the Etruria pottery.

The art of the Renaissance was many-sided, being exemplified not only in the decoration more or less dependent on architecture, but in every direction in which taste and skill could enter, as for instance—jewellery, tapestry, metal-work, enamel, glass, inlaid work, and bookbinding. Not only was the art of the period many-sided, but that of the individual was scarcely less so; thus Michael Angelo was at once an architect, sculptor, and a painter, and great in all. Benvenuto Cellini, the sculptor, together with Ghirlandajo, La Francia, Holbein, and many others whom we naturally think of as painters, were also workers in gold and designers of jewellery of exquisite taste. Raffaelle, one of the greatest artists of all time, the painter of the Madonna di San Sisto, a work that alone would secure him immortal fame, did not disdain to paint decorative panels or to supply designs for the pottery painter. Whatever was of art had their fullest sympathy.

The Renaissance metal-work is often of excellent design, and many of the examples are amongst the priceless treasures of the various museums of Europe. The Italians excelled in this; for many years Lombardy was the great armoury of Europe, and the art that was primarily bestowed upon weapons of war [1] found abundant exercise also on lanterns, candelabra, keys (as in Fig. 146), cressets, hinges, knockers, coffers, jewel caskets, the fronts of balconies, and the like. The variation in design is almost infinite, and many fine specimens still remain in Venice, Verona, and other cities.

In our own country much excellent work of the same kind may be seen; as, for instance, the grilles and gates of the choir of St. Paul's Cathedral, and several other London churches have very good iron-work; of these we may mention St. Mary-at-Hill, All Hallows, Barking, St. Mary Woolnoth, and St. Andrew Undershaft. A good deal

---

[1] Weapons of war seem at all times to have been the medium for the exhibition of elaborate art; the ancient Greek, the savage of the South Sea Islands, the skilful craftsman of India, the armourer of mediæval and renaissance days, all alike count no time or labour excessive spent in beautifying instruments of warfare.

Fig. 146.

of excellent iron-work may also be seen in the gates of
various public buildings of secular character; and many
of the old private residences scattered about the older

suburbs of London, such as Hampstead, Stoke Newington, Chelsea, Stratford-le-Bow, and Clapham, have very fine entrance gates.

A great deal of fine Italian metal-work may be seen in the South Kensington Museum, and there, too, are now preserved the gates that formerly adorned the gardens of Hampton Court Palace. These magnificent specimens of iron-work are the creation of Huntingdon Shaw, a Nottingham man, and date from about the year 1695. These most admirable examples of English wrought iron were, after some hundred and fifty years of service, perishing from exposure to the weather, and were therefore securely housed, where from henceforth every possible care will be taken of them. Fig. 147 is an illustration of one of them. The workmanship is excellent, and each gate or grille is of different design in its details; one has the rose of England as a centre, another the thistle, while the figure shown has the Irish harp. Others have the initials of William of Orange and of his consort. The capabilities of the material are well understood, the structural necessity of forming a barrier and a security is well provided for, and yet the structure is not unnecessarily ponderous; while the necessary strength once obtained, the accessory ornament grows most naturally from the leading and essential forms. The king commissioned the work, but very unfortunately died before remunerating Shaw, and the Parliament repudiated all obligation to pay for it—a fact that gives it a somewhat tragic interest, as the artist died at the comparatively early age of fifty-one, his end being hastened by the dis-

FIG. 147.

appointment and injustice he had met with. Practically, therefore, as we admire this collection—twelve of these screens being produced by Shaw, and each thirteen feet wide and over ten feet high—we are regarding the results of thus much time, labour, and taste that were practically stolen from him. Shaw was buried at Hampton Church, and he is described on a mural tablet there as "an artist in his own way," a somewhat depreciatory way of implying that as he neither painted pictures nor sculptured statues, his claim to any sort of recognition as an art-worker was rather dubious, but that they would in all charity give him the benefit of the doubt.

Many excellent books on decorative metal-work have been published in England, France, Germany, Belgium, and Italy. Of these we need here but mention, as an aid to the student, the following: Hefner Alteneck's work on the metal-work of the Middle Ages and the Renaissance, entitled "Eisenwerke oder Ornamentik der Schmiedekunst des Mittelalters und der Renaissance," containing eighty-four engraved plates of examples; Wyatt's "Ornamental Metal Work" in gold, silver, iron, brass, etc., from the twelfth to the nineteenth centuries, with a history of the art in Italy, England, France, Germany, and Spain—a folio volume with fifty large plates in gold and colours of the choicest examples; King's "Orfevrerie et Ouvrages en Metal du Moyen Age," giving in two volumes of folio size two hundred plates of measured drawings, and details of every variety of ecclesiastical and domestic metal-work. Ebbetts' folio volume, "Examples of the Decorative Wrought-Iron Work of the Seventeenth and

Eighteenth Centuries," containing seventy examples of measured drawings of large and small gates, screens, grilles, panels, balustrading, etc., including the great gates and screens from Hampton Court Palace, and specimens from St. Paul's Cathedral, Westminster Abbey, Carshalton, and Loughton Halls, together with a large number of gates from London and its suburbs; and Burty's " Chefs-D'Œuvre of the Industrial Arts," including pottery, glass, metal-work, gold and silver work, tapestry, etc., and having some two hundred and twenty illustrations.

Tarsia-work, or tarsiatura—designs worked in inlaid wood, either stained or of different natural colours—was at one time much used in decoration. It originated in Florence, but soon spread through Italy and France. In this latter country it was termed Marqueterie. In the sixteenth century Cologne was very famous for its tarsia-work, and in England we have numerous examples of it in old furniture, on clock fronts, the flaps of bureaux, the doors of cabinets, and such-like available flat surfaces. It was scarcely indigenous art, and only came into fashion with divers other Dutch things in the reign of William and Mary. Many of the designs consist of more or less naturalistic representations of birds and flowers, and occasionally we find landscapes or scroll-work. In Germany and Italy simple designs of a geometrical character in ebony [1] and ivory were much in vogue. Boule-

---

[1] Ebony was first introduced into Europe in any considerable quantity after the year 1695, on the settlement of Ceylon by the

work[1] is a modification of this, in which metal is employed. The work derives its name from André Charles Boule, a Frenchman, born in the year 1642, who if not the absolute originator of it—a point on which some little doubt exists—at all events greatly developed its possibilities. Boule executed a great deal of work under the direction of Louis XIV. for the rising splendour of Versailles, and, naturally, the work that was sealed with the approval of the monarch was in demand by all the grand seigneurs of the court. The great Colbert, the king's minister of finance, amongst many other services to the state and to art, founded the famous Gobelins tapestry works, and established an Academy[2] under the royal patronage, where painting, sculpture, and decorative art were studied and encouraged to serve the state, and Boule was placed in a responsible position herein, quartered in the Louvre, and made director of the royal furniture department. He

Dutch, and the subsequent appearance of the wood as an article of commerce. Prior to this the supplies were small and intermittent. Riesner, a famous maker of furniture, derives his title of *ébéniste* from this, a favourite material of his, though he also used rose-wood, holly, tulip tree, and other woods in the beautiful marquetry produced by him.

[1] Often called Buhl-work. At the period in which the artist lived orthography was not by any means one of the exact sciences, and in various old books we may find such variations as Buhl, Boulle, Boul, and Boule. The balance of evidence from various official documents leans towards the last of these.

[2] In negotiating a treaty between France and Morocco, he insisted that the latter State should supply yearly a certain number of skins of the famous Morocco leather for the binding of the books in the royal library. This is but one characteristic instance of the way in which he was ever alert to utilise all things and all men for the honour and dignity of France and the monarch whom he served.

had great talent as a designer in several directions; but the work with which his name is specially identified consists of arabesques and other decorative forms cut out of one material and inserted in another, these two materials being ordinarily tortoise-shell and brass. In the earlier examples the shell was used simply as it was, but in later examples we find that the bed upon which it was placed was either painted scarlet or was gilt, thus giving to the translucent tortoise-shell a richer effect. The forms were produced by placing three or four thicknesses of each material together and then sawing through the whole mass, so that the forms on the brass or on the shell were the same, and each was interchangeable with the other, the solids of one fitting to the openings of the other. The brass portion of the design when made up was often elaborately chased. Gold, silver, the red brass that results from a large proportion of copper, yellow brass, or the pale silvery brass that other alloys create, horn, ivory, mother-of-pearl, have all been employed. Given taste in design, a good eye for colour, and perfect execution, it will be seen that excellent results may be achieved with such materials, but the omission of any of these three qualifications is fatal.

The splendour and artistic character of the book-binding of the Renaissance epoch was another marked feature. During the whole of the sixteenth century we find books gorgeously bound, and popes, cardinals, princes, and nobles vying with each other in the richness and beauty of their collections of books and bindings. One often hears of the Grolier bindings, and many of the beautiful volumes

R

identified with his name remain unsurpassed. Grolier himself was a great collector and had a magnificent library, but his books were bound not by himself but by others under his directions and supervision. He was a great patron of art in many ways. He died in 1565, but his library was not dispersed until more than a century afterwards. Henry II. and Francis I., amongst the monarchs of France, were great book collectors, and had them sumptuously bound with their devices and other decorations.

James I. of England was an enthusiastic lover of fine binding, and the British Museum contains many beautiful examples of work done for this sovereign, as well as specimens of all the best work of this kind produced either on the Continent or in England.[1] Some very good examples may also be seen in the South Kensington Museum. The student may take note of the following specimens:—

---

[1] It is entirely hopeless in a page or two, or for the matter of that in a volume or two, to give any notion of the various schools of book-binding, or to even barely catalogue the names of famous craftsmen, but the student will of course take every opportunity of seeing fine work in the national and other collections. The following books may be referred to as giving good illustrations of fine bindings: Stockbauer's "Abdildungen von Mustereinbänden aus der Bluthezeit der Buchbin-derkunst," containing forty plates exhibiting some fine specimens, chiefly by French and Italian binders of the sixteenth century ; and " Les Reliures d'Art a la Bibliothèque Nationale," by Henri Bouchot, with forty-eight plates of choice specimens. He may advantageously refer, too, to such books as Tuckett's " Specimens of Ancient and Modern Bindings," the " Monuments Inédits ou peu Connus " of Libri, Techener's " Histoire de la Bibliophilie," the " Album de Reliure " of Julien, and Zaehnsdorf's book on the subject.

Officium Beatæ Mariæ Virginis. Antwerp, 1625. In binding of olive morocco; the back and sides ornamented with gilt tooling, fastened with silver clasps.

Lutheran Bible, printed at Jena, 1564. Binding covered with gold tooling, a coat of arms emblazoned on either side; the edges gilt and gauffré, with birds and flowers, and the same coat of arms. Dated 1583.

Mar. Fabii Quintiliani Declamationes. Lyons, 1530. In binding of dark brown calf; on each side a medallion of Charles V., his shield, device, and motto.

"Questio de distinctione Attributorum Dei." In red calf binding, with gold tooling; shield of arms in colours on the centre of each side, the edges gilt and gauffré. Sixteenth century.

Arme (Andrea dall') Emblemi e Sonetti. Oblong small quarto. In the original binding, the sides covered with gold tooling; fan pattern in corners. Sixteenth century.

Manuscript, on vellum, in Italian, relating to the Riario family, in morocco leather binding, executed at Rome, with the arms of a cardinal as the centre ornament on either side. Date of MS., 1683.

Martyrologium Romanum. Venice, 1673. Bound in crimson morocco, with gilt tooling, fan pattern in corners; gilt metal clasps.

Psalmorum Davidis translatio. R. Stephens, 1556. Grolier binding in morocco of different colours, with gilt leaves, gauffré.

Missale Romanum. Antwerp, 1577. In brown calf binding, with gilt tooling and coloured strap-work in the Grolier style.

Psalmorum Liber. Lyons, 1542. In brown calf binding in the Grolier style, with strap-work of coloured leather, the edges gilt and stamped.

L'Office de la Vierge Marie. Paris, 1596. 12mo. Bound in olive morocco, tooled and gilt with devices of Marguerite de Valois.

Enamelling on metal has had a wide range of application. Though several processes have been employed, the central idea in all enamel-work is the adornment of a metal surface by means of vitreous colours fused upon it by means of great heat. The two broad divisions are as follows : translucent colours that enable us to see the metal beneath, and those that from their opacity entirely conceal it. In the first of these the metal itself enters largely into the decorative effect, being engraved or in bas-relief, and the transparent enamel merely gives an added richness to what is already an artistic production ; this is termed translucid on relief. In the second it is the colour itself that gives the decorative effect, the metal beneath being merely the supporting surface. This latter system of enamelling is again subdivided. When the spaces to receive the vitreous material are cut into the surface of the metal, the process is termed champlevé ; but when the surface is undisturbed, and the cells to contain the colouring matter are formed upon it by narrow bands of metal, it is known as cloisonné. Enamelling as a decorative process was in use by the Gauls, Britons, and Celts,[1] and many good examples of its use by these

---

[1] In a treatise by a Greek writer, Philostratus, he refers to this in a way that shows that the art was unknown to the Greeks and

peoples have been recovered and preserved. It was also a favourite art-medium in Byzantine work, the process used being the cloisonné; and Limoges, in the west of France, was a great centre for works in champlevé. These were chiefly employed in the service of the church, in the decoration of shrines and reliquaries, crosses, pastoral staves, and other objects of ecclesiastical use. Later on Limoges became famous for its painted enamels. In these the whole plate of metal was covered with black enamel, and then the design was painted in opaque white and grey upon it; such portions as were to be coloured were glazed over with transparent enamel, and the lights were often emphasized with touches of gold. A great taste for work in "grisaille" sprang up, when strong colour was either very sparingly used or entirely absent, the whole design being worked in a neutral grey. The effect was very delicate and refined. It will be seen that, except in the common ground of vitreous material on metal, these various methods widely differ, as while some of them entail a good deal of metal working and the inlay of small masses of colour, this last process is as distinctly painting as though it were worked on a sheet of paper or a piece of canvas. The enamel-painters of Limoges were producing excellent work for over three hundred years, and many examples may be met with in various museums in England and on the Continent.

The stained glass of the Renaissance period was ordi-

Romans, and tells his readers that "the barbarians living near the ocean" were able to "pour colours on hot brass so that these adhere and become like stone, and preserve the design represented."

narily too pictorial in treatment to be decoratively sound.
Donatello, Ghiberti, and Perugino amongst others designed for glass-work. It is labour misplaced and genius
misapplied when a stained-glass window loses its distinctive idiosyncrasy and has no other ambition than to emu-
late an oil picture. In the subject of any fresco or oil
picture we can arrange the lights and shades to fall in
any required direction, but in a painting on glass the
light must necessarily come immediately from the rear in
a way that entirely falsifies any light and shade that is
therein represented. Moreover the function of a window
is essentially to give light, and this primary aim is
thwarted when the heavy shadows and dark backgrounds
that would be strictly in place in a picture are transferred to this transparent medium. Beauty of form and
richness of luminous colour are open to the glass painter,
and these give an ample field for beautiful results, as the
magnificent windows of the Gothic of the thirteenth century abundantly testify. The resources of glass painting
are more limited than those of oil, and in endeavouring
unsuccessfully to compete with this medium of expression
it loses at the same time much of its distinctive charm.[1]

---

[1] The following works may advantageously be consulted : Warring-
ton's " History of Stained Glass, from the Earliest Period of the Art
to the Present Time," containing twenty-six coloured plates, with
text, imperial folio. Westlake's " History of Design in Stained
Glass," in three volumes. Vol. i. comprising from the earliest
times to the thirteenth century ; vol. ii., fourteenth-century work in
England, France, Germany, and Italy ; vol. iii., fifteenth-century
work ditto, heraldry, monograms, quarries, etc. The book contains
nearly three hundred illustrations. The work of Franks on " Orna-

Another failing in these pictorial renderings is that the composition is often taken across a whole window, irrespective of any necessary architectural members. No painter or sculptor would so treat a subject extending over a series of distinct spaces, but would always arrange that each panel should be complete in itself, even though forming only a portion of the illustration of some legend or other subject. This is natural and reasonable, and there is no justification for a departure from it in glass painting. By so doing we seem, as in Fig. 148, to be regarding the event depicted through the bars of a cage, the dog cut in half by the mullion bar being a notable illustration of this false style of working. Such an elaborate use of perspective is a mistake also, as the representation is correct only from one point of view, and

mental Glazing Quarries, collected and arranged from Ancient Examples," gives over one hundred interesting illustrations.

The three following works it will be seen do not deal exclusively with stained glass, but they are books that should be seen : Gailhabaud's "L'Architecture du V. au XVII. Siecle, et les Arts qui en dependent, la Sculpture, la Peinture sur Verre, la Mosaique, etc.," four hundred fine plates, folio. It illustrates the gems of architecture and its dependent arts, not only in France, but also in Italy, England, Spain, Flanders, Germany, Arabia, etc. The examples comprise ecclesiastical, monastic, civil, municipal, and military edifices ; details in stone, wood, metal, ivory, etc. ; many plates of mural painting, stained glass, mosaics, etc., printed in colours ; ecclesiastical and domestic furniture, etc. Waring's book on "The Arts Connected with Architecture," illustrated by examples in Central Italy of stained glass, fresco ornament, marble and enamel inlay, wood inlay, etc., from the thirteenth to the fifteenth century ; and Shaw's "Decorative Arts of the Middle Ages," giving good examples of ancient enamel, metal-work, wood-carving, stained glass, etc. It is well illustrated.

it is alien to the stern simplicity of treatment that best becomes designs for glass-work. The subject represented in Fig. 148 is the driving of the money-changers from the Temple, a subject capable of excellent treatment as a

Fig. 148.

fresco, but scarcely capable of satisfactory introduction in a stained-glass window. It is unfortunate that our closing comments on the Renaissance should be of an unfavourable nature, as it may leave a false impression on the

mind of the student; our last words, therefore, shall dwell
not on the greater or less success of any particular application of art, but on the whole field covered, and of this
we may without risk of contradiction say that, taking
this broad view, we find a magnificent power of drawing
and a striking ingenuity of design in the work of the
Renaissance. It stands to reason that amidst so much
work, the product of many minds in many countries, there
are degrees of excellence; and we naturally find that on
the abandonment of old traditions of work, the new liberty
became in some cases a license that was abused. Both
on its own merits and as a striking example of the
principle of æstheticism, beauty for its own sake, this
period is of the highest interest in the development of
decorative art.

CHAPTER VI.

WE turn our attention, in conclusion, to art that has been produced under entirely different limitations, the offspring of different creeds, the result of different processes of work, the outcome of other art-traditions, and commence with the art of Islam. We must here at once point out, what on a moment's reflection is evident enough, that this is a term of wide comprehension. If we deal with the art that has been executed under the influence of Christianity, we at once find ourselves confronted by the work of many centuries, executed in countries far remote from each other; and in like manner Mohammedan art, though it has its set principles, has differing developments, so that the art of Moorish Spain is not that of Persia or of India.

All Eastern art that is done under Mohammedan influences loses, irreparably, the highest charm, for the creed of Islam forbids the representation of any living thing. Architecture may flourish still, as we see in the grace of the palace of Alhambra in Granada, in the stately mosque of Cordova, or in the magnificent Taj Mahal of Agra, but the decoration employed must be of the most conventional and arbitrary character, and this consists largely of intricate strap-work and geometrical design. The enjoyment of the old Gothic carver in the wayside weeds is impossible for them; no clustering capitals of hawthorn, no wreathings of the graceful maple are seen in their work; and the joy of the old Greeks in the olive, the acanthus, and the bay has no counterpart in the art of Islam. Painting, therefore, and sculpture in their higher developments are wholly banished; while shut out from all the higher possibilities of art, they have developed all that was accessible to them to a degree that no other men have ever done, the Celtic illuminations and stone carvings being the nearest approximation to the wealth of fancy and intricacy of detail shown in the simple elements beyond which they were forbidden to pass. Of this richness of design, the pattern shown in Fig. 26 may be regarded as a fair example.

John Ruskin, one of the greatest of art critics, calls, in one of his books, the art of the Alhambra detestable.[1] The word is a strong one, and we would venture to say wholly misplaced. Whatever we may think of the Mohammedan religion, it has most potent sway over its followers. Doubtless the designers of the beautiful Moorish, Persian, and Indian work that we may see in our museums and elsewhere could have, under different influences, produced work as fine on other lines; the limitation is not of their own seeking, but is laid upon them by religious obligation. Even, however, where we cannot help considering that strong feeling has led to exaggeration of statement, such statements from men of influence and thought have at least this good in them, that they compel thought in others. It is so much the custom to accept ideas at second-hand, and to allow our thinking to be done for us by other people, so much the habit to bow down before precedent, that a writer who arouses our antagonism by the strength of his assertions, though he may compel our dissent, does us an inconceivable service.

The great plain of Arabia, lying beyond Roman influence and its persecuting orthodoxy, became in the sixth century a refuge for men of all opinions, political or religious, who found themselves out of touch with

---

[1] Wornum, in his "Analysis of Ornament," writes: "a more beautiful simply ornamental style than perhaps any that had preceded it." Owen Jones, in his "Grammar of Ornament," writes: "The Alhambra is at the very summit of perfection of Moorish art, as is the Parthenon of Greek art."

dominant ideas. A considerable emigration of Jews
from Palestine, Nestorians, Manicheans, Gnostics, Magian
followers of Zoroaster, and others found in this no-man's
land a refuge highly favourable to religious liberty. The
Arabs recognised with pleasure the descent from Abraham
common to themselves, the Jews, and the Christians in
their midst, and many of them accepted one or other
of the newly introduced faiths. But the bitterness of
religious strife from which the strangers in their wilds
thought to have fled broke out anew, divisions and sub-
divisions cleft them apart, abstruse arguments as to the
nature of angels, the power of evil, the Incarnation, and
the like formed ground for interminable wrangling; and
the Arab, turning aside from a spectacle so unedifying,
returned to his simple idol-worship.

In the midst of this unrest was born Mohammed, a
man of good family, and a traveller who mixed freely
with men of all opinions, a man of intense thoughtfulness
and earnestness. For years it was his custom to retire
each year for a month to a mountain cave for rest and
meditation. Here, apart from warring strifes and the
petty life of man, the great book of Nature was spread
before him, the truths that he had gathered from the
Hebrew Scriptures fed his hungry spirit, and conscious of
the living soul within him and the necessity to teach
a better way to his idolatrous fellow-countrymen, he
brushed aside the tangled maze of theological subtleties
that the warring Christians had reared and proclaimed
the central truth, the greatness and unity of God.

"Mahomet was in his fortieth year when, having

withdrawn to a cavern in Mount Hara, near Mecca, during this Ramadhan, to pass the month in prayer, and meditation on those great questions, he one day told his wife Kadijah, who with his household was with him or near him this year, that by the unspeakable special favour of Heaven he had now found it all out; was in doubt and darkness no longer, but saw it all. That all these idols and formulas were nothing—miserable bits of wood; that there was one God in and over all; and we must leave all idols and look to Him. That God is great; and that there is nothing else great! He is the Reality. Wooden idols are not real; He is real. He made us at first; sustains us yet; we and all things are but the shadow of Him; a transitory garment veiling the eternal splendour. 'Allah akbar, God is great;' and then also 'Islam,' that we must submit to God. That our whole strength lies in resigned submission to Him, whatsoever He do to us. For this world and for the other!

"Such light had come, as it could, to illuminate the darkness of this wild Arab soul. A confused dazzling splendour as of life and heaven, in the great darkness which threatened to be death; he called it revelation and the angel Gabriel;—who of us yet can know what to call it? That Mahomet's whole soul, set in flame with this grand truth vouchsafed to him, should feel as if it were important, and the only important thing, was very natural. That Providence had unspeakably honoured him by revealing it, saving him from death and darkness; that he therefore was bound to make known the same to all creatures: this is what was meant by 'Mahomet is the Prophet of God.' " [1]

To get men thus to believe on him was the initial difficulty, yet in this alone lay success. It meant faith that the preacher was a true man—"a man who," to quote Arnold's graphic words, "had really communed with the Supreme, and undoubtingly believed, not that fact only, but also that Heaven had selected him as its instrument in raising and reforming his fellow-men. This being granted, this condition fulfilled, faith was easy and natural to those enthusiastic children of the sun. Here was a man who said that God visited him through the intervention of angels, and told him this or that; this man's life was plainly, according to Arab standards, virtuous and noble; it was consistently ruled by some powerful spirit within; he refused no responsibility; shrank from no depth or height of trust reposed in him; was ready to lead if they would follow; to teach authoritatively if they would listen: was it very wonderful if they took him at his word, hailed the voice of God as speaking by his mouth, and rapturously bade him lead them whither he would? He has read carelessly the annals of mankind who does not know that when the passion of loyalty comes to be transfigured in the light of religious faith, no enterprise is too great for those under its potent influence, no form of suffering or death can deter, no human sagacity can calculate the consequences of the resulting movements."

---

[1] Carlyle.

For some considerable time, nevertheless, belief in the new religion was of slow growth. Persecution was brought to bear against it; attempts to assassinate Mohammed were made, and he withdrew for awhile to Medina, where he had several devoted followers. This is the Hegira,[1] or flight from Mecca, that forms the recognised era of all Mohammedan countries. It marks the turning-point, when Mohammed, finding persuasion in vain, drew the sword, and placed himself at the head of his adherents.

We need scarcely pause to say that we are no apologists for Islamism. In its cruelty and sensuality, any comparison with Christianity becomes impossible. But what we have desired to do is not to dwell upon it as it impresses ourselves, but as we should imagine it impresses its followers. It is the influence of the creed of Islam upon those who accept it that now concerns us, and of course more especially its influence upon art.

The success of the movement in its rapidity and far-reaching thoroughness must in great measure be ascribed to the fact that the utter corruption, religious and political, of the expiring Eastern Empire could offer no resistance to an attack that we may not uncharitably say carried with it not only the zeal of the followers of the new creed, but also promised an easy transfer of untold wealth from the effeminate hands that were powerless to defend it, to those that were quite ready

---

[1] In Arabic, el Hijrah : literally, the going forth, which it will be noted is not quite the same thing as flight.

to appropriate it as lawful spoil of the infidel, while death had no terror, since it was but the gate to Paradise, a bliss that, apart from all previous shortcomings, was the inalienable right of all who fell in strife against the enemies of Islam.

As the influence spread, those who came beneath it in turn sent forth their hosts, and in a very short space of time Syria, Persia, and Northern Africa were all as Mohammedan as Arabia. Scarcely a hundred years had elapsed from the first promulgation before we find the new creed in firm possession from Spain to the banks of the Ganges.

The Arabs themselves, a warlike and nomadic race, children of the desert, had no national art of their own. Hence in their conquests they at first adopted with little change the buildings they found to hand, but erased from them all naturalistic representations. Later on new ambitions arose with increased power, and the Byzantine artists and architects were pressed into the service of the conquerors, and required to accommodate their skill to the new requirements and limitations.

Thus, for instance, the Mosque Teyloum at Cairo, built in 876, was the work of a Christian architect whom the Sultan clapped into prison to enable him to prepare his designs under the advantage of strict retirement, plus the stimulus of knowing that a considerably worse fate would befall him if he did not rise to the occasion. In the mosques of Cairo and in some of the Sicilian remains this Greek influence is very evident, the fret, anthemion, and other classic types under some

S

degree of modification being clearly recognisable, while the decorations of the Alhambra are almost purely Saracenic. It must be borne in mind that while the great mosques of the East are mostly of the seventh or eighth centuries, the Alhambra is of the fourteenth, a sufficiently long interval to allow of a full development and individuality of style. The Mosque of Omar at Jerusalem dates from the year 637; of Amrou at Cairo, 642; of Damascus, 705. In these early buildings a great use was made of the columns and other wreckage and plunder from old Classic and Christian temples and churches, and in the Mosque Teyloum a good deal even of the new work executed by Arab workmen or impressed Christian artisans is very classic in feeling, the Greek architect probably not being able to clear his mind of old traditions of work. On the site of the mosque of Damascus was originally a Roman temple, but this was afterwards converted into a Christian church, dedicated to St. John the Baptist. The Mohammedans pulled it down and rebuilt it to suit their own requirements,[1] the result being that it is now a

---

[1] The all-important condition was the Kibleh that indicated the direction of Mecca. This once fixed, all that was needed was an enclosed space and an outer court for ablution. As the Christian churches were built on an axis due east and west, it was but rarely that they met the Kibleh requirement, and no European building could do so, since all are considerably north of Mecca, though an exception was made at Constantinople, where the magnificent church of Santa Sophia was spared, and a compromise arranged. In a mosque the axis of the building is not a fixed east and west, but may vary greatly from this, as the one essential is that it should

strange blend of Roman, Christian, and Arabic details. Of the hundreds of pillars in the mosque at Cordova, by far the greater number have Roman or Byzantine capitals.

The decorative art of Islam is chiefly a rich surface decoration,[1] and of this the frontispiece gives an excellent idea. The walls are covered with diaper-like forms in an inexhaustible variety of conventional patterns, the general constructive lines of the design being of geometric character and the filling-in consisting of very conventional foliate and floral forms. The scheme of colour is very rich and harmonious, a great use being made also of gold. Such architectural features as doorways, windows, and niches are emphasized, as our frontispiece clearly shows, by broad bands of ornament, and amidst all are inscribed with great ingenuity and decorative charm numerous sentences from the Koran

---

point to Mecca; it may therefore be due north and south, or any other of the possibilities of the compass.

[1] For excellent examples see " Architecture Arabe " of Coste; Girault de Prangey's " Monumens arabes d'Egypte," and his " Essai sur l'Architecture des Arabes en Espagne, en Sicile, et en Barbarie "; Gally Knight's " Saracenic Remains in Sicily "; Laborde's " Voyage, pittoresque et historique de l'Espagne "; Caveda's " Geschichte der Baukunst in Spanien "; the charming three volumes of Goury and Owen Jones on the Alhambra; Coste et Flandin's " Voyage en Perse "; Murphy's " Arabian Antiquities of Spain," a folio volume richly illustrated; Hessemer's " Arabische Bau-verzierungen "; Bisson's " Choix d'Ornaments Arabes de l'Alhambra "; Parvillec's " Architecture et Decoration Turques," a folio volume, with many illustrations, mostly printed in colours; the " Espana Artistica y Monumental " of Perez de Villa-Amil, three grand volumes, folio; Prisse d'Avenne's "L'Art Arabe"; Bourgoin's " Les Arts Arabes," a finely illustrated folio volume.

or the poets. These inscriptions are a very characteristic feature in Mohammedan art.[1] The Cufic or Arabic letters lend themselves readily to graceful treatment, and we find these texts from the sacred writings of the Mohammedans or passages from other authors very freely introduced, not only in mural decoration, but in metal-work, as in Fig. 149, on textile fabrics, tile-work and pottery, arms, and in fact wherever any opportunity for their introduction occurs.

If we turn to the Alhambra, which may be considered as a typical example of Mohammedan art at its finest, we find these inscriptions most freely introduced. They at once please the eye by their beauty of form, and reward the mind by their beauty of sentiment. They are either extracts from the Koran, or sentences of elevated thought from other writers, or poems in praise of the building itself or of its owners. One of the most freely used is the well-known "There is no Conqueror but God," the reply of Ibnu l'-Ahmar to the acclamation of his subjects when they saluted him as conqueror on the surrender of Seville. Others of like nature are the following:—

" God is the best of protectors ; He is the most compassionate of the compassionate."

" Praise be given to God the only one."

" Praise be given to God. There is no power or strength but in God."

---

[1] In the book of Sir Thomas Herbert, " Some Yeares Travels into Africa and Asia," a book published in London in the year 1677, the palace at Spahawn, *i.e.* Isphahan, is described as being " painted with blew and gold, imbroidered with posies of Arabick, which after the grotesco manner makes it shew very pleasant."

"There is no Deity but Allah; Mohammed is his messenger."

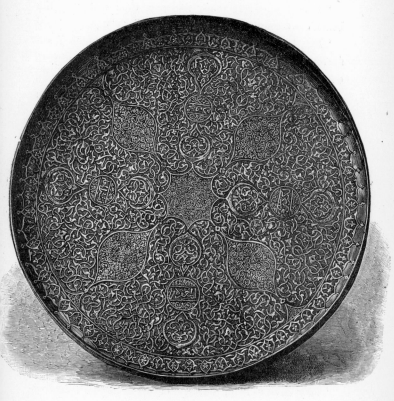

Fig. 149.

"Durability is God's."

"O God! Thine is the praise for ever; and Thine are the thanks for ever."

Illustrations of inscriptions in praise of the building itself may be seen in the following sentences :—

" Look attentively at my elegance, thou wilt reap the benefit of a commentary on decoration."

" For, by Allah ! the elegant buildings by which I am surrounded surpass all other buildings in the propitious omen attending their foundation."

" Apartments are there enfolding so many wonders, that the eyes of the spectator remain for ever fixed upon them; provided he be gifted with a mind to estimate them."

" How many delightful prospects—how many objects in the contemplation of which a highly gifted mind finds the gratification of its utmost wishes."

" Markets they are where those provided with money are paid in beauty, and where the judge of elegance is perpetually sitting to pronounce sentence."

Sentences, in conclusion, in praise of the earthly rulers may also be found. Thus :—

" Brightly doth our Sultan, like the full moon, shine in the high regions of the empire. May his praiseworthy deeds for ever last, and his radiant light never tarnish."

" Glory to our Lord, the warlike and just Sultan Abú-Abdillah Al-ghani-billah."

" May divine help, solidity of empire, and splendid victory over the enemy fall to the lot of our Lord Abúl-hajáj, commander of the Moslems ! "

" May power everlasting and imperishable glory be the lot of the owner of this palace."

We may here turn aside for awhile and dwell for a

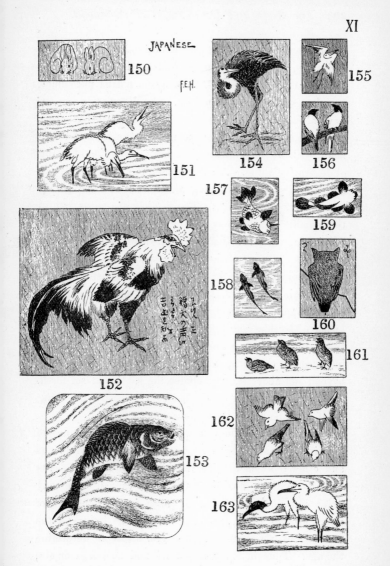

JAPANESE

F.E.H.

150

151

152

153

XI

154

155

156

157

158

159

160

161

162

163

263

short space on this feature in design, the use of inscriptions, of which Mohammedan art is the most conspicuous exemplar, but which is by no means uncommon
in other systems of decoration. An inscription, as we
have already pointed out in our remarks on the Assyrian
arrowhead, may be merely a most matter-of-fact statement, without the slightest pretence or intention of being
of decorative value. All such—and the reader will find
no difficulty in identifying them—are at once placed
outside our pale; but in many other instances, as in
the notable illustrations that we have given from the
Alhambra, they are distinctly intended to enhance the
beauty and interest of the work on which they occur.

The Roman letters in ordinary use, excellent as they
are in their blunt straightforwardness, do not lend themselves happily to decorative requirements, but many of the
forms of Gothic and Lombardic alphabets do, and it is
these that we most ordinarily find in use in illuminations,
inscriptions on bells, and the like. Apart from this,
beyond and above it, is of course the sentiment set forth.
It does not suffice to set forth a thing prettily, the thing
itself must be worth the setting.

The ancients made a considerable decorative use of
inscriptions, and many antique Greek and Roman rings
and other trinkets are inscribed with kindly sentiments
that made them doubtless the more valued. We may
point out, too, that indirectly such inscriptions are of
value, as they often, from the form of the letters or the
presence of the letters themselves, assist to determine
the age. Thus in early Greek we find no omega or eta,

and in later Greek the koppa and the digamma fell into disuse, while the forms of the letters changed very much at various periods. The same thing is as evident in later times ; a thirteenth-century Gothic alphabet is quite different in its forms from one of the fifteenth century.

While the Arabic and Cufic inscriptions please the eye by their graceful setting forth, and awaken interest by their curious and complex character, many of them being so arranged as to read from either direction, this love of complexity is a feature that may readily be carried too far, as it is evident that an inscription that is illegible, or only decipherable after great trouble has been expended upon it, fails in its primary object, and might preferably be exchanged for ornament pure and simple.

The characters employed, we need scarcely point out, should be suitable in style to the position in which they are to be placed ; thus an inscription in Roman letters in a design permeated with mediæval feeling, or a legend in fourteenth-century characters across the classic façade of the British Museum, would be equally open to adverse criticism. A very happy and particularly appropriate inscription may be seen in the classic quotation in praise of the virtues of water, duly inscribed in Greek characters on the Corinthian portico of the Pump-room at Bath.

The marked power of the Latin language of expressing much in a little compass, fits it in an especial degree for inscriptions ; and though, on the one hand, the use of Latin or Greek is a bar to the unlearned, on the other these appeal at once to the educated of all civilized lands. While, therefore, the legend on the village pump may well be in the vulgar tongue, we recognise the value of the classic languages on the public buildings of our great cities. Thus, for instance, in the International Exhibition held in London in the year 1862, around the great window ran the beautiful legend, "Gloria in excelsis Deo et in terra pax," while round the arch of the western gallery, in the midst of all the triumphs of human skill and the utilisation of natural products to the needs of man, was the grand acknowledgment of the source of all, "Domini est terra et plenitudo ejus." On the other hand, in that portion of the building specially devoted to home exhibits, the poorest and lowliest might read around the base of the great eastern dome the equally grand acknowledgment set forth in the simple language of our English Bible, "Lord, both riches and honour come of Thee, Thou reignest over all: in Thy hand is power and might, and in Thy hand it is to make great." Latin, from its long association with the services of the Church, and its use as the language of the learned in early times, when scholarship was scarcely found outside the ranks of the ecclesiastics, is especially appropriate again for use in Church work;[1] while the introduction of Latin mottos in heraldic devices is another happy illustration of its use in mediæval and modern times.

Inscriptions are freely found upon the bells cast in the Middle Ages; in some cases these are prosaic and matter-

---

[1] Thus, for example, " Item one chalis syluer and gylte havyng wrytten abowte the cuppe Laudabo dominum in ecclesia sanctorum, and on the foote Totus mundus est ecclesia."— Inventory Lincoln Cathedral.

of-fact enough,[1] while others in matter and manner come fully within the limit imposed by our title. The variety of lettering used upon bells is somewhat remarkable, and many of the forms used are of admirable decorative effect. On early bells the inscriptions are frequently wholly in Lombardic capitals; later on we get every variety of Gothic, and this in turn was succeeded by lettering of the Roman type. The inscriptions are often dedicatory in character, to God, to the Virgin, and to the saints; at other times invocatory, or expressive of loyalty, or suggested by the use of the bells. As examples, we may instance, "Sancta Agatha, ora pro nobis;" "Ye people all that hear me ring, be faithful to your God and king;" "Mankind, like us, too oft is found possessed of nought but empty sound;" "Would men, like us, join and agree, they'd live in tuneful harmony."

A very common inscription is the following: "I sweetly tolling men do call to taste on meats that feed the soul." Elsewhere we find, "Our sounding is to each a call to serve the Lord, both great and small;" "I to the church the living call, and to the grave do summon all;" "The fleeting hour I tell, I summon all to pray, I toll the funeral knell, I hail the festal day;" "I call the living, mourn the dead, I tell when days and years are fled, for

---

[1] As at Stoke Rivers—

"Our Soundes is good, our shapes is neat,
Its Davis cast us so compleat."

Or at Himbleton Church—

"John Martin of Worcester he made wee,
Be it known to all that do wee see."

joy and grief, for prayer and praise, to heaven my tuneful voice I raise."

Sometimes an inscription takes two or more bells of a peal to complete it. For instance, at St. Austell it takes eight bells to produce the following (we number the portion contributed by each bell to the whole):—

1. By music minds an equal temper know,
2. Nor swell too high, nor sink too low.
3. Music the fiercest grief can charm,
4. And Fate's severest rage disarm.
5. Music can soften pain to ease,
6. And make despair and madness please;
7. Our joys below it can improve,
8. And antedate the joys above.

The interesting allusion in the book of the prophet Zechariah to a coming day of blessing and dedication, when even the bells and bridles of the horses should be inscribed "Holiness unto the Lord," points to an analogous use of inscriptions on bells that would be quite familiar to his hearers centuries before the Christian era.

During the Middle Ages great use was also made of inscriptions on rings. These were generally placed on the outer surface of the ring in the fourteenth and fifteenth centuries, and on the inner surface in the sixteenth and seventeenth. Such are termed "posy rings," and many of these mottos or "posies" [1] are charming in their epigrammatic quaintness, in their sentiment and appropriateness. These mottos were ordinarily placed in the plain gold circle of the wedding ring, though not exclu-

---

[1] " Is this a prologue, or the posy of a ring?"—SHAKESPEARE.

sively confined to these pledges of troth.[1] Such legends were ordinarily of a religious character. The following examples from old wedding rings will sufficiently illustrate this, and also show the kindly, wholesome tone that is so characteristic of them : " In thee my choice I do rejoice ; " " Let me in thee most happy be ; " " United heartés death only partes ; " " Noe heart more true than mine to you ; " " Where hearts agree there God will be ; " " True love is lyfe to man and wyfe ; " " In thee my choyce how I rejoyce." In one hundred and ten examples before us as we write we find that eighty-five are thrown into this rhyming form. On one plain gold ring in our collection we find the inscription, " The gift of a faithfull frend " ; and while we would not for a moment imply that husband and wife may not be the best and most faithful of friends, such an inscription so far differs from the general character of those found as to call for notice.

Many of the devices adopted by the old printers were very quaint and ingenious. The famous J. Daye, for example, in the sixteenth century, instead of merely affixing his name to his work, used an emblematical woodcut of the rising sun, and the motto, " Arise, for it is Day ! " and the great love of the Middle Ages for these conceits, rebuses, plays upon words, and such-like devices affords us many illustrations of like character. Of these

---

[1] On an old gold ring in our collection, that from its size and style, the traces of blue enamel upon it, and a diamond cut in the form of a heart, may be considered as equivalent to a modern " engagement " ring, we find the propitiatory motto, " I am sent to Salute."

Mrs. Bury Palliser's book on "Historic Devices and Badges" gives hundreds of interesting examples, and we cannot do better than refer those of our readers who are interested in the subject to its pages.

Inscriptions as an element in the design may frequently be met with on our coinage, giving some interesting historical allusions or other source of interest beyond the bare enumeration of such more or less necessary facts as names, titles, dates, or values as one ordinarily expects to find on coins. Queen Elizabeth's motto, "Rosa sine Spina," was, for instance, a happy reference to the cessation of civil strife and the blending of York and Lancaster into the house of Tudor, and its occurrence on the money in circulation was a constant reminder to all of the welcome fact.

"Posui Deum adjutorem meum,"—I have taken God for my helper,—was an especially favourite inscription, as we find it on the coinage of Edward III., Richard II., Henry IV. and V., Edward IV., Richard III., Henry VII. and VIII., Elizabeth and Edward VI., and in the plural form on the money of Philip and Mary.

Other examples are the "Auxilium meum a Domino" on the rose-nobles of Richard II., the "Christus vincit, Christus signat, Christus imperat" of Henry V., and the "Sit nomen Domine benedictum" on the groats of Henry VI. Charles I., a man of culture, artistic taste, and refinement, placed, amongst others, the following mottos on his coinage : "Cultores sui Deus protegit,"—God will protect His worshippers; "Amor populi præsidium regis,"—The love of the people is the defence of the king; "Floreat concordia regna,"—With concord kingdoms flourish; "Justitia thronum firmat,"—Justice strengthens the throne.

On divers medals, seals, and coins we find an ornamental arrangement based on the initials or letters of the king's name, or of the place where the coin was struck. Thus, on some of the coins of Alfred the Great we find a monogrammatic arrangement based on the word Londinia, crude enough in arrangement, but distinctly decorative in intention.

The custom of introducing inscriptions on their work was largely in vogue with the earlier English potters, and any one visiting such collections of ceramic ware as that in the Museum of Practical Geology, or the excellent Willett collection in the Corporation Museum, Brighton, will find abundant store of illustrations.

> " To observations which ourselves we make,
> We grow more partial for the observer's sake."
> —Pope.

Failing this personal hunting up of examples, the reader may turn advantageously to such an excellent work as that of Solon, "The Art of the Old English Potter," where many interesting examples will be found and much valuable information on the whole subject of Early English ceramic art very pleasantly picked up.

As we have just given a quotation in support of the value of personal observation, we may for the consolation of those who are denied this great advantage refer them to the equally true words of Johnson : "Knowledge is of two kinds : we know a subject ourselves, or we know where we can find information on it."

The inscriptions on this early pottery are ordinarily feeble in sentiment and feeble in execution, while the spelling is outrageous; all points indicating that many of the early potters were men of little or no education. Nevertheless, the use they made of these inscriptions as a decorative feature brings them well within our view. Such inscriptions as, " Break me not, I pray, in youer hast, for I to none will give destast," or " Earth I am, et is most trwe; desdan me not, for so ar you," or " Come, brother, shall we join? Give me your twopence, here is mine," are characteristic.

During the Middle Ages the use of inscriptions on almost every object of use [1] or ornament was a very marked feature, one that is now but rarely seen, but which might advantageously to some extent be revived. The writings of our old authors are full of excellent passages suitable for such purposes,[2] and it appears to

---

[1] The following, for instance, are from mediæval trenchers :—

" Feede mynde with myrth, thy mawe with meate,
And eate to lyue not lyue to eate,
For gorging doth offende thy healthe,
Thy god, thy soule, thy witt, thy wealth.

At meate or a meale make myrth with geast,
Of absent folkes reporte the best,
Mirth pleaseth with ciuilitie,
The rest is but scurrilitye."

[2] In the excellent book by Tymms and Wyatt, on "The Art of Illuminating," this is very well worked out. Scores of excellent passages are given from the writings of George Herbert, Milton, Shakespeare, Ben Jonson, Gay, Young, Bacon, and other old writers, and classified for the embellishment of various rooms—dining-room, bedroom, study, schoolroom, museum, counting-house, and so forth.

us that a pleasant, interesting, and profitable old custom might very well take its place anew in the thousand and one decorative opportunities of daily life—opportunities at present very inadequately met by the "Cave Canem" on a doormat, the "Mizpah" often placed upon a ring, or some such motto as "Waste not, want not," entwined amidst the ears of corn around a bread-trencher. A thing, we must remember, however, is not necessarily good because it is old. Thus, one may have one's curiosity and interest somewhat roughly repelled by reading along the front of an old half-timbered house in Cheshire the unsympathetic inscription, "Walke, knave, what lookest at?" a very gratuitous rebuff, and not by any means a precedent to be followed in selecting some pleasant form of welcome for one's visitors.

The study of illumination—a subject that requires a whole volume to itself to do justice to it—naturally comes in this section. The student who desires to investigate the study at length should consult the following works: Shaw's "Illuminated Manuscripts of the Middle Ages"; the volume of Noel Humphreys on "The Illuminations of the Middle Ages"; the excellent work of Tymms and Wyatt on "The Art of Illuminating," and Waagen's "Treasures of Art in Great Britain." There are, of course, many other excellent books on the subject, but those named are very readily accessible. After a course of reading such works, and getting a general notion of the various periods, and so forth, the student will then put himself in the way of seeing original work in the magnificent collections at the British Museum, at South

T

Kensington Museum, and elsewhere. The most ancient volume extant is a copy of Virgil in the Vatican Library, dating from the fourth or fifth century. The Byzantine school produced very splendid works from about the seventh to the thirteenth century, and in the West the Carlovingian school and the magnificent works of the monks of Iona fully rivalled them in beauty of design and faultless workmanship. The English school from Anglo-Saxon times onward until the advent of printing is replete with beautiful work.

Many of the finest English MSS. of the tenth and eleventh centuries were the work of the monks of Winchester, though there were many other famous scriptoria. The general characteristic of the work of this period is the elaboration of the bordering, the free use of gold, and the richness of colouring, together with a considerable use of animal forms. In the twelfth century the capitals frequently extended over the whole page, the letters being often a foot or more in length. In the fourteenth and fifteenth centuries the art takes a very high position, the design and execution alike being superb. The number and variety of MSS. extant of this period is so great that it is impossible to generalise all in a sentence or two. In the sixteenth century a great change comes over the method of work; the capitals and lettering generally are now ordinarily of the Roman instead of the Gothic type, and the decorative work is either purely naturalistic or a strange blend of both naturalistic and conventional ornament in the same composition; so that in a panel or bordering we find a lily or other flower, butterflies, snails, etc., direct transcripts of the natural form, and yet twining amongst them the most conventional scroll-work. These are often painted upon a golden ground, and this gives great richness; but they are often depicted with their shadows thrown upon it, an effect which cannot be defended as a wholesome decorative treatment.

In a great deal of the modern amateur illuminated work that one sees, the student is in woeful need of the knowledge that study of past work should give. Had the well-intentioned but too easily satisfied beginner seen something of the glorious work of his mediæval predecessors in the field, though the shock to self-esteem might be considerable, the after-result would be most valuable. Most beginners fail in almost all directions where failure is possible to them—bad spacing, bad proportion, bad design, bad colour, bad drawing. One very common failing is to so wrap everything up in feeble ornament that legibility is lost sight of. The old illuminators never fell into this error; the text itself was the primary consideration, and its adornment a secondary matter. Note, for instance, in Fig. 164, how clearly, in the midst of all its enrichment, the letter itself tells out, and this we should see yet more distinctly if instead of the black and white of our illustration we had the potent aid of colour to give still more emphasis to the forms.

Interesting as the whole subject of illumination would be, had we space to pursue it, it is impossible here to do more than make the baldest reference to it. We resume, therefore, the consideration of Mohammedan art that these parenthetic references to the general use of inscriptions in art have for a space interrupted. The noblest examples of Mohammedan art are found in Spain. Granada was for seven centuries a Moorish kingdom, and during that long period many noble buildings were erected, notably the magnificent mosques at Cordova and Seville, and the fortress-palace of the Alhambra. " Poets, historians, travellers, and artists, of all degrees of competence," says Hannay, " have laboured on this wondrous Moorish ornamentation, and have done their best to convey some idea of it to readers who have never seen it, by pen, by brush, and by pencil. At the end, however, one sees it all very dimly indeed. Owen Jones explains with care how by drawing straight lines, to cut one another in this or in that way, the basis of the Moorish ornamentation can be laid bare. One knows that he is right; but for all that his explanation leaves one with a general impression of chess-boards gone mad. He gives drawings which a mole could see to be admirable of their kind; but he had to leave the sun and air and the space of Granada behind, and without them the form of the decoration is *caput mortuum*. Ford comments with excellent sagacity on the good fortune of a people who could use an alphabet which is itself an ornament. The motto of Ibnu-l-ahmar, the founder, ' Ila la gháliba illa Allah ' (There is no conqueror but God), which is everywhere written up, makes in itself a fine decoration. One notes the fact, and one agrees with Spanish Ford; but it is in a languid sort of way, and one remains nearly as far as ever from realizing what the thing is really like. You may talk about intersecting straight lines and the use

of primary colours, and the advantage of having a Cufic
alphabet to write inscriptions with; but you will never
enable any one of us who has not seen it to realize what
the ornamentation of the Alhambra is, nor will you show

Fig. 164.

men of another race, brought up under another sun, to
reproduce it."

It is a subject of immense thankfulness that we have
any Alhambra at all. Charles V. had part of it pulled
away to make room for a palace of his own, a palace that

was never finished after all. Another king used it as a prison. Afterwards it was handed over as a residence to officers and hangers-on of the court. Another king actually set galley-slaves to work to pull it down, for the mere purpose of keeping them employed. General Sebastiani, the leader of a party of French invaders, on his evacuation of the place, proposed to blow up the whole thing; and if a Spaniard had not had the good fortune to cut the burning fuse, centuries of neglect and spoliation would have been consummated in a final destruction that one could imagine even a Hun, a Goth, or a Vandal would have hesitated at.

Religious prohibition notwithstanding, we occasionally find representations of animal life. In the Alhambra itself, in one of the rooms we find human figures painted, and it has been suggested in excuse or explanation that they were the work of a renegade Christian. But if we admit that they were painted there during the Moorish occupancy (and it is of course quite possible that they were not), the excuse is of no value; as if the Moors believed the representation of such figures to be inherently wrong, it could not become right to them, even if done by some one else. If the reader really believes that on religious grounds the stealing of pears is wrong, he cannot conscientiously enjoy the fruit, because he has persuaded or forced a man who has no such scruples to procure it for him. It may be that such a prohibition was only maintained up to a certain date, and was held to be rather expedient than essential, as we know that the Mussulmans are divided into two great sects, that of the Sunnites being entirely opposed to images, while that of the Shiites admits them. One of the inner courts of the Alhambra, the Court of Lions, derives its name from a fountain in the centre, the basin being supported by a ring of lions, not of a very natural character certainly, but still sufficiently so to bring them within the religious prohibition; while the inscription round the fountain betrays the fact that it was want of power, not want of will, nor the restraint imposed by Mohammedan precepts, that prevented their being more lifelike than they really are, as the portion of the inscription relating to them runs as follows: " Truly what else is this fountain but a beneficent cloud pouring out its abundant supplies over the lions beneath? Like the hands of the Caliph when he rises betimes to distribute amongst his soldiers, the lions of war, their bounteous reward. O, thou who beholdest here these crouching lions, fear not, for life is lacking to enable them to show their fury!" A sufficiently needless caution, as all will agree who have seen the originals in the Casa Real, or the casts of them in the Alhambra Court in the Crystal Palace at Sydenham.

The Sicilian Moors made a very notable use of animal forms in their ornament. These invaders brought with them from Africa and Asia a knowledge of many creatures, such as the giraffe, gazelle, elephant, cheetah, and parrot, and all these appear freely, together with the dog, eagle, swan, and other more familiar forms, in their textiles and other art products. In the tenth century one of the Moorish kings of Sicily captured Corinth and Athens, and brought back with him to Palermo Greek weavers and other skilled workmen, and this naturally led to new modifications, a great use of the vine and other Byzantine types being evident, and the griffin, centaur, sphinx, and other monsters found in classic work reappear in the Sicilian or suggest new forms as bizarre. Many interesting examples of these textile fabrics may be seen in the South Kensington Museum. In the excellent handbook of Dr. Rock, published by the Museum authorities, this free use of such forbidden forms is very clearly recognised, as for example in the following passage amongst others that might be quoted: "However much against what looks like a heedlessness of the teaching of the Koran, it is certain that the Saracens, those of the upper classes in particular, felt no difficulty in wearing robes upon which animals and the likenesses of created things were woven; with the strictest of their princes a double-headed eagle, possibly borrowed from the crusaders, was a royal heraldic device. Stuffs figured with birds and beasts, with trees and flowers, were not the less on that account of Saracenic workmanship, and meant for Moslem wear."

A great use is made in Mohammedan art of tile-work, either for pavements or for mural decorations. In the frontispiece, for instance, we notice that the dado is of tile-work, and in this position it is of very extensive application. The designs are ordinarily of distinctly geometric character, but we find not only in tile-work but in many other kinds of decoration a great use made of what is termed counterchange. We should have been disposed to regard this as a strictly technical term had we not come upon the following use of it in a poem of Tennyson, where he speaks of—

> " Witch elms that counterchange the floor
> Of this flat lawn with dusk and bright."

This term is applied to a pattern in which the unit of repeat and the ground are of the same form, and Eastern ingenuity has developed a surprising variety of patterns that fulfil this requirement. Very beautiful wall tiles from Damascus, with floral patterns upon them, may be seen in the South Kensington Museum and in other collections.

The Persians belong to the Shiite section,[1] and in their various decorations the forms employed are of considerably more naturalistic character than is the case in typical Mohammedan work, and one readily recognises on the pottery, embroideries, and arabesques many natural forms, such as the hyacinth, iris, and rose. The founders and original supporters of the Mohammedan creed were but rude Bedouins, who gradually imbibed some ideas of culture from the more artistic countries that came beneath their sway; and while the Arabs subdued the Persians by force of arms, the art culture of the latter was not crushed out by the limitations of the new creed. The relationship between the two peoples seems to have

---

[1] " Now concerning their Religion (if such I may term it, being as one says rather a confused hotch-potch or mass of superstition) at this day it varies not from the Turks in any particle of the Alcoran : yet account they one the other Hereticks, being no less divided in their profession than we and the Papalins," says Herbert in his account of the Persians in his " Some Yeares Travels into Africa and Asia the Great."

been similar to that of Rome and Greece, where on the one side we get the conquering physical form and little or no artistic ability, while on the other we have the intellectual gifts that the conquerors gladly availed themselves of. It is known that during the Moorish occupation of Spain there was a very considerable Persian colony in that country, the city of Rioja being assigned to them as a place of residence, and the Alhambra and other so-called Moorish work owed doubtless much of its beauty and refinement to this Persian influence. A reference to such books as Texier's "Arménie et la Perse," or Flandin and Coste's "Voyage en Perse," both beautifully illustrated works, will at once show how artistic a people the Persians were;[1] while such buildings as the mosque at Tabreez, the tomb of the Sultan Khodabendah at Sultanieh, the palace of Sultan Husein at Isphahan, all figured in these works, are most interesting, both from the beauty and richness of their decoration, and from its marked resemblance to that of the Alhambra, allowance being made for the fact that the Persians in Spain were foreigners more or less working out the behests of their employers, and of necessity under various religious and

---

[1] The student may also advantageously see Collinot and Beamont's book, "Ornements de la Perse"; while amongst the "Portfolios of Industrial Art," published by the South Kensington Museum people, will be found one dealing with Persian art, and giving examples of pottery, carpets, damasks, etc. Other good sets in the series that we may take this opportunity of referring to are those on Indian, Italian, Sicilian, Flemish, and Saracenic art. All the sheets are of imperial quarto size, and are reproduced from the original objects in the Museum by photo-lithography.

Fig. 165.

other limitations that were less irksome to them in their own land. Greek art is at its best in Greece, Persian art in Persia, Japanese art in Japan; the principle involved in these three statements may be taken to be of universal application. A French designer brought to Manchester or Stoke-upon-Trent rapidly deteriorates in art-power. The environment is of potent influence. People have even been known to speak disrespectfully of the bagpipes when transported from the heathery crags of Caledonia to the sea-front at Brighton or Eastbourne; while the man who has plucked oranges from the tree never fails to point out to the man who has only drawn his supplies from Covent Garden that, practically, he can scarcely be said to know what an orange really is at all.

Indian art produced under Mohammedan influence naturally exhibits the general characteristics of that wrought under the common faith in other lands; but we are equally naturally prepared to find that the severer forms rigid orthodoxy requires give place in some degree to the greater freedom and grace of Persian art-ideas. The close proximity of India and Persia, and intimate intercourse between the two peoples, readily accounts for this. Some of the ruins of Mohammedan art around Delhi are unapproachable in their beauty of design and exquisite finish of workmanship. The Taj Mahal at Agra, commenced in 1630 and finished in 1647, marks the period of decadence; and the ornament upon it, though of most elaborate character and execution, is not of so pure a type as in the earlier work. The whole is composed of polished white marble richly inlaid. It was erected by

Shah Jehan to the memory of his beloved wife, Noor
Mahal. When she lay dying, he assured her, in the
passionate anguish of his grief, that as while alive she
had surpassed all in loveliness and virtue, so after her
death should she have an unequalled monument. It was
his intention to have built a mausoleum for himself of
similar magnificence upon the other bank of the Jumna,
and to have connected them by a marble bridge; but the
troubles of his reign prevented so imposing a design, and
his remains therefore rest by the side of her to whom he
was so attached. This sentimental association of ideas with
the building has naturally given it an added interest to
many, and the fact that much of the inlay is in precious
stones appeals to a somewhat vulgar wonder with others.
In some cases a single flower is composed of hundreds
of jewels,[1] but we need scarcely say that the result is not
by any means necessarily a success. The Sultan employed Europeans to aid in the planning and carrying out
of the work, hence the lack of purity of Eastern feeling.
The Italian-Indian of Agra was no more a real success
than the English-Japanese that we see too much of. A
similar curious illustration of this working out of a style
by alien hands is seen in the fact that the whole European shawl trade of the highest class was for many
years almost entirely given up to the production of
things in imitation of Oriental fabrics. There was, however, infinitely greater variety of design in the genuine

---

[1] " The gold branches, hung with emerald leaves,
    Blossomed with pearls, and rich with ruby fruit."
                                        —Southey.

things than in their Western counterfeits, and they were also superior in colour and in texture. Indian shawls show one notable feature—the general effect is always rich and harmonious, as whatever the choice and disposition of the detail one part never interferes with the whole by insisting on particular attention to itself. Some Indian specimens are made up almost entirely of the so-called pine form, and yet it is so unobtrusive in its treatment that its presence might well be overlooked, while the colour-sense of the Orientals preserves them from the crude vulgarity that the Western craftsmen does not always escape. The less-skilled European endeavours to create an Indian effect by unduly emphasizing and dwelling upon typical Indian forms, and by substituting mere strength of colour for the harmonious blending that gives it its charm. In the same way it appears to us a fatal mistake to establish schools of art under South Kensington influence in India. A people that for a thousand years has produced a distinct and excellent style of design, is now, in deference to supposed European requirements, grafting upon it a senseless copying of Western art, and destroying the charming individuality of their own work. One of the saddest sights, we think, in the Colonial Exhibition was a series of studies from the Indian Schools of Art from poor Renaissance casts, greatly wanting in themselves in any grace or beauty, and mere poison to the poor Hindus set to work upon them.

In India we find many phases of art; for though we naturally think of the land as a whole, it is a gathering

together of many kingdoms and peoples, it is under the
influence of several forms of religious belief, and the
examples of art scattered throughout its length and
breadth are of very varying date. It is really no more

Fig. 166.

reasonable to expect to find the art of India alike throughout its vast area, than to expect the art of London and
Constantinople, or Madrid and Moscow, to be identical.
In many works distinctly Mohammedan Hindu forms,
both decorative and structural, are introduced; and

similarly in many parts of India we find Hindu buildings adopting, with more or less success, Mohammedan types of decoration and construction. At the same time each has its distinctive character, and in most cases this is decisively enough marked. The polytheistic character of the religion of the followers of Vishnu and Siva reflects itself in their work, and covers their temples with the carvings of countless divinities. Buddhist art, again, has its easily recognisable peculiarities. The creed is a far purer one than either of the others that we have named, and the work has a solid grandeur that is very striking.

Buddhism took its rise about 600 B.C. through what is termed the great Renunciation of Prince Siddartha, of the race of Saka, an old dynasty in Northern Bengal, who forsook everything of earthly grandeur, and wandered from city to city teaching and preaching. The lofty religious precepts he inculcated were formulated into a definite creed that rapidly spread throughout India, and has now countless adherents also in China, Burmah, Siam, Thibet, and Japan. His followers bestowed upon him the name of Gautama Buddha. The Mohammedan invasion of India dates from about 1000 A.D. All the great monuments in India before this are of Buddhist origin.

Some four hundred and eighty millions of our race are this day living or dying in the faith of Gautama; and in this faith, for over twenty centuries, have countless millions of men found solace and support. "Most other creeds are youthful," writes Edwin Arnold, the author of that noble poem, "The Light of Asia," that deals with the great Renunciation with matchless power and beauty, "compared with this venerable religion, which has in it the eternity of a universal hope, the immortality of a boundless love, an indestructible element of faith in final good. The extravagances which disfigure the record and practice of Buddhism are to be referred to that inevitable degradation which priesthoods always inflict upon great ideas committed to their charge. The power and sublimity of Gautama's original doctrines should be estimated by their influence, not by their interpreters."

One of the most marked peculiarities of Hindu work is the profusion of decoration. Of this, Fig. 165 may be taken as a fair illustration. Every surface is so lavishly carved with conventional floral forms, with animals, or the representations of the many deities, that one often feels that the very amount is a drawback, and that the whole would gain greatly in effect if the value of contrast in the form of occasional bands of plain surface had been more appreciated. In architectural work one especially feels the need of a more massive and simpler treatment. The *modus operandi* that does well enough for an ivory or sandal-wood box is deficient in dignity when applied to a temple. In an Egyptian or Greek temple the strength and solidity of the mass is the chief character, and to this essential all enrichment is subservient. In India the leading forms are too often lost in the perplexity and multiplicity of the decorative details, the sense of scale is destroyed, and what should be distinctly an accessory goes far to become a principal. The attributes of the gods are often so peculiar that their representations are necessarily very conventional, as we may see very well in

U

Fig. 166; but the animal forms introduced, such as elephants, are generally very well expressed. Indian art often owes much of its effect to the repetition of units that are themselves of a very simple character. We have seen this already in Fig. 10—a group of vases—and we may note the same thing equally well in Fig. 167. This complexity of effect, produced by such simplicity of means, sometimes gives place to a great intricacy and elaboration of line. Many of the Indian embroideries are conspicuous illustrations of this richness of treatment, and other good examples arise in stone carving, from the necessity of admitting air and light and yet preserving privacy, as in the window opening shown in Fig. 168.

The India Museum at South Kensington is a magnificent collection of examples of every kind of decorative work, stone and wood carving, jewellery, pottery, metal-work, woven fabrics, embroidery, ivory-work, etc., and to this the student will turn, sketch-book in hand, to attempt to note something at least of the wealth of beauty that hundreds of hours of study will still leave apparently as inexhaustible as ever.[1]

Chinese and Japanese ornament is of great antiquity. The singularly conservative character of the Celestials

[1] Amongst the excellent handbooks published by the Science and Art Department, will be found one by Sir George Birdwood, C.S.I., on " The Industrial Arts of India," a book that the reader in search of fuller information than is here possible may very advantageously refer to. Other admirable volumes in this series are those on Textile Fabrics, Ivories, Majolica, Japanese Pottery, Tapestry, the Industrial Arts in Spain, the Saracens in Egypt, and that on Persian Art. All are most reasonable in cost and freely illustrated.

has led to the repetition for centuries of some few simple types, but unfortunately this same spirit of conservatism

Fig. 167.

has led to the almost entire exclusion of the outer barbarian. Much, therefore, still requires to be worked out before we shall possess a competent historic knowledge of Chinese art. The South Kensington Museum has a very fairly good collection of examples of various kinds, some being purchases, while others are generally to be found on extended loan. The book of Lemercier, "Les Ornements de la Chine," and Owen Jones's "Examples of Chinese Ornament," should each be seen by the student. Both are freely illustrated by chromo-lithography, the latter containing nearly a thousand examples from objects in the South Kensington and other collections. Of Chinese porcelain some fine specimens may be seen in the Asiatic Saloon at the British Museum. Apart from pottery, Chinese art ordinarily displays itself in bronzes, carvings in jade, steatite, and wood, in enamels, personal adornments and armour, in more or less pictorial representations on rice paper and other materials, and in dress fabrics.

The Chinese have a great love of the grotesque. One of the best illustrations of this will be found in their varied treatment of the dragon, the emblem of the Imperial power. We have already, in Fig. 95, given an example of this. Dwarfs, dogs, and other forms are also freely pressed into the service. They have an evident love for nature, and butterflies, flowers, and other natural forms recur, though in the majority of cases the treatment is stiff and conventional. A great use is also made of inscriptions. Their colour sense is decidedly good. Geometrical forms are freely employed, and a great use is made of frets; these, however, are not continuous and regular like those of the Greeks, but are often broken in

Fig. 168.

line in a very arbitrary and capricious way. Examples of these may be seen in Figs. 15, 16, 18, 19, 20, 21. In these, as in almost everything else, we find that they will resort to almost any irregularity rather than get symmetry and an even balance of parts.

There is no more pleasing feature in the works of the Japanese artists than their evident enjoyment of nature —an enjoyment that appears continually. In such work consists the true strength of the Japanese draughtsman ; and the invariable truth of drawing and colour proves that this small and, until lately, isolated nation possesses an artistic power that no nation on earth, with all the aid of museums, schools of art, government grants, and all the rest of it, can excel. It is the intense appreciation of the life-habits of the creatures, and his evident delight in his work, which gives the Japanese this high position and pre-eminent skill. All is admirably suited to decoration in the way it is treated. The force and freedom, and the absolute fidelity to nature in the whole, is a constant delight; and the simplest Japanese object shows this enjoyment of nature in its degree as thoroughly as the most profusely ornamented and costly. These people can draw ; they have both the observant and appreciative eye and the ready hand ; no complexity of structure, no sharp foreshortening is shirked by them, and all the beauty that their eyes delight in, their hands transfer unfailingly to paper.

In looking over a collection of Japanese drawings in our possession, we are at once struck by the closeness of observation, and the wonderful facility with which a

great deal is expressed by means so slight, a few touches
put on with master-hand conveying at once some incident
of daily life, or it may be some scene of mountain, wood-
land, or surging flood. In one of these drawings we see
a couple of wrestlers represented in eighteen entirely
different positions, from the preliminary grip to the final
overthrow, and each is full of spirit and life. If any of
our readers fail to realize what power of drawing this
means, they may very advantageously try even half a
dozen renderings of the same theme, when we may venture to affirm that they will rise from their task with a
considerable accession of respect for Japanese draughtsmanship.

Another illustration represents men diving after fish,
and is, equally with the last, replete with quaint humour,
excellent drawing, and foreshortening of the figures, and
variety of incident. The trees and herbage introduced
are equally happy in effect, and the fishes full of life and
motion.

Yet another quaintly delightful drawing deals with the
very simple incident of a man proposing to carry a bale
of goods on his shoulder; and here again we get nine
perfectly distinct drawings, dating from the time he first
lays hold of it on the ground till he marches triumphantly
off with his load, the intermediate drawings showing the
trouble he had to get a good grip of it, and the various
ways he tried of carrying before he hit on the right
one.

Japanese art is now fashionable, and we may but seem
to be joining in the general applause and swimming with

the stream. We can therefore only say that our admiration is a thing of no recent date. It must be borne in mind, too, that this popular applause, though in some cases of little or no critical value, in this case springs from the true estimation first expressed by those whose opinions were really worth regarding, and this esteem will remain when the votaries of mere fashion will have deserted Japan and all its ways, and raised another idol on the empty throne: for the art of these people is no dead thing, but a vital force.

The decorative art of the Japanese shows the same general characteristics as the pictorial,—in fact, there is no broad line of distinction. The due amount of conventionalism or naturalism that a decorative composition calls for under varying circumstances has been, and still remains, one of the most difficult problems of the designer. Tokio has one set of principles, and South Kensington another; and instead of endeavouring to conform to the practice of Japan, or requiring the Japanese to conform to ours, we may well endeavour to derive what is good from each, and find, it may be, an equal pleasure from results so diverse. When Owen Jones prepared his excellent "Grammar of Ornament,"—which, however, is much less a grammar than a goodly store of illustrations,—Japanese art was practically unknown in England, and finds no place in his book. Since then the country has been opened up to Europeans, and the West has been delighted with an art so fresh and striking; the result has been that some enthusiasts would have us in matters decorative all turn Japanese, turn our backs once for all upon the teachings of the past, and burn all text-books that do not support this view.[1]

English art training has been deficient in the power of seizing on the salient points and expressing them with the charming freedom and unlaboured grace shown by the Japanese. The Englishman trusts to precedent and convention, while the Japanese goes direct to Nature, and embodies in his resulting work the delight he has himself felt, and the principles he has there learnt.

Thus the Orientals, possessing little knowledge of machinery and much experience of artistic handwork, having found out the charm that springs from the repetition of some simple stellate or floral form, at once give freedom and life to their designs by producing this unit at irregular intervals over the ground, instead of adhering to a methodical and geometrical arrangement. The Western system appeals to our love of precision, exactness, order, and is so far characteristic; while the Eastern, the art of India, Persia, Japan, is no less typical. When we look on a meadow in spring strewn over with its countless buttercups, a sea of waving gold, or gaze on some clear night into the deep vault of heaven and see

---

[1] "A narrow-minded man would never do anything noble; he would also be narrow in his work and actions. They must remember that there was such a thing as bigotry in art, as well as in other things. The bigot in art was the one-sided man who could see beauty in only one particular phase of art. Some pinned their faith to the classical expression, and others to the mediæval expression of ideas, each ignoring the beautiful in whatever did not tally exactly with his own peculiar views. They should avoid such a pit-fall as this."— RAWLE, Address to Students, Nottingham School of Art.

the myriads of stars scattered over the limitless expanse of mystery spread out before us, the sense of their countless profusion appeals strongly to us; and this delight in mystery and profusion is eminently characteristic of the Eastern races. Much of our sense of awe at the contemplation of the starry host of heaven, much of our pleasure in the mass of golden blossoms in the meadow, would be lost if we saw that stars or flowers were all exactly alike in size, were all disposed at regular intervals, so that by counting so many rows up the meadow and so many rows across, we could bring out a definite arithmetical result, or if the great dome above could be laid out in rectangles, like a plot of building land.

The eighth proposition in the general principles laid down by Owen Jones at the commencement of his " Grammar of Ornament " runs as follows : " All ornament should be based upon a geometrical construction." Here is a perfectly clear and simple rule ; but if we accept it in all its rigidity, we must, there and then, dismiss as a heresy all the quaint beauty of Japanese art; we cannot at once pin our faith on Owen Jones and on Hishigava Monobu. The fact is beyond dispute that many writers would exact from us in things artistic a too rigid and a too narrow obedience. In matters of the law of the state, a man can be dragged before the statute book and judged at once therefrom, and in questions of the moral law the still severer tribunal of a man's conscience will declare him guilty or not guilty; but in art matters we need a wider charity and freer scope than the lawmakers are always willing to yield us.

Ornamental art has its canons, no doubt, though the whole subject is full of difficulty, and matters have not reached the cut-and-dried stage that some authorities would have us believe. It is no doubt true, that where the trumpet gives uncertain sound, men cannot prepare themselves for the battle; but the same treasure-house of wisdom that teaches us this warns us equally against crying "peace, peace," where there is no peace.

Few, we fancy, of our multitudinous art students could give the beautiful sweep of flying birds, or the graceful foreshortening and variety of line-direction in a shoal of fish, as the Japanese do. On Plate XI. we have taken one section only of this nature-study—animal forms. Most of our readers, we suppose, had in their younger days a fit of keeping rabbits; it comes as naturally as the idea of being a sailor or an engineer, and runs its course as regularly as the measles or other such incidents of our childhood; and all, we are sure, will at once feel how admirably true to nature are the two rabbits we have figured from a Japanese source—all expressed, too, with the very minimum of labour in simple outline. How admirable, again, the groups of wading birds in the rippling water, either intently watching for their prey, swallowing it with that peculiar jerking and constriction of the neck that is so true to nature, or indulging in those lengthy fits of contemplation that appear so character-istic of these wading birds, and which, again, is so happily caught by the artist. The flying stork, again, with its head thrown well back and its outstretched legs, is capitally rendered; while the various studies of fish are equally admirable in their graceful undulations. The quaint-looking owl, too, that perches with his back to us, is thoroughly and sufficiently expressed by the simplest of lines; while the feeble, fluttering quail, and the grandly-plumed "rooster," are full of expressive drawing and natural character.

All these illustrations are from authentic sources, from books, fans, and similar articles in our collection. It is necessary to give this voucher for their accuracy, as a great deal of spurious Japanese, manufactured in Birmingham, Paris, etc., is now flooding the market; while, on the other hand, the commercial instinct is playing havoc with a good deal of genuine Japanese work—work, that is to say, done in Japan and by Japanese, but produced in enormous quantities, and at a very low rate of payment, for the European market. Any one who will take the trouble to compare the Japanese work of a few years ago even with much of the present stuff turned out will realize readily enough that artistically their association with enterprising Europeans and Americans has not been by any means an unmixed blessing, whatever it may have been commercially. Many charming examples may be seen in the South Kensington and British Museums. They afford a marked contrast, indeed, with much that may be seen in the shop-windows. The same unfortunate influence we have seen is at work amongst the skilled art-workers of India.

A few bold lines, a few vigorous sweeps of the brush, but those few put on with consummate knowledge and unfailing art-instinct, suffice to give the most life-like impression when the designer so chooses it; while at other times the loving labour of months or years is spent to produce the result. The following passage from " Seas and Lands," by Sir Edwin Arnold, so happily illustrates the subject that we gladly avail ourselves of it. " On the screen in my bedroom are two turtles swimming in the sea, wrought upon the flimsiest of paper, with certainly not more than three brushes full of Indian ink. The first brush swept in the forms of the reptiles, and the vague veil of the sea wave half covering them. The second delineated, by soft half tints, the mail-plates of their carapaces, their bending flippers, their horny-plated heads, their shadowed bellies. The third, charged with the last and deepest wash, gave, by instantaneous touches, life and motion to the creatures, made the water seem to follow their gliding shells, and the fins appear to fold as their stroke is finished—effected, in a word, just enough for the imagination to complete the irresistible suggestion, so that there is a picture in it, perpetually delightful, which perhaps occupied three minutes at most of the artist's time." In another passage the same author writes : " Artistic genius runs through all their crafts, making their commonest domestic joinery almost like jeweller's work for finish, their mat-making as delicate as silk-weaving, their tubs and pails and buckets as exquisite in completeness as ivory-work. And the strange thing is that they have the two styles rarely found combined, one of which is characterised by this same exquisite finish, while the other is that swift, suggestive impressionism so constantly seen in their ordinary drawings and designs. Where they will complete a thing, nothing can be completer; the microscope itself could find no flaw in the patient, faithful article turned out. When, again, they merely desire to arouse the imagination, one sweep of the brush, one turn of the dexterous wrist, and they have indicated twenty leagues of blue distance, or limned a bird's wing in the very act of beating."

The love of art appears to be ingrained in the Japanese. In that beautiful country, life passes under easier and more graceful conditions than in these islands of the West. The cruel tyranny of fashion and the senseless cry after novelty are unknown, and in their place is the changeless law of love and beauty for its own sake.[1] "The government, sharing the national passion for beauty in nature and art, plants seats just at those spots in its public gardens and highways where the view is perfect of Fujiyama or of the sea, or of some range of wooded hills,[2] and it is common along the bye-roads to find

---

[1] "Whether it be the coolie setting out minute maple trees on the slopes of a miniature Fujiyama, the maiden setting gew-gews in her raven tresses, your 'boy' arranging flowers for your table, the journeymen painter daubing colour on the commonest fan, all alike know the mysterious secret, and act upon it. You cannot live a week in Japan without noticing that it is deeply rooted in the people's instincts. I verily believe that, with some inclinings of the head and not a few soft interjaculatory reflexions, a Japanese could put a postage stamp on an envelope artistically."—Piggott.

[2] Ruskin very truly says: "Beautiful art can only be produced by people who have beautiful things about them, and leisure to look at them; and unless you provide some elements of beauty for your workmen to be surrounded by, you will find that no elements of beauty can be invented by them."

official notices telling you where to stop for the best prospect, or how to find the most lovely clump of plum or cherry blossom. In the same spirit the peasant and the artisan, when the wife sets a flowering plant [1] on the tansu, looks upon it almost in the light of a good meal, and might grudge money for fish or rice rather than for that." [2] The art of Japan sprang doubtless from China. Centuries ago this influence began, and her ideals of art, her processes and traditions of style, have been those upon which the art of Japan was nurtured ; and the artistic practice of Tokio to-day is the outcome of a thousand years of this dominating influence. Why we at the present day see so great a difference in the results is that China has still to a great extent adhered to conservatism of practice and the routine of conventionalism, while Japan has used these as but stepping-stones to freedom. It is but another version of the

---

[1] " The arrangement of cut branches, leaves, and flowers for interior decoration, should rank among the applied arts of Japan, so carefully is the subject studied, and so charming the result obtained. It is an art with fixed canons, on which innumerable treatises are printed, long and patient courses of study are devoted—cultivated by high and low, rich and poor, and taught by regular tutors and professors. The intense love of nature innate in every Japanese, finds here a congenial form of expression which is open to dwellers in town and country alike. The highways and byeways of the cities are supplied with numerous flower markets, and places set apart for open competitions. Prizes under set rules and regulations are awarded to successful candidates, and no private or public reception takes place without the aid of a duly qualified professor being called in to arrange the inevitable floral decorations."— LIBERTY.

[2] Arnold.

liberation of art from the trammels imposed in Egypt and Assyria and its development into the matchless work of the Greeks. The strong individuality that we now see in Japanese art has arisen from two potent factors, isolation and feudalism.

Soon after the discovery of Japan by the Portuguese traveller Mendez Pinto in the year 1542, Jesuit missionaries entered the country, and by 1587 the converts from Buddhism to Roman Catholicism numbered some six hundred thousand. At this time some Spanish Franciscan monks appeared on the scene, and political and religious discord soon followed. The Japanese ruler took alarm at the papal claim to universal sovereignty, and the Buddhist priesthood and the English and Dutch Protestant traders fanned the flame of suspicion and jealousy. This was done so effectually that in 1614 a proclamation was issued by the government against the missionaries, and, as this was contemptuously ignored by the priests and their converts, a general and sanguinary persecution began. This was met by armed resistance, and after a struggle of many years Christianity was absolutely stamped out, and all foreigners[1] were banished from the country, the government imposing in addition severe restrictions on their own people, as it was naturally deemed almost as important that the Japanese should not visit the foreigner, as that the foreigner should not visit Japan. Hence all vessels of

---

[1] Except a few Chinese and Dutch merchants who were allowed to remain at certain points, on submitting to the most ignominious and humiliating restrictions.

sea-going capabilities were destroyed and a rigid limit of size imposed upon the ship-builder. This state of things lasted for over two centuries, and it was only in the year 1853 that Japan was reopened to the foreigner.

The Mikados have ruled in uninterrupted succession for over two thousand years. In the third century of our era the conquest of Corea by the Japanese brought them into touch with the Chinese, a nation at that time of more advanced culture than themselves, and to this they owe the introduction of Buddhism and doubtless many other things, and presumably amongst these a considerable degree of art-influence. In the twelfth century a powerful nobleman, the Shogun Yorimoto, usurped the governing power, and the Mikado had but its semblance left to him. This dual system of government lasted until our own day, the Mikado being a semi-sacred and almost mythical being to his subjects, while the actual power was wielded by the great nobles, or Daimios. The power of these Daimios has been broken within the recollection of most of our readers, and the sovereign of Japan is now both nominally and actually ruler of his people. These political changes exercised great influence on the art of Japan.

Throughout the Middle Ages and down to the year 1868, the principle of feudalism was supreme, and each feudal lord reigned a little potentate in his district, and having his vassals, and amongst these his art-craftsmen, living under his protection; and it was under these conditions, the amount of time and labour spent being immaterial, and sustenance assured, that the craftsmen of the clan produced noble works of art. On the break-up of the Daimio power these priceless examples were scattered, and were eagerly purchased by the appreciative foreigners at sums that may perhaps be best expressed in the formula " an old song." The Japanese have now fully realized the value of their antiquities, and are on the watch to prevent their leaving the country. They are even endeavouring, where it is at all possible, to re-purchase them. The rigid isolation of the nation kept its art untainted, and the political system favoured its production, until the collapse came, and the impoverishment of the nobles, and the impossibility of carrying away bulky impedimenta, compelled them to dispose of their heirlooms and art treasures. Immense quantities of lacquer-work, bronze, wood, and ivory carvings and ceramic ware were then thrown upon the market at any sacrifice.

The chief ruling clan and the great nobles all vied with each other in the encouragement of art, and at their great gatherings exhibitions of artistic skill were always welcome.

Floral forms have a great importance in Japanese art ; these are not used in haphazard fashion, but in accordance with various meanings and traditions. Hence this is one reason of the failure in England to copy Japanese work, since it is copying without understanding the underlying motive, and without any real knowledge of the things introduced. The pine-tree is an emblem of longevity, hence it naturally occurs freely in designs on objects to be presented to friends and others, and may

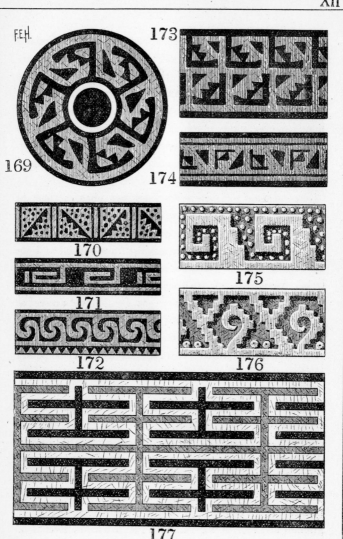

ANCIENT AMERICAN AND POLYNESIAN FRET-PATTERNS.

be translated colloquially into our formula, " Wishing you many happy returns of the day." The chrysan- themum is the emblem of the Imperial power. Other plants bearing various meanings, that we need not here pause to dwell upon, are the peony, bamboo, willow, maple, cherry, plum, peach, iris, nelumbium, wistaria, and daffodil. These are perhaps the most commonly found, but the list might very readily be considerably length- ened.

Japanese art exhibits several distinct phases; thus, in the ninth and tenth centuries the forms are sharply outlined and great care is given to minute detail. In the next century a reaction against this set in, and we get much greater freedom and boldness of treatment. Other variations of treatment that we need not par- ticularize will be found, until at length we arrive at the art of the present day. This is naturally most in evidence, and is characterized especially by simplicity of treatment, boldness of draughtsmanship, close study of nature, and a love of the grotesque or humorous.

This love of the grotesque is constantly cropping out in Japanese art, and there seems to be no limit to the fertility of the imagination exercised, or to the extrava- gance of the ideas conjured up. These grotesques readily divide themselves into two classes: those in which ordi- nary objects are presented to us, but with some added quaintness; and, secondly, conceptions of the super- natural and visionary, in which a whole mythology of gnomes and spirits is given with inexhaustible invention.

Amongst these examples of quaint renderings of

natural forms we may instance some few as illustrations, though it must be borne in mind that the supply is inexhaustible. In one drawing, for example, we see a grand procession of grasshoppers, the king grasshopper being borne in state in a sedan-chair, and around him are carried the various insignia of rank; in another example we have a similar procession, the actors in it being foxes. In the South Kensington Museum may be seen carvings of a monkey playing with a skull, two frogs playing leap-frog, a frog sitting on a large leaf and having an umbrella under his arm. The small carvings known as netsukés offer a great field for grotesque treatment. "Until very recently a netsuké was a term which included, in the minds of all foreigners, every carving below a certain size, and it is only a comparatively small class who now know the contrary. In reality a netsuké is a toggle affixed by a cord to the tobacco pouch, or the pipe, or the inro, to prevent it from slipping through the sash or waistband. In early times it probably had little, if any, ornamentation, but gradually, as it was one of the few articles upon a Japanese's dress which admitted of it, ornamentation was added. But so long as it was utilised as a toggle it never lost its original idea, or its form; so that whenever we see a netsuké without compactness, or with extraneous excrescences which would catch the folds of the dress, or break off, it may be taken for certain that it is of modern date and has been made for the outside market."[1] They are worked in

---

[1] Huish.

wood, ivory, horn, jade, metal, porcelain, onyx, and other suitable materials. Many of them were the work of men whose success in this field made them famous, and though to most of us the names of Tadatoshi, Tomochika, Shiuzan, or Miwa convey no meaning, their work, and that of many others equally well known to collectors, is much sought after and prized. The artists tell their story with the greatest clearness and point, while nothing is too solemn or too trivial to be safe from humorous treatment.

The creed of Japan ennobles the people by its purity, and " the race has evolved a high form of natural religion, known as ' Shinto '—' the way of the gods '—which teaches simplicity, courtesy in social life, and careful attention to the least detail in life's surroundings. Shinto teaches the fundamental tenets of true politeness, in that it inculcates reverence to parents as one of the highest virtues, and the family circle fosters the germs of the great national trait of ceremonious politeness. There is no oath or offensive word with which to express dissatisfaction in the Japanese vocabulary, save recent acquisitions supplied by Western civilization at the Treaty Ports. Deference to age is universal with the young; and it is considered a privilege as well as an evidence of filial duty, to study the wants and wishes of the parents even before the necessities of the progeny of those who may have households of their own. 'Keep this mirror— my picture—and thy destiny will endure as long as heaven and earth,' were the injunctions delivered to Jimmu-Tenno, the first Mikado, the first head of the

Shinto faith; and the Shinto faith has survived both
the introduction of Buddhism in the third century, and
Roman Catholicism in the sixteenth century; Buddhism
adapting itself and amalgamating itself with the indigenous cult; Roman Catholicism being obliterated and
swept away.   The national social 'Tea Ceremony,'
known as the 'Cha-no-ya,' which specially cultivates
hospitality, courtesy, purity, and tranquillity, comes of
Shinto origin, and largely influenced the applied arts, as
the rigid ceremonious rules of the 'Cha-no-ya' make it
compulsory on the part of every guest to bestow compli-
mentary and minute inspection on each utensil used, and
on each object and surrounding in the room." [1]

"In Japan the two chief religions of the country,
Shintoism and Buddhism, have been more completely
fused together than in China, chiefly owing to the compromise effected by Kobo-Daïshi (in the ninth century),
who proved that both religions were merely various reve-
lations of the same deity.   Every one therefore adores
the gods for whom he feels a special liking, without
regard to their origin.   Idols are unknown to real
Shintoism.   The bare temple contains nothing but a
simple altar with the sword, mirror, and the Gohei.   The
first denotes the palladium of the nation, the sacred
sword which the sun-goddess bestowed on her grandson.
The second is an imitation of the mirror which the same
goddess gave to her descendants, that they might always
behold in it their mother's soul and find the truth.   The

[1] Liberty.

Gohei, a collection of white strips of paper, folded in a peculiar manner, and attached to a wooden rod, was originally nothing but a mere dust-broom in the temple, afterwards used to clear the air of impurities during the prayers. Finally it came to be placed upon the altar as a symbol of the godhead's purity." [1]

Outside the definite religious teaching, even as in Christian England, a large amount of superstitious belief in goblins, wraiths, and the like has grown up, and influences the art and the life, though even here the sense of fun and incongruity finds abundant exercise. In one drawing we see the god of thunder rummaging in a basket for his storm-cloud. In another drawing in our possession we have the Japanese god of the winds in mid-air directing a mighty blast from the distended wind-bag on his back; while in yet another instance another storm-god has in either hand a short staff with which he hammers away at a ring of tambourines and thus produces the rolling thunder, while an attendant with a big box of hail in his left hand plentifully disperses handsful around. "The favourites of the people and perpetual butt of their wanton wit," writes Christian Bahnson, a Danish authority on matters anthropological, "are especially the god of contentment, the ever-joyous Hotei, with his fat paunch and his sack, and Dai-koku, god of wealth, with his rice-sack and miner's pick-axe, with which he extracts riches from the bowels of the earth. The others are not spared. Yebis, god of trade and fishing, the

---

[1] Bahnson.

cithern-playing Ben-ten, and the reverend old Dju-ro-
djin with his stag, are often seen in situations little
consistent with their divine dignity." Many of the
representations of spirits that appear to various mortals
are of the weirdest forms.

Japanese art has been so frequently dealt with of late
years by various writers that the student may readily
be bewildered amidst such a choice of guides. The few
we mention are all worthy of attention. Sir Rutherford
Alcock's " Art and Industries of Japan," Audsley's
" Ornamental Arts of Japan," and Dr. Dresser's work
entitled " Japan ; its Architecture, Art, and Art Industries," should be referred to. Audsley and Bowes'
" Keramic Art of Japan," containing sixty-three plates
(thirty-five of which are in gold and colours), and nearly
two hundred pages of text, with numerous wood engravings printed in colours, the whole being produced from
the original Japanese works, should be seen ; as also
should the excellent book of Anderson on the " Pictorial
Arts of Japan," a work illustrated by eighty plates
executed by chromo-lithography, photogravure, and native
engravings on wood and copper, and about one hundred
and fifty figures printed with the text, reproducing works
by representative artists, from the seventh century to
the present day. The " Grammar of Japanese Ornament and Design," illustrated by sixty-five plates, many
in colours and gold, representing all classes of natural
and conventional forms, drawn from the originals, with
introductory, descriptive, and analytical text, by T. W.
Cutler, should also be referred to ; and to these we may

add "L'Art Japonais, Ancien et Moderne"; a History of the Art of Japan, comprising the Arts of painting, architecture, sculpture in bronze, ivory, and wood, lacquer-work, metal-work, arms, fabrics, embroidery, engraving in black and colours, ceramics, etc., with letterpress in French, by M. Louise Gonse, Directeur de la Gazette des Beaux Arts, illustrated with sixty-four full-page engravings (thirty of which are in colours, thirteen etchings, twenty-one heliogravure), and over seven hundred engravings scattered through the text. In conclusion we may mention the "Japanische Vorbilder" of von H. Dolmetsch, containing many plates, printed in gold and colours, of most careful reproductions of textiles, paintings, ceramic paintings, diaper and other patterns.[1]

The subject is one replete with interest, and the only painful side to it is that the Japanese, in their desire to utilise to the full the benefits of Western civilization, are allowing themselves to be influenced adversely in artistic matters, and endeavouring to engraft upon their indigenous art entirely alien methods and tradi-tions. Fortunately some of their better men see this danger, and are now striving with zealous patriotism to

---

[1] Other books which deal with the country as a whole rather than dwell upon the artistic side alone may be read with interest and profit, as they often give an excellent insight into the character of the people, and enable us to see much that bears upon art, even though that be not the primary intention. Amongst such books we may mention Arnold's "Seas and Lands," "Japan and her People," by Steinmetz, "Unbeaten Tracks in Japan," by Miss Bird, "Japan, Historical and Descriptive," by Eden, "The Manners and Customs of Japan," by Humbert, "Tales of Old Japan," by Witford, and "Japan, Past and Present," by Buhicrosan, a Japanese author.

keep in the country the noble examples of native workmanship that were being disposed of as old-fashioned
lumber. Whatever may be the value of our Western art,
even its most devoted adherents surely would shudder
at the notion of a Japan South-Kensingtonised, though
the attempt to bring Calcutta, Bombay, and Poonah
into sympathy with stages 9*a*, 12*b*, and all the rest of
the routine of the Science and Art Department, is not a
very hopeful symptom.

In Mexico and Peru we find strange remains of a
bygone civilization, the decoration being of the most
bizarre description, and, to European taste, of most unsatisfactory type. It appears impossible to clear away the
thick darkness that enshrouds the origin of these races.
It is impossible, with our present materials, to say
whether these are two independent civilizations, or
whether one was derived from the other, and if so,
which was the parent and which the offspring. It
is equally impossible to say whether these civilizations
were indigenous, or whether they owed anything to
influences imported from the old world. No chronological table of the various remains is yet possible,
nor can it be said whether the works are those of one
race, or whether successive waves of immigration have
modified the type forms.

It is distinctly curious that several of the typical forms
of the old world, such as the scroll or the fret, are found
under barbarous modifications in the art of Mexico and
Peru, though the thousands of miles of ocean between
Assyria or Greece and these lands of the far West at

first sight appear impassable. The more, however, we study the records of the past, the more evident it becomes that there was much more communication between the various peoples of antiquity than we perhaps on casual consideration find possible to realize; and if we once frankly accept the idea that the population of the world all sprang from one centre in Western Asia it is needless to wonder whether it would be possible for men from thence to get to Central America when we actually find them there. As generation after generation of men gradually spread over the world, the traditions and ideas that they carried with them would also have an ever-widening distribution, and one can scarcely doubt but that the key pattern on the rude Aztec pottery or on the bordering of a pavement in Nineveh have a common parentage.

The monuments of remote antiquity, whether we find them in the old world or the new, show a marked similarity.[1] It is impossible to conclude that there have been no points of contact between these widely separated races, impossible to conceive that the human mind everywhere naturally gravitates towards a stone circle or a pyramid. It is much more reasonable to suppose that this similarity has arisen from some common source in the remote past. In the writings of the Chinese, amongst the traditions of the North American Indians, and stamped

---

[1] The colossal earthwork at Silbury Hill in Wiltshire, the mighty pyramids on the banks of the Nile, the many-storied pyramids of Xochicalco or Tehuantepec in Central America are but variants of the same idea.

on the clay tablets of ancient Assyria, is found the story of a mighty deluge that overswept the earth, and in which one family alone escaped destruction, in the far-distant childhood of the world. Columbus, Pizarro, Cortes, all set forth to the new world ; but though it was new indeed to them, they found it the home of many civilized races, and of others whose mysterious monuments amidst the tangle of the tropical vegetation still remain an unsolved problem. Nor need we see an impassable barrier to still earlier races in the three thousand miles of restless ocean that stretch between the old world and the new, since it was not necessary to cross the Atlantic at all, as there was a very much easier route by way of Siberia and the narrow strait (only thirty-six miles wide at the narrowest part), with its numerous island resting-places, that lies between Asia and America. We naturally now-a-days associate with Siberia the idea of a frost-bound penal settlement, but there are numerous geological indications that this was once a bright and fruitful land, as indeed it is much more nearly so to-day than popular belief credits. Great crops of grain are gathered-in each year, and the vine ripens its fruit in the open air.

The ancient Mexican buildings are profusely covered with carved ornament, this ornament being ordinarily either very imperfectly rendered figures of men or animals, or, more commonly still, various rude geometric devices and scrolls.

The circle often appears in Mexican ornament, and it is very natural that this should be so, since adoration of the sun was one phase of the worship of these ancient people, and amongst all sun-worshippers the circle is used as a symbol of the creed.

The fret forms found in Mexican and Peruvian work, instead of being continuous, as in most old-world examples (as in Figs. 11, 13, 14), are in small detached portions. On Plate XII. we have instances of this in Figs. 171, 175, 176. The step-like arrangement is peculiar to these new-world frets, and gives them a very peculiar appearance. On Plate IX., Figs. 131, 132, are examples of Peruvian grotesque pottery from specimens in the British Museum. The two we have sketched from this collection are fairly typical illustrations of the sort of thing. Many others may be found of equally quaint character.

Serpent-worship was a cult in ancient America; but whether this was a natural instinct, or derived from the similar worship of which traces may be found all round the world, it is hopeless to surmise. The great temple in the capital city of Mexico was built entirely of large stones fashioned like interlacing snakes; and amongst the ruins of Yucatan, at Uxinal, is a structure having two massive walls of stone 128 feet long and 70 feet apart. The sides facing each other are carved with gigantic serpents which run the whole length of the walls. Bernal Diaz, in his account of the march of Cortez to Mexico, says: "We to-day arrived at a place called Terraguco, which we named the town of the serpents, on account of the enormous figures of those reptiles which we found in their temples, and which they worshipped as gods."

The rattlesnake was the species most ordinarily

represented by the Mexicans. Squire, in his "Serpent-Worship in America," a most interesting work full of valuable information,[1] mentions a case where on a wall 163 feet long two colossal serpents run from end to end, entwining the various ornaments that are carved throughout its length. These serpents, adorned with crests of feathers and furnished with the curious tail-appendages of the rattlesnake, would be monsters indeed were they unrolled. At Chichenitza, in Central America, we find on either side of the foot of a flight of steps a serpent's head, ten feet long, with extended jaws and protruding tongue. A coiled rattlesnake carved in stone may be seen amongst the Mexican antiquities in the British Museum. See also Fig. 91, where we find one crowned.

The aboriginal Indians of America shared in this superstitious reverence for the rattlesnake, and worshipped under this guise the great Spirit. In Ohio may yet be seen an earthwork or embankment in the form of a serpent. Its head rests on a hill, and its body winds down the slope in graceful undulations and terminates in a triple coil. If fully extended its length would be over one thousand feet. The embankment varies in height and breadth, being at its centre five feet high and thirty feet broad, and gradually diminishing from thence to the head and tail.

Even amongst the most primitive people we still

---

[1] For general information the student may also refer to "Prehistoric America," by the Marquis de Nadaillac, translated by N. D'Anyers and edited by W. H. Dall, and containing over two hundred woodcuts and illustrations of antiquities.

find the love of decorative design. We have in our own collection some charming specimens of bead-work, the work of North American Indians. Other curious examples of Indian skill will be seen in the pipes exhumed from the grave-mounds of Ohio. Perhaps the best collection in England of these may be found in the Blackmore Museum at Salisbury. The figures of beasts, birds, and reptiles are carved with great skill and fidelity to nature, the attitudes assumed being very characteristic, and the habits of the various creatures admirably indicated. Hundreds of examples may be seen in various ethnographical collections, and amongst the animals carved we remember noting the otter, puma, bear, wolf, beaver, squirrel, racoon, crow, swallow, hawk, heron, buzzard, toucan, turtle, seal, frog, and rattlesnake. Amongst these pipe designs we also find human heads; these are marked with flowing lines and patterns representing either tattooed or painted designs. The Indian cast of physiognomy is capitally given.

Tattooing is a custom of great antiquity; we see illustrations of men thus adorned in some of the tombs at Thebes, and Cæsar in his Commentaries speaks of the Britons as being tattooed. The effect is produced by puncturing the skin in the desired pattern, either the pointed instrument itself being rubbed with some permanent stain that at each puncture it carries into the tissues, or this colouring matter is rubbed in afterwards. Captain Cook, in his excellent account of his voyage to the South Seas, thus describes the procedure in Otaheite : " They stain their bodies by indenting or pricking the flesh with a small instrument made of bone, cut into short teeth ; which indentings they fill up with a dark blue or blackish mixture prepared from the smoke of an oily nut. This operation is exceedingly painful,[1] and leaves an indelible mark." [2]

Sir Edwin Arnold [3] is quite enthusiastic on the splendid designs that may be seen on the natives of Japan. "The jinrikisha pullers in particular are sometimes gorgeously pictorial from nape to heel, and you may study for an hour the volutes, arabesques, flowers, gods, dragons, and poetical inscriptions on the back of your coolie as you bowl along, without exhausting the wealth of design and colouring upon the saffron surface of his skin." It is, however, to the countless islands of Polynesia and to New Zealand that we turn for the finest examples of this decorative treatment of the human body. The following

---

[1] John Rutherford, an English sailor, captured by the New Zealanders in 1816, wrote an account of various experiences of his captivity. Amongst other things he was tattooed, and so severe was the scarifying that he lost his sight for three days and did not fully recover for six weeks.

[2] This indelible character has led to its use in England, though it is not regarded as an added charm by the tattooees who come under the following section of the Mutiny Act : "On the first and on every subsequent conviction for desertion, the court martial, in addition to any other punishment, may order the offender to be marked on the left side, two inches below the armpit, with the letter D : such letter not to be less than an inch long, and to be marked upon the skin with some ink, or gunpowder, or other preparation, so as to be visible and conspicuous, and not liable to be obliterated." Notwithstanding its penal associations, many soldiers and sailors have a taste for being tattooed, and such markings are a useful means of identification in case of need.

[3] "Seas and Lands."

passage from the book of a Mr. Earle, who resided in New Zealand for nine years, at a time when there were very few English in the country,[1] and when the native customs were in full force, shows very clearly the importance attached to the art. He says: "The art of tattooing has been brought to such perfection here, that whenever we have seen a New Zealander with skin thus ornamented, we have admired him. It is looked upon as answering the same purposes as clothes. When a chief throws off his mats, he seems as proud of displaying the beautiful ornaments figured on his skin as a first-rate exquisite is in exhibiting himself in his last fashionable attire. It is an essential part of warlike preparation. The whole of the district of Ko-ro-ra-di-Ka was preparing for the approaching war. Their cannon, muskets, powder, and ball increased daily; and a very ingenious artist, named Aranghie, arrived to carry on this important branch of his art, which was soon placed in requisition; for all the mighty men in the neighbourhood were one by one under his operating hands. As this professor was a near neighbour of mine, I frequently paid him a visit in his studio; and he returned the compliment whenever he had time to spare. He was considered by his countrymen a perfect master of the art of tattooing; and men of the highest rank and importance were in the habit of travelling long journeys in order to put their skins under his skilful hands. Indeed, so largely were his works

[1] Mr. Earle's book was published in 1829. One of the illustrations represents a chief recumbent under the hands of the artist tattooer.

esteemed, that I have seen many of his drawings exhibited even after death. A neighbour of mine very lately killed a chief who had been tattooed by Aranghie, and, appreciating the artist's work so highly, he skinned the chieftain's thighs, and covered his cartouch-box with it! I was astonished to see with what boldness and precision Aranghie drew his designs upon the skin, and what beautiful ornaments he produced; no rule and compasses could be more correct than the lines and circles he formed. So unrivalled is he in his profession, that a highly finished face of a chief from the hands of this artist is as greatly prized in New Zealand as a head from the hands of Sir Thomas Lawrence is amongst us. This professor was merely a slave; but by skill and industry he raised himself to an equality with the greatest men of his country; and as every chief who employed him always made him some handsome present, he soon became a man of wealth, and was constantly surrounded by important personages."

The influence of civilization is now far reaching, and the picturesque individuality of the various peoples is ever growing less and less. The cantonal costumes of Switzerland, the quaint dresses of the Norwegian, Spanish, and Italian peasantry are dying out of use, and in the course of a few generations the chimney-pot hat will reign supreme over a conquered world. The Sioux and the Blackfoot Indian don coat and trousers; the Japanese forswears the picturesque costume of his forefathers in order that he may take his place in the dead level of tailordom.

Even in the neolithic days, when our prehistoric ances-
tors, the men of the stone period, were chipping flints
into arrowheads and chisels, the soft clay of their rude
vessels afforded opportunity for ornament, and in the
whole field of ethnographical research no tribe is found
so low in the scale of humanity as to yield no illustration
of this love for decoration. The claims of religion and of
war are ordinarily paramount, and it is in these two
directions that we most naturally look for illustrations
of decoration. The religion may be the rankest idolatry
or fetish-worship, still to the holders of the creed it is
as truly a recognition of a higher power, shaping the
destinies of men,[1] as pontifical High Mass at St. Peter's,
and as such receives the highest honour possible to
the worshipper. The pursuit of war is also a matter
of immense importance, as the existence of the tribe

[1] We so naturally associate the idea of this idolatry with South
Sea Islanders, the natives of tropical Africa, and such-like folk, that
the following passage from the book "Wisdom" is very striking.
The writer describes the carpenter felling timber, forming part of it
into vessels of service, using part as fuel, and then diligently making
the rest into his deity, having carved it carefully, "and formed it by
the skill of his understanding, and fashioned it to the image of a
man; or made it like some vile beast, laying it over with vermilion,
and with paint colouring it red, and covering every spot therein:
and when he had made a convenient room for it, set it in a wall, and
made it fast with iron: for he provided for it that it might not fall,
knowing that it was unable to help itself (for it is an image, and hath
need of help): then maketh he prayer for his goods, for his wife
and children, and is not ashamed to speak to that which hath no life.
For health, he calleth upon that which is weak: for life, prayeth to
that which is dead: for aid, humbly beseecheth that which hath
least means to help: and for a good journey, he asketh of that which
cannot set a foot forward."

depends on its ability to hold its own against all comers, and therefore every care and honour is bestowed upon the shield and spear. The design shown in Fig. 177 on Plate XII. from a shield from the Solomon Islands is a really excellent piece of work, and far superior, as an example of a fret pattern, to the Mexican and Peruvian examples on the same plate. The original, to be seen in the ethnographical collection in the British Museum, is worked in black, dull red, and white, and in the same collection many other most interesting examples may be found.

To man the simple formula, "Let us eat and drink, for to-morrow we die," is not enough for his needs. It may suffice for the lower animals; but even the lowest savage is a man made in the image of God, and the dark recesses of his mind are lit up with aspirations that mere animalism will not satisfy. In the simple zigzags on the pottery dug out of some prehistoric barrow or the choicest examples of the ceramic art of Hellas, we alike see the desire to create forms of beauty, and the difference between the carved prow of a South Sea canoe and the sculptures of the shrine of Athene Parthenos is only a difference of degree and not of kind. That we may not ourselves think a given thing beautiful is beside the mark. We have been educated on other lines and have had other opportunities, and the only fair way to view a thing that appears to us rude, archaic, barbarous, is not to estimate it from our own prepossessions at all, but to frankly see in it the endeavours of a man whose environment was in every possible way different from our own, to attain to some ideal of beauty in his mind. Judged by this common-sense principle, the efforts of every age and of every race are of interest, and all fall naturally into their appointed place in the history and development of Ornament.

> " What is writ, is writ. —
> Would it were worthier ! "

HISTORICAL LANDMARKS.

"Footprints on the Sands of Time."

In some cases, and especially in the earliest dates, the figures given are only approximate, as in these exceptional cases it has been impossible to obtain absolute certainty.

Menes, founder of Memphis . . . . . B.C.	4400
Entenna, king of Babylon . . . . . ,,	4200
Sargon I. reigns . . . . ,,	3750
Khufu, builder of first Pyramid . . B.C. 3733 to	3700
Kha-f-Ra, builder of the second Pyramid . . B.C.	3666
Men-kau-Ra, builder of the third Pyramid . . ,,	3633
Usertsen III., great builder, Thebes, Memphis, etc. ,,	2333
The founding of Carthage . . . . . ,,	1800
Assyria independent of Babylon . . . . ,,	1700
Thothmes III. erected obelisk, now called Cleopatra's Needle . . . . ,,	1600
Amenophis III., colossal statues at Thebes . . ,,	1500
Rameses I. reigned from . . . . B.C. 1400 to	1366
Seti I. built great Hall of Columns at Karnak, etc. B.C.	1366
Rameses II., great temple-builder, Abu Simbel, etc. ,,	1333
Shalmaneser I. founded Nimroud . . . . ,,	1290
Ashur-nasir-pal came to the throne . . . ,,	885
,, ,, built great palace of Nimroud . ,,	885
Sargon III. came to the throne . . . . ,,	722
,, built great palace at Khorsabad . . ,,	722

Tyre besieged by the Assyrians	B.C.	719
Sennacherib built palace of Kyonjik	,,	705
Earliest known coin, struck in Lydia	,,	700
Esarhaddon builds great palace at Nimroud	,,	681
,, —conquest of Egypt	,,	672
Thebes sacked by the Assyrians	,,	666
Psammeticus came to the throne	,,	666
Temple at Corinth	,,	655
Nineveh destroyed by the Medes and Persians	,,	609
Nebuchadnezzar II., great temple-builder	,,	605
Rise of Buddhism	,,	600
Capture of Jerusalem by Nebuchadnezzar	,,	597
Earliest coinage of Athens	,,	590
Tyre taken by Nebuchadnezzar	,,	572
Cyrus founds Passargadæ	,,	560
Babylon captured by Cyrus	,,	539
Cambyses conquers Egypt	,,	527
Darius builds palace at Persepolis	,,	521
Temple at Ægina	,,	508
Phidias, Athenian sculptor, born	,,	500
Xerxes, great buildings at Susa	,,	485
Sack of Athens by the Persians	,,	480
Temple at Agrigentum	,,	480
Temple of Theseus, Athens	,,	469
Temple of Zeus at Olympia	,,	460
Parthenon, commenced B.C. 444, finished	,,	438
Phidias, sculptor, died	,,	432
First Temple of Diana at Ephesus burnt	,,	356
Mausolus, Prince of Caria, died	,,	353
Monument of Lysicrates, Athens	,,	335
Conquest of Egypt by Greece	,,	332
Tyre taken by Alexander the Great	,,	332
Conquest of Etruria by Rome	,,	285
First Roman war against Carthage	,,	264

Rochester Cathedral rebuilt by Gundulph . . . 1077
Hereford Cathedral commenced 1079
Durham Cathedral commenced 1090
Canterbury Cathedral commenced 1106
Capture of Majorca by the Pisans 1115
City of Mexico founded 1125
Fountains and Rivaulx Abbeys founded 1132
Bayeux Cathedral commenced 1183
Temple Church, London 1185
Salisbury Cathedral commenced 1220
Mosque of Cordova converted into Cathedral . . . 1238
Palace of Alhambra commenced 1248
Strasburg Cathedral commenced 1277
Nicola Pisano, Italian sculptor, died . . . 1280
Eleanor crosses erected 1291, 1294
Alhambra finished 1314
Luca della Robbia, potter, born 1400
Ravenna captured by the Venetians 1440
Constantinople conquered by Mohammed II. . . . 1453
Constantine Palæologus, last Emperor of Constanti-
    nople, slain 1453
Lorenzo Ghiberti, Florentine sculptor, died . . . 1455
Re-conquest of Granada by Spaniards . . . 1492
Luca della Robbia died 1481
Palais de Justice at Rouen built . . . 1493 to 1499
Bath Abbey Church . . . . . . 1500 to 1539
Henry VII.'s Chapel, Westminster . . . 1502 to 1519
Cathedral of St. Peter, Rome, commenced . . . 1506
Bernard Palissy, the potter, born 1510
Egypt came under dominion of the Turks . . . 1517
Spanish conquest of Mexico 1519
Wolsey building Hampton Court Palace . 1520 to 1540
Torrigiano, Italian sculptor, died 1522
Peter Vischer, sculptor and metal-worker, died . . 1529

Conquest of Peru by Pizarro 1534
Holbein, painter and designer, died 1543
Jean Goujon, French sculptor, died 1572
Bernard Palissy died 1590
Extirpation of Christians in Japan 1622
Decree of expulsion against all foreigners in Japan . 1624
Grinling Gibbons born 1648
Inigo Jones, English architect, died 1652
First stone laid of new Cathedral of St. Paul, London . 1675
St. Paul's Cathedral finished 1710
Grinling Gibbons died 1720
Sir Christopher Wren died 1723
Chelsea pottery established 1745
Worcester pottery established 1751
Derby pottery established 1751
Excavations commenced at Pompeii 1755
Lowestoft pottery established 1756
British Museum opened January 15th 1759
Wedgwood established Etruria works 1769
Bristol pottery established 1774
Elgin marbles placed in British Museum . . . 1816
Botta exploring Kyonjik and Khorsabad . . . 1842
Palaces of Sennacherib, Esarhaddon, and Ashur-bani-
    pal discovered by Layard 1845
Welby Pugin died 1852
Re-opening of Japan to the rest of the world . . . 1853
Rawlinson excavating at Babylon 1854
Mausoleum of Halicarnassus, remains 1856
Blacas collection bought for nation 1866
Wood's excavations at Ephesus . . . 1869 to 1874
Castellani collection bought for nation 1872
Rassam excavating in Assyria 1878
Cleopatra's Needle brought to London 1878

INDEX.

"This is the true beginning of our end."

Abou Simbel, 25.
Acanthus, 43, 118, 133, 134, 140, 251.
Accessory not to be made principal, 289.
Acropolis, destruction at the, 71.
Adam Krafft, art-worker, 190.
Adam, the brothers, 227.
Ægina, Doric temple, 80.
Æsthetic decoration, 17, 92.
Agnus Dei, 152.
Ahmes, temple-builder, 25.
Albert Hall mosaics, 137.
Albert Memorial, 165.
Albert Memorial Chapel, Windsor, 138.
Albertolli on Roman art, 118.
Alcock's "Art and Industries of Japan," 313.
Alexander and Darius mosaic, 127.
Alhambra, 251, 258, 260, 276, 277, 278, 282.
Alphabets suitable for inscriptions, 264.
Alternation as a principle in design, 32.
Amen-hotep, temple-builder, 25.
Amrou, mosque of, at Cairo, 258.
Anachronisms in art, 190.
"Analysis of Ornament," Wornum, 97, 252.
Ancient Egypt, 23.
"Ancient Timber Houses in England," Clayton, 212.
Anderson, "Pictorial Arts of Japan," 313.
Angelic forms, 202.
Anglo-Saxon, 144, 274.
Angoulême, Byzantine work at, 132.
Animal forms in art, 38, 109, 127, 134, 144, 152, 158, 169, 184, 188, 196, 279, 299, 309, 320.
Anthemion form, 32, 55, 89, 122, 134, 218, 257.
Anthropomorphic pillars, 38.
Antiquity not necessarily excellence, 218.
Antonelli, "Antique Ornaments," 220.
Anubis, 39, 78.

Ape, sacred animal, 39.
Apis cult, 159.
Application or adaptation, 93.
Arab art, 144, 257.
Arabesques, 122, 124, 218, 219, 280.
Arabic characters in inscriptions, 260, 265.
Arabs conquer Egypt, 26.
Aratus, "Phænomena" of, 76.
Arcading, 176.
Archaic work, 31.
Archeistic work, 31.
Archelous, representation of, 160.
"Architectural Antiquities of Great Britain," 212.
Architectural character of Egyptian ornament, 24.
Architectural forms as ornament, 203.
"Architectural Remains," Richardson, 212.
"Architectura Numismatica," 102.
"Architecture Arabe," Coste, 259.
Arch of Severus, 116; of Titus, 116.
Arch, use of the, 114, 216.
"Armenie et la Perse," Texier, 282.
Arnold, Sir Edwin, on Japanese art, 301.
Arnold on Mohammed, 255.
Arnold, "Seas and Lands," 314, 321.
Arrowhead inscriptions, 52.
"Art and Industries of Japan," Alcock, 313.
Art at second hand, 11.
Art difficult, but criticism easy, 17.
"Art of Illuminating," Tymms and Wyatt, 272, 273.
"Art of the Old English Potter," Solon, 271.
Ashanti, fetish-tree of, 58.
Ashur-nasir-pal, 44.
Asiatic Saloon, British Museum, 292.
Asp, Egyptian, 40.
Assyrian Empire, 44.
Athens, coins of, 104.
Atherstone on fall of Nineveh, 45.
Atlantes, 39.
Audsley, "Ornamental Arts of Japan," 313.

332

z

"The conclusion of the whole matter."